Britain and the H-Bomb

Also by Lorna Arnold

A VERY SPECIAL RELATIONSHIP: British Atomic Weapons Trials in Australia

WINDSCALE 1957: Anatomy of a Nuclear Accident

Britain and the H-Bomb

Lorna Arnold

with Katherine Pyne

Foreword by Professor Lawrence Freedman

To Ken,
with best wishes
Lorna.

Best wishes Ken
Kate Pyne
3rd July 2001

palgrave

First published 2001 by
PALGRAVE
Houndmills, Basingstoke, Hampshire RG21 6XS and
175 Fifth Avenue, New York, N.Y. 10010
Companies and representatives throughout the world

PALGRAVE is the new global academic imprint of
St. Martin's Press LLC Scholarly and Reference Division and
Palgrave Publishers Ltd (formerly Macmillan Press Ltd).

Outside North America
ISBN 0–333–73685–0 hardback
ISBN 0–333–94742–8 paperback

In North America
ISBN 0–312–23518–6 hardback

This book is printed on paper suitable for recycling and made from fully managed and sustained forest sources.

A catalogue record for this book is available from the British Library.

Library of Congress Cataloging-in-Publication Data
Arnold, Lorna.
    Britain and the H-Bomb / Lorna Arnold ; foreword by
    Lawrence Freedman.
        p. cm.
    Includes bibliographical references and index.
    ISBN 0–312–23518–6
    1. Hydrogen bomb—Great Britain. 2. Great Britain—
    —Military policy. I. Title.
    UG1282.A8 A76 2000
    355.8'25119'0941—dc21
                                                    00–036898

10   9   8   7   6   5   4   3   2   1
10   09 08 07 06 05 04 03 02 01

Printed and bound in Great Britain by
Antony Rowe Ltd, Chippenham, Wiltshire

To David Holloway
in admiration and friendship

Contents

List of Plates

Foreword

In this rich, informative and lucid analysis of the development of the British H-Bomb in the 1950s, Lorna Arnold has provided yet another valuable contribution to the nuclear history of this country, in addition to those she has already made both independently and in collaboration with the late Margaret Gowing. A number of scholars have already analysed the policy-making process which preceded the decision to follow the superpowers into the development and production of thermonuclear weapons in July 1954. Such a decision is not the end of the story but only the beginning. In 1957 and 1958 four weapon trials were conducted in the Pacific and this is largely the story of those tests. This was a remarkably challenging undertaking – in many ways more so than the development of an atomic bomb, for now there was great ignorance about how the Americans were going about their nuclear business, and Fuchs, one of the few British scientists to have had known about early American calculations, had been revealed as a spy. Lorna Arnold's distinctive contribution is to bring this project to life, setting out the obstacles that faced those charged with turning this aspiration into a reality, from the scientific and engineering challenges to Treasury parsimony. With affection and respect, she explains the special talents and the singular personalities of the responsible individuals, especially Penney and Cook. All this is against the background of public unease at the questions of morality and safety raised by the thermonuclear age, high-level diplomacy as attempts were made to reconstruct the special nuclear relationship and the pressure of test ban diplomacy. Such a book cannot answer the question of whether Britain was right to travel in this direction, but it does put back into centre stage those who considered it their duty to ensure that it did become the third thermonuclear power

LAWRENCE FREEDMAN
King's College, London University

Preface

Scope and purpose

In 1952 Britain – having played a crucial part during World War II in creating the world's first atomic weapons – became the world's third atomic power.

Significantly, Britain came after the superpowers and before any other nation, and was the only European member of NATO with atomic weapons. Rather than setting the agenda Britain acted in response to a situation created by the superpowers, and one in which it felt uniquely vulnerable. Britain's objectives, its modes of thinking and its resources differed greatly from theirs. Britain wanted, as soon as possible, a minimal, low-cost but effective weapons programme which would provide a credible, independent deterrent, contribute to the strength of Western defence and – not least in importance – give Britain political leverage in Anglo-American relations. In 1957 Britain was again to be the third power, in developing the H-bomb.

Much valuable work has been done by historians on this strategic and political background. Our chief concern is with the nuclear weapons programme itself, how it was carried out and by whom. A great deal less is known about the British than the United States and even the Soviet programmes; we have tried to fill some gaps and to dispel some misconceptions about the work of the British weaponeers faced with the urgent demands of national defence policy in the 1950s.

Britain's H-bombs were conceived and fabricated at Aldermaston, a wartime airfield in rural Berkshire, and were tested in four weapon trials, code-named *Grapple*, in the Pacific in 1957 and 1958. We should have liked to write more about these dramatic events and the experiences of the thousands of test participants, many of them young National Service men most of whom had never been abroad, or flown in an aircraft, before their long flight to and across America, then to Hawaii and finally to Christmas Island. That would be another book and we are chiefly concerned with the trials as part of the R&D programme.

The role of weapons trials

The role of weapon trials – and so their success or failure – was and is little understood. Trials were essential in developing nuclear warheads and the information needed from them changed as development proceeded.[1] The first might simply confirm that the device would produce a real nuclear explosion.

More questions would then follow. Could the design be improved to give a larger yield? Could the required yield be obtained from a smaller device, or one using less (expensive) fissile material? Could it be made into a gravity bomb, or one carried by a torpedo or a ballistic missile? How could it be made safer to store and handle? After fission weapons the same questions, and a host of new ones, would arise for H-bombs and boosted bombs. At least one test might well be needed for each question and it would take a series to explore even a few lines of enquiry. But the British weaponeers did not have the luxury of numerous trials as both time and resources were very short.

Trials could have other ancillary purposes as they afforded unique opportunities for civil defence studies of thermal, blast and radiation effects on structures and materials, for biological experiments and for military training. These all featured in some British A-bomb trials in Australia, but were ruled out at the *Grapple* trials by constraints of time and cost.

An atmospheric test might also have a political and propaganda purpose, as did the huge 58-megaton Soviet explosion which coincided with an intense East–West crisis in Berlin in October 1961.

Who was the father of the British H-bomb?

People sometimes ask who were the British counterparts of Teller and Ulam, famous as the inventors of the first H-bomb, and of Sakharov and Khariton in the Soviet Union. It has been suggested that William Penney, the director of Aldermaston, was 'the father of the British H-bomb'; three other men have been named – William Cook, K. V. Roberts and J. B. Taylor; and claims have also been made for the physicist John Ward. We have found no 'Eureka' answers. What Norris Bradbury, the second director of Los Alamos, said of the American H-bomb is at least as true of the British H-bomb, 'Well, who invented it? No single individual probably invented it'. In a laboratory there is 'constant interplay between people. And then the way is found.'[2]

The record

Records of this important project are voluminous but nevertheless incomplete and fragmented. Many crucial meetings and discussions went unrecorded, perhaps for reasons of secrecy. In Whitehall the Prime Minister himself had ordered that officials should write nothing down about the project if it could be avoided.

Many useful papers have undoubtedly been destroyed[3] deliberately or inadvertently. In a radical but well-intentioned reorganization of Aldermaston's records 40 years ago, files were broken up and unsatisfactorily reassembled in some 6,500 synthetic new files which lack archival integrity, and in the process Penney's and Cook's directorate files were demolished. These are gaps in our scientific history that cannot be filled.

One senior Aldermaston scientist, at the centre of developments in the 1950s, thought that many strands of the nuclear weapons story would be difficult to disentangle, and impossible for anyone working solely from documents. He was, he said, one of only three people knowing certain important aspects.[4] All three have since died. None of the British weaponeers, even Penney – unlike their American or Soviet counterparts – has ever published memoirs, or articles about what they did at Aldermaston. They worked in the anonymous traditions of the civil service; their achievement was considered a corporate achievement and only very exceptionally did anyone claim individual credit for a personal contribution to it.

Sadly, less and less first-hand evidence is available. We are all the more grateful for the help generously given to us by the scientists and engineers whose names are listed below, in interviews, correspondence and conversation. We were, unfortunately, too late to talk to either Lord Penney or Sir William Cook, and some others whose recollections would have been invaluable.

Words and meanings

When the British scientists began work on the H-bomb they did not know clearly what they were trying to make. They knew that a 'superbomb' with a megaton or multi-megaton yield involved using a fission explosion to create conditions in which thermonuclear reactions – fusion – could take place in isotopes of hydrogen (see Appendix 1). But how? Many ideas were examined. The terms 'superbomb', 'hydrogen bomb', 'H-bomb', 'thermonuclear bomb' and 'megaton bomb' were used rather loosely, as well as terms like 'intermediate' and 'hybrid'. Was a megaton bomb necessarily a hydrogen bomb? It seemed clear that a multi-megaton bomb would have to be an H-bomb (such yields were otherwise theoretically impossible). But could a megaton bomb (or a bomb 'in the megaton range') be just a very big fission bomb? Was a boosted bomb a thermonuclear bomb or not? There were complaints that people used the same words to mean different things and different words to mean the same thing.

Whatever they called it, what the government wanted in 1954 was a megaton explosion as soon as possible, achieved by whatever technical means, to demonstrate Britain's ability to make such weapons, and to meet military requirements. Military requirements were for megaton warheads: first, as gravity bombs; then as powered guided bombs, for the RAF's V bomber force; and later for a medium-range ballistic missile (under development). Eventually, a multi-megaton warhead was wanted. The scientists and engineers would have to solve the problems of meeting these requirements within the limited time and resources likely to be available to them.

Fission weapons were comparatively simple devices, employing a single nuclear reaction. The H-bomb was a very different matter. To quote a Soviet weaponeer,[5] it was '... one of the most perplexing challenges ever tackled in the history of mankind. The physical processes involved in the detonation of the thermonuclear charges were so extraordinarily complex that physicists could develop the required concepts only by attaining a high level of mathematical modelling and comprehension of these subtle processes'. This book tells how the British scientists and engineers met the challenge.

Acknowledgements

We thank many past and present members of staff of Aldermaston and the Ministry of Defence for much help in interviews, conversations and correspondence, especially the late Ken Allen, Jim Biltcliffe, John Challens, the late John Corner, the late Sir Sam Curran, David Dearden, Les Elliott, Lord Flowers, Alan Fraser, Ken Johnston, Peter Jones, Bill Lord, the late Victor Macklen, Mike McTaggart, Clive Marsh, the late Charlie Martin, the late Frank Morgan, Eric Pendlebury, Herbert Pike, Peter Roberts, Leslie Russell, the late Bill Saxby, Ron Siddons, Bryan Taylor, John Ward and Tony Wilson.

Two of the task force commanders, Marshal of the Royal Air Force Sir John Grandy and the late Air Vice-Marshal Wilfrid Oulton, kindly gave us interviews.

We owe a great debt of gratitude to British, American and Russian historians working in the nuclear field (though consultation with colleagues was limited by the nature of our task).

The help of Anne Marshall and the staff of AWE Corporate Archives at Aldermaston has been much appreciated. Many thanks are due to Melanie Kingdon, who typed the early drafts, and Valerie Marson, who expertly produced the final typescript.

Katherine Pyne – who subsequently, in 1996, became the technical historian at Aldermaston (the first such appointment) – made a very special and greatly valued contribution to the book during two arduous years of research.

Finally, many thanks to Alison Howson and Keith Povey of the publishers for their expert and kindly help in making this book a reality.

The author was given full access to official documents. She alone is responsible for the statements made and the views expressed.

Part I
Setting the Agenda

1
Stellar Forces

The scientific study of the sun and other stars – astrophysics – began some 80 years ago. In 1920 the great astronomer A. S. Eddington, addressing the British Association for the Advancement of Science, said:

A star is drawing on some vast reservoir of energy by means unknown to us. This reservoir can hardly be other than the subatomic energy which, it is known, exists independently in all matter. ... The store is well nigh inexhaustible, if only it could be tapped ... F. W. Aston's experiments seem to leave no doubt that all the elements are constituted out of hydrogen atoms (protons) bound together with negative electrons. But . . . the mass of the helium atom is less than the sum of the masses of the four hydrogen atoms which enter into it. There is a loss of mass in the synthesis amounting to about one part in 120. ... Now mass cannot be annihilated, and the deficit can only represent the electrical energy set free in the transmutation. We can therefore at once calculate the quantity of energy liberated when helium is made out of hydrogen. If five per cent of a star's mass consists initially of hydrogen atoms, which are gradually being combined to form more complex elements ... we need look no further for the source of a star's energy. ... If indeed the subatomic energy in the stars is being freely used to maintain their great furnaces, it seems to bring a little nearer to fulfilment our dream of controlling this latent power for the well-being of the human race or for its suicide.[1]

The idea of fusion was pursued by a young Russian physicist, Georgii Gamow, and by Robert Atkinson, an English astronomer, and Fritz Houtermans, a German physicist. They suggested that stellar energy was derived from the collision of atomic nuclei. Gamow thought that in the exceedingly high temperatures in the interior of stars, atomic nuclei – normally kept apart by mutual electrical repulsion – might occasionally collide

3

and fuse, releasing vast amounts of energy.[2] In 1929 Atkinson and Houtermans published a paper which many regard as the true beginning of thermonuclear research.[3]

In 1933 Gamow – exuberant, full of life and fond of practical jokes – left Russia for the United States. There, at George Washington University in Washington DC, he began pure thermonuclear research. He was soon joined by Edward Teller, a brilliant and ambitious young Hungarian refugee scientist with 'a smouldering passion for achievement in physics'.[4] They and their colleagues concluded that the most likely element for thermonuclear reactions was hydrogen, the lightest element and with the lowest electrical charge.

Experimental work began at the Cavendish in Cambridge in 1933 when Rutherford received a small amount of heavy water[5] from Gilbert Lewis in the United States. Working with Oliphant and Harteck, Rutherford managed to isolate and to fuse deuterium (heavy hydrogen) atoms, producing atoms of helium and releasing neutrons and energy. Tritium, a heavier isotope of hydrogen, was also produced, releasing protons and even more energy. The momentous implications were not yet apparent.[6]

The next big advance was in the United States, when Georgii Gamow, Edward Teller and another *émigré* scientist, Hans Bethe, began applying nuclear physics to questions of stellar evolution. They were concerned with nuclear reactions[7] between nuclei of hydrogen (H–H) and deuterium (D–D). Fusion of deuterium nuclei (deuterons) looked promising.

Then in 1937, in his last published paper, Rutherford noted the probability of another reaction (D–T) between deuterium and the tritium produced in the D–D reaction. This again was of immense but unforeseeable significance to thermonuclear weapon development.

During 1938, at Cornell University, Hans Bethe, 'a virtuoso in the field of mathematical physics',[8] investigated every conceivable nuclear reaction and identified those which generate energy in the sun and other stars. But no way was known to science of creating temperatures on earth comparable to those at the heart of the sun, until the discovery of uranium fission by Hahn and Strassmann in December 1938. This opened up possibilities of developing immensely powerful atomic (fission) bombs, which were to lead to the later development of vastly more powerful thermonuclear (fusion) bombs.

It was a stupendous thought that the explosion of an atomic bomb – if it could be achieved – might create, for a fraction of a millionth of a second, temperatures comparable to those at the centre of the sun. In these conditions light atoms could fuse and in doing so release colossal amounts of energy. In May 1941 Tokaturo Hagiwara,[9] a physicist at Kyoto University, postulated that a uranium-235 explosion could start a thermonuclear reaction between hydrogen atoms, but his idea had no practical consequences. A year later, in New York, Enrico Fermi, a brilliant *émigré* physicist from Rome, made a similar suggestion to his colleague at Columbia University, Edward Teller. Now that there seemed some prospect of an atomic bomb, Fermi said, it might be possible to use it to initiate the fusion of deuterium nuclei. Their conversation foreshadowed the advent of the H-bomb 10 years later.

2
The First Superbomb Project – the United States

Long before the first atomic bomb – or even the laboratory at Los Alamos – existed, some American scientists were already thinking about a superbomb a thousand times more powerful. In the summer of 1942 a group of theoretical physicists gathered at Berkeley;[1] they included Robert Oppenheimer, Hans Bethe, Robert Serber, Emil Konopinski, John H van Vleck and Edward Teller. They concluded that a much more powerful reaction than nuclear fission might be produced by a thermonuclear fusion of deuterium. Konopinski then made a suggestion, crucially significant later, that the ignition temperature could be lowered by adding tritium (a heavier and more reactive isotope of hydrogen). The T–D thermonuclear reaction, Bethe said, would release nearly five times as much energy as the D–D reaction. But tritium was very difficult and extremely costly to manufacture. This idea was not followed up immediately.

So, before Los Alamos was set up, fundamental understanding of the fast thermonuclear reaction had been reached, and when Los Alamos was established in 1943 under the leadership of the polymath physicist Robert Oppenheimer, its plans included a 'Super' research programme directed by Teller. When the Super programme was reviewed early in 1944,[2] it again appeared that igniting deuterium might be too difficult. If so, Konopinski's idea could be used: even a little tritium would have a dramatic effect. But production of tritium – by irradiating lithium in a reactor – would significantly reduce plutonium output. This, and outstanding theoretical problems, meant that developing the Super would take much longer than originally supposed. Meanwhile atomic bombs were wanted quickly and were more difficult than expected. Moreover the Super itself would totally depend on perfecting efficient atomic bombs. High priority for atomic bomb development was therefore both logical and unavoidable.

But work on the Super continued and in May 1944[3] experimental production of tritium was approved. John von Neumann suggested a device with a

D–T mixture inside the fissile material. He assumed that thermonuclear ignition of the D–T mixture would result from heating and compression in an atomic explosion; then fast neutrons released by the thermonuclear reaction would increase the number of fissions in the atomic bomb and enhance its yield. This idea foreshadowed the later development of boosted bombs.

After the war ended with the two atomic bombs on Hiroshima and Nagasaki, there was a great exodus of scientists from Los Alamos. Such luminaries as Oppenheimer, Bethe, Weisskopf, von Neumann and Teller all returned to their university careers. The future objectives and even the survival of Los Alamos were uncertain.[4] Some people thought that, with its wartime mission completed, it should be closed down, or preserved as a monument of man's inhumanity to man. But thanks to the vision and determination of Norris Bradbury, the new director of the laboratory, it survived with a renewed sense of purpose and direction.

The conference on the Super – April 1946

In April 1946 a conference at Los Alamos,[5] chaired by Teller, reviewed progress on the Super. Thirty-one scientists were present, including two members of the British mission who were still at Los Alamos. They were the Swiss-born Egon Bretscher (who had been making D–T calculations) and the German-born Klaus Fuchs, who was later (in 1950) arrested as a Soviet spy. Both were shortly to leave Los Alamos to become division heads at the new atomic research establishment at Harwell, near Oxford.

Fuchs was a versatile and original scientist, with extraordinary physical insight and great mathematical fluency. He had made important contributions especially in isotope separation and implosion. In early 1946 he was looking at the possibility of using a gun-type primary, boosted on the lines proposed by von Neumann, to improve the working of the Super.[6] He proposed to place the D–T mixture outside the uranium-235, in a radiation-heated tamper of beryllium oxide, where he calculated it would still be subject to heating and ionization implosion, so establishing conditions for its thermonuclear ignition. To confine the radiation within the tamper volume, he suggested enclosing the system inside a radiation-impervious case. Separation of the atomic charge and the thermonuclear fuel, and compression of the latter by radiation travelling from the former, clearly constitute radiation implosion. On 28 May 1946 Fuchs and von Neumann jointly filed a patent application.[7]

This remarkable design was the first physical scheme to use the radiation implosion principle, and was far ahead of its time. Mathematical modelling of the physical processes involved was not then sufficiently advanced to develop it further. It took five years for its enormous conceptual potential to be developed by Teller and Ulam.

To return to the April 1946 meeting: Teller and others described the super-bomb design – later called 'the classical Super' – that he and his group had developed. It was an idea rather than a design, and lacking in detail. The idea was to place some thermonuclear material – deuterium – next to a fission bomb, and to let it ignite after the uranium bomb had exploded, Ulam remembered,[8] but it was by no means easy to see how such an arrangement would ignite and not just splutter and fizzle out.

The question, was there a specific design that would work, was unanswered. Studies so far merely showed how difficult the problems were. The immense complexity and variety of the processes involved would demand extensive mathematical analysis – perhaps the hardest mathematical task ever undertaken – which might then be inconclusive. However, the scientists present at the conference believed that, after much work, a superbomb on these lines could be made.

Besides the need for better understanding of the basic physical processes, the requirements for material and engineering resources would be formidable, absorbing a considerable share of all the resources available for atomic energy work in the near future. Even a feasibility programme would compete for resources needed to improve and expand the small stockpile of A-bombs. A special reactor for tritium production, and other new facilities, would probably have to be built. So Bradbury recommended that Los Alamos should limit its thermonuclear work to theoretical studies and some laboratory experimentation; tritium should be requested only in small amounts for that purpose.

Much greater scientific effort was needed than for the first fission weapons, but by mid-1946 Los Alamos had lost many of its theoreticians and had only eight left. However, they were powerfully assisted by consultants, sometimes on brief visits, sometimes working at the laboratory for months at a time.[9] They included Bethe, Fermi, Gamow and Teller. From 1943 on, work at Los Alamos on thermonuclear weapons never stopped. Between 1946 and 1949, theoretical division effort under Carson Mark was about equally divided between A-bomb design, in which great advances were made, and thermonuclear work. By early 1947 thermonuclear studies had become focused on two concepts – the Super and *Alarm Clock*, an apparently simpler device suggested by Teller in August 1946, with alternate spherical layers of fissile and thermonuclear materials. A year later he proposed using a new thermonuclear fuel, lithium-6 deuteride. However, the problems seemed insurmountable. The Super and the *Alarm Clock* might be important one day, Bradbury thought, but for the present he was more concerned with improving and testing A-bombs for the stockpile.

In 1950 there was still no prospect of developing a practicable superbomb. Apparently it would require a major endeavour over some years. It might be as powerful as a megaton but no one yet knew how, even with a fission explosion, to obtain the temperatures and pressures necessary to start and sustain a thermonuclear reaction. Even if it *could* be done, could a superbomb be made small enough to carry in an aircraft? Perhaps it would have to be shipborne or delivered by railroad (or, said Oppenheimer, 'by ox-cart').[10]

The great American debate

The first Soviet A-bomb test was a rude shock. It was detected in September 1949 when radioactive debris was picked up by filters on United States aircraft making monitoring flights.[11] The American atomic monopoly was ended, far earlier than American politicians or the public had imagined. (Scientists who were more aware of Soviet scientific capabilities were less surprised.) The effect on political and public opinion in the United States was cataclysmic.

What should be the American response?[12] The Atomic Energy Commissioners consulted the General Advisory Committee. The GAC – set up, with the AEC, by the 1946 Atomic Energy Act – included the most eminent nuclear scientists, with Oppenheimer as chairman.

President Truman knew nothing about the superbomb, but when told about it he was immediately interested and wanted the issue to come up to the White House as quickly as possible.[13] Meanwhile, at Berkeley, E. O. Lawrence and two colleagues[14] agreed that the thermonuclear weapon would be the appropriate response to the Soviet test. Visiting Los Alamos early in October 1949 they found that the scientists there were still a long way from knowing if a thermonuclear reaction was possible, even further from knowing how to achieve it. The design of a weapon would have to await long and complicated calculations by Ulam, and then a thermonuclear experiment which Teller proposed for inclusion in a weapon test series in 1951.

Lawrence and his colleague Alvarez[15] made it their immediate mission to persuade the AEC to construct a reactor to produce tritium, since Teller believed large quantities would be needed. The AEC chairman, David Lilienthal, was uninterested, and disliked their ardour for such devastating weapons. But Alvarez and Teller, experienced lobbyists, talked to Senator Brien McMahon, the chairman of the powerful Joint Congressional Committee on Atomic Energy (JCAE). All three saw the threat of a Soviet H-bomb hanging by a thread over a defenceless America,[16] and they convinced the Joint Chiefs of Staff and the JCAE that 'we must have a Super and we must have it fast'. But the technical prospects for the Super were little better than they had been years before.

The GAC scientists were divided. Some opposed any all-out effort that would disrupt A-bomb development and Oppenheimer was not sure that the superbomb (which he called a miserable thing)[17] would work. But it had caught the imagination of the politicians and the military. The AEC commissioners – except for the enthusiastic Lewis Strauss – were doubtful about it, and were preoccupied with an atomic expansion programme just approved by the President.[18]

A special GAC meeting at the end of October[19] was to consider whether the Commission was 'doing things which might well be curtailed or stopped, and also what further things [it] ought to do to serve the paramount objective of the common defense and security'. Civil defence and expanded weapon production topped the agenda; as to the Super, the AEC wanted to know if the nation would use such a weapon if it could be built, and how it would compare to fission bombs in military value.

The GAC met on 28, 29 and 30 October.[20] Bethe confined his comments to technical feasibility; convinced that after a war with such weapons the world would not be worth preserving even for the victors, he had decided not to take part in the Super project. Robert Serber was sure that the Super would not work. The GAC report was unable to endorse a high priority for the Super. The fundamental studies were not complete; until they were, the AEC could not begin to consider the formidable engineering problems. The outcome was unpredictable, but an 'imaginative and concerted attack on the problem [had] a better than even chance of producing the weapon within five years'.[21] However, the GAC was unanimous in hoping that its development could be avoided since its virtually unlimited potential would make possible a policy of exterminating civilian populations. Oppenheimer and four other members called it a weapon of genocide and advised its complete and unconditional renunciation. Fermi and Rabi said it was 'necessarily an evil thing in any light',[22] and thought the United States should invite the nations of the world to join in a pledge renouncing it.

The AEC chairman, David Lilienthal, was pleased by the GAC report[23] but realised that the JCAE was determined to have the Super. Its chairman, Senator McMahon, saw war with the Soviet Union as inevitable and the Super as the only defence. The views of AEC commissioners differed.[24] One thought the military value of the Super was doubtful even if the Soviet Union developed it too; it would be better to reopen discussions of international control. One suggested that the President should tell the Kremlin through secret diplomatic channels that the United States did not want to develop the Super if there was any hope of international control and the elimination of weapons of mass destruction. Another believed that a policy of 'announce and renounce' would not impress the Soviets. (In retrospect, it appears that he was right.)[25] Strauss said it was inconsistent to develop more powerful fission weapons but reject the Super. Lilienthal reported to President Truman on 9 November, giving the views of the commissioners, and appending the full report of the GAC.

In early November Teller arrived in Washington to see McMahon, who told him about the GAC report (which, he said, made him sick).[26] A group from the JCAE[27] had recently visited Los Alamos and was fired with enthusiasm for the Super. Several scientists were also missionaries for the project, but opinion among the scientists was very diverse. Some believed that Teller's enthusiasm was running counter to his scientific judgement.[28] Ulam observed 'weird and unnatural things going on in Washington',[29] and thought that some opposition to the Super might even be due to Teller's passionate advocacy.

McMahon[30] wrote a long letter to the President about the decision to be made on the Super. 'If we let the Russians get the Super first', he said, 'catastrophe becomes all but certain'. He admitted the horror of the weapon but believed it might save the country from enemy attack, and could well be decisive against tactical targets as well as population centres. He could see no moral dividing line between a big explosion causing heavy damage and many smaller explosions causing equal or greater damage.

Various studies began. The Joint Chiefs of Staff thought it essential to determine the feasibility of a Super.[31] It might act as a deterrent to war. A Soviet monopoly of the Super would be intolerable, and the advantages of developing it decisively outweighed the possible social, psychological and moral objections.

An AEC study estimated that the costs would be heavy.[32] New reactors to produce the required tritium might cost $150 million, and a heavy water plant for deuterium production at least $8 million. It questioned the military value of the Super; were there enough targets for such destructive weapons? In early December 1949 Oppenheimer told the AEC[33] that, after reconsidering their October report, none of the GAC members wished to change his views. Their arguments included the dubious diplomatic and military value of the Super, the danger that American atmospheric tests actually might assist Soviet development, the diversion of valuable resources, and the undermining of the nation's moral values.

Security leaks had begun to open the subject up as a public issue.[34] On 1 November 1949 a Senator had mentioned it on television; an article appeared in the *Washington Post* on 18 November. On 15 January 1950 an influential radio commentator, Drew Pearson, said that the question of the Super had engrossed the capital. On 17 January a well-informed account by the noted journalist James Reston appeared in the *New York Times*. The newspaper reported a speech by the Nobel laureate, Harold Urey, the discoverer of heavy water, who backed the 'E. O. Lawrence – Strauss' position.[35]

By late January 1950 the President had not yet made a decision. The tide of public opinion was running in the Super's favour.[36]

Then in England, with fatal timing, on 27 January 1950 Klaus Fuchs confessed to espionage activities between 1942 and 1949 and was arrested. The

GAC held a special meeting on 30 January[37] to assess what he knew and what he could have passed on to the USSR, and concluded that it could have been a great deal.

The President decides

Meanwhile President Truman had asked a special committee of the National Security Council (the NSC)[38] to evaluate the Super in political and military terms as well as technical. At the NSC committee meeting the Fuchs affair was 'in the back of everyone's minds, but not dominant'. Truman met the three members – Secretary of State Acheson, Secretary of Defense Johnson, and Lilienthal, the outgoing AEC chairman – on 31 January 1950. Lilienthal, in the minority, advised an enquiry into the basic question: what was the best way to further common defence and security? The AEC had no information to support the weapons requirement that the military and the JCAE now recommended. Lilienthal considered complete reliance on weapons of mass destruction as an instrument of foreign policy to be a fundamental weakness in the nation's position.

The President argued that, though no one wanted to use it, the United States had to have the H-bomb, if only for bargaining purposes with the USSR. He was already beginning to build up a large and threatening nuclear arsenal that no President intended to use except for political leverage. Later that day, 31 January 1950, he announced his decision to proceed with the development of the H-bomb in the following terms:

> It is part of my responsibility as Commander-in-Chief of the Armed Forces to see to it that our country is able to defend itself against any possible aggressor. Accordingly I have directed the Atomic Energy Commission to continue its work on all forms of atomic weapons, including the so-called hydrogen or superbomb. Like all other work in the field of atomic weapons, it is being and will be carried forward on a basis consistent with the overall objectives of our program for peace and security.[39]

The debate was over and the programme gathered momentum. Anyone hearing Brien McMahon's rousing speech to the Senate on 2 February 1950 – the day that Fuchs was arrested in England – would have understood the H-bomb to be a piece of hardware almost ready for production. In reality it was still a highly theoretical concept, based on very few hard data, and the most knowledgeable scientists on the GAC were extremely sceptical about it. But the determined advocacy of Teller and Lawrence, and Teller's immense self-confidence, had convinced the politicians and the military that, but for an obstructive GAC and an over-cautious Los Alamos, a new weapon of unlimited potential was theirs for the asking. As Bethe wrote later, Teller led Los Alamos, and the country, into an adventurous programme on the basis of calculations which he must have known were very incomplete.[40]

The Super

Teller's Super was basically a tank or pipe full of liquid deuterium (deuterium is a gas at normal temperatures) with an atomic bomb at one end.[41] This bomb would be a large, powerful uranium gun (not an implosion device) with an unheard-of yield, several hundred kilotons. Some tritium would have to be added to the deuterium at the atom bomb end of the pipe since, it was generally agreed, a propagating reaction in deuterium alone would be impossible at the temperatures achievable. A flood of neutrons from the atomic bomb explosion would initiate the thermonuclear reactions. The whole assembly might yield 40 megatons but the yield was theoretically unlimited. If it worked, however, it would be so heavy and cumbersome that it was difficult to imagine how it could be made into a deliverable weapon. The more modest design, *Alarm Clock*,[42] had a layer of lithium deuteride placed round the fissile core of an atomic bomb to boost the yield, and little or no tritium would be needed. This idea was similar to the Soviet 'layer cake' model (see Chapter 3).

The outlook was hardly promising but worse was to come in June 1950.[43] The mathematician Stanislaw Ulam and his colleague C. J. Everett, using slide rules and desk calculators, completed a lengthy mathematical calculation of the initial progress of a thermonuclear reaction in a mass of deuterium or deuterium–tritium mixture. They studied the multiplicative (or branching) processes in steps of 10^{-8} sec (hundredths of millions of a second) and cross-sections of 10^{-24} cm^2. Their work was finished months before the results began coming in from von Neumann's new Princeton computer (MANIAC) and the duplicate version being built at Los Alamos by Nicholas Metropolis.

Ulam and Everett established that, to ignite a tank of liquid deuterium with heat from an atomic bomb, unrealistic quantities of tritium would be needed. Bitterly disappointed and pale with fury, Teller (Ulam said)[44] shed tears of frustration. But Ulam's and Everett's results were soon supported by the MANIAC results. Ulam began another series of calculations with Fermi on the propagation of thermonuclear reactions.[45] Together they produced a report which was to prove basic to the technology of thermonuclear explosions. Meantime, though things looked bad for the Super, even if modified, Teller continued to be very active politically and was pressing for a second weapons laboratory.

Testing times

Work was going forward at Los Alamos for a new weapon test series, *Greenhouse*, in the spring of 1951.[46] One shot, code-named *Item*, was called the Booster because it was a fission bomb with small amounts of gaseous deuterium and tritium added to the core to boost the yield. Another shot, code-named *George*, was the Cylinder – a device thought up by Teller, based in fact on the design that Fuchs and von Neumann had patented four years earlier. The Cylinder was described as an experiment in which a nuclear explosion would send material down a tube and cause a small thermonuclear reaction in deuterium; it would use the energy of a 500-kiloton atomic bomb to ignite a reaction in an ounce of deuterium and tritium placed in a small adjoining chamber. It was sure to work; 'using a huge atomic bomb to ignite a little vial of deuterium and tritium was like using a blast furnace to light a match'.[47] The basic goal of the Super programme was, of course, to use a relatively small amount of fission fuel to ignite a relatively large mass of thermonuclear fuel. But as yet no one had made a 500-kiloton bomb. Teller's thoughts about the configuration of the Cylinder turned out later to be very important.[48] How to convey energy from an exploding fission bomb to ignite D–T *outside* the bomb? He realised that the explosion's main product is electromagnetic radiation, especially X-rays, which move much faster than neutrons or hydrodynamic shock. These X-rays could transport energy through a radiation channel to a capsule of D–T in an adjoining chamber, where the thermonuclear reactions could be observed.

Towards the end of 1950, despite all the effort at Los Alamos, prospects for a hydrogen bomb were still poor. GAC meetings in September and October 1950[49] noted that little progress had been made, in marked contrast to the striking advances in fission weapons. Teller could offer nothing but a desperate determination. It looked as if Los Alamos might be squandering talent, time and resources on a fruitless enterprise. However a dramatic change was imminent.

'It will change the course of history'

In December 1950 Ulam thought of a way to increase implosion compression by orders of magnitude beyond what could be achieved by high explosives.[50] He proposed using the shock wave and neutron flux from an atomic bomb to implode another atomic bomb. A fission bomb explosion, he said, produces a neutron gas, together with other fission fragment nuclei, at densities comparable to ordinary solids. To use fission for compression would require staging; one bomb (a 'primary') would set off a 'secondary', and in theory any number of assemblies in succession. (But this was not a new idea, and whether Ulam knew it or not, it had been around for at least three years.) Ulam soon saw how to use this 'iterative scheme', to implode a secondary containing thermonuclear fuel. 'It is a totally different scheme', he told his wife Françoise, 'and it will change the course of history.'[51] She was appalled.

He went to see Carson Mark, then Norris Bradbury, and next day Edward Teller. Though not convinced at once, Teller soon became enthusiastic. He produced a brilliant adaptation of Ulam's concept – to use radiation rather than neutrons or material shock to implode the secondary.[52] As Carson Mark commented later, 'The fact that Edward thought of radiation was natural because he had been involved in much more detailed work on the *George* shot than had Ulam.'[53] (But Teller knew about the 1946 Fuchs-von Neumann patent and, when Fuchs was arrested, was very anxious – as was Bethe – lest he had given it to the USSR.)[54] In Mark's opinion, planning the *Greenhouse* experiments led Teller to the idea of radiation implosion. Intensive work with colleagues followed and on 9 March a joint report on work done by Teller and Ulam was issued,[55] describing staging and emphasising high compression. The third breakthrough idea – incorporating a fissile component in the secondary – seems to have originated also with Teller and a young colleague de Hoffmann.[56]

The credit for the American H-bomb has been much debated. Teller was apparently reluctant to share the credit for the historic invention on which he had been working single-mindedly for so many years, but he did later describe the achievement as the work of many people.[57] His relationship with Ulam was, however, difficult.

The *Greenhouse* tests took place successfully in May 1951. Teller was there at Eniwetok, so were E. O. Lawrence, Gordon Dean (the AEC chairman) and Herbert York. The *George* shot on 8 May was the largest fission explosion to date – 225 kilotons – and it ignited 'the first small thermonuclear flame ever to burn on earth'.[58]

Turning point at Princeton

The new design ideas and supporting calculations were submitted in June 1951 to a conference at the Princeton Institute for Advanced Study.[59] The AEC commissioners and members of the GAC were there, and other scientists including Bethe, von Neumann and senior Los Alamos staff. Teller presented the new design with passionate eloquence. At the end of two days everyone was convinced that for the first time there was something feasible in the way of an idea, removing the scientific and technical objections to the Super which the GAC had quite properly raised in late 1949. The ethical objections made then were not now mentioned. The proposed weapon no longer seemed to be 'an evil thing', but 'technically sweet', in Oppenheimer's words. 'I cannot very well imagine', he said, 'if we had known in late 1949 what we got to know by early 1951 that the tone of our report would have been the same.'

The weekend Princeton conference of June 1951 marked a turning point in the thermonuclear quest. The *Greenhouse* shot provided much needed experimental data, and was to fulfil the role of a pilot plant in thermonuclear development. Bradbury reported confidently on prospects for the new Super, the materials required, possible yields, and plans for testing in the 1952 *Ivy* series.

Mike

There was much to be done at Los Alamos and by industry to turn the Teller–Ulam design into a test device. Teller offered to stay at Los Alamos to take responsibility for thermonuclear development, but Bradbury was unwilling to put this erratic star in charge, fearing to lose many of his division heads. The man appointed to direct the programme was Marshall Holloway, a first-rate experimental physicist and head of weapon development at Los Alamos.[60] Teller refused alternative offers at Los Alamos and decided to quit.

Holloway and his team, and Carson Mark and his theoretical division, were brilliantly successful in designing and building the test device for *Ivy Mike*.[61] Holloway's Theoretical Megaton Group first met on 5 October 1951, two days after *Joe 2*, the second Soviet A-bomb test, had been detected, and two weeks before the third Soviet test (*Joe 3*). Holloway's team decided that *Mike's* thermonuclear fuel should be liquid deuterium, not solid lithium deuteride, because the thermonuclear burning process is much easier to study in pure deuterium – also apparently because adequate supplies of lithium deuteride were not yet available. The disadvantage was that deuterium, a gas at normal temperatures, requires a cryogenic apparatus to keep it in the liquid state. Lithium deuteride is much easier to handle, and produces tritium and deuterium *in situ*, within the bomb, when required.

The target date for the *Mike* test was late October 1952, though Teller had urged July. But – apart from the immense amount of work to be done in 'imagining abstract concepts into physical reality',[62] for which a year was hardly enough – summer brought monsoons to the Marshall Islands.

Clearly, the test gadget would be huge.[63] A primary of sufficient yield would be almost four feet in diameter. The secondary was to be a double-walled bottle like a giant thermos flask (called a 'dewar') containing liquid deuterium with a plutonium component inside it. The whole assembly would be in a big steel cylinder with thick walls. The steel casing would be lined with material which would absorb the flood of X-rays and would be ionised to a hot plasma, which would exert pressure to implode the secondary and start the thermonuclear process.

Holloway adopted a technique (long known to shipwrights and marine engineers as 'lofting'),[64] using a giant draughtsman's board made of plywood sheets on the floor of a large building. The full-scale drawing was too big to be seen at ground level and a viewing balcony was built. Meanwhile arrangements were being made with the industrial firms that would make the components. The basic design was frozen in mid-January 1952 but by March it had to be unfrozen for major redesign, and it was completed only just in time to meet the test date of 1 November. Co-ordinating the work of production[65] – of liquid deuterium, dewar flasks, bomb casings, uranium castings, pumps, and so on – meant constant travel across the continent from Albuquerque to Buffalo and Boston. Components were being shipped all over the country; some never came to Los Alamos but went directly overseas. *Mike* was never put together in the United States. A full-scale mock-up, assembled in July 1952 in Buffalo, was used for training and rehearsals.

The final device consisted of a tapered steel cylinder, lined with lead, with an inner polythene lining. At one end was the fission bomb; at the other was suspended the deuterium dewar, surrounded by a heavy uranium-238 tamper. Inside the deuterium dewar was a cylindrical plutonium device, enclosing a chamber into which a few grams of tritium gas could be fed. The huge gadget was expected to have a total yield of 1 to 10 megatons; the most likely being 5 megatons – equal to all the explosives used during World War II.

There were some political doubts[66] about carrying out the test only three days before the presidential election, and some people thought that it should be postponed, to seek an agreement with the USSR to end testing. However President Truman, who was not seeking re-election, would not change the date, unless technical reasons required. But they did not, and presidential approval was given on 29 October 1952 for the *Mike* shot on 31 October/ 1 November.

Mike was a surface shot. The device, 20 feet tall and weighing 62 tons, was housed in a large steel frame structure, erected on a small coral island called Elugelab. An elaborate array of instruments was set up to measure the performance of the device. Shortly before the target date one of the physicists, Marshall Rosenbluth, had misgivings about the fission primary, thinking it might pre-detonate, and he suggested changing the core.[67] A new core arrived by cargo plane with a few days to spare. Rosenbluth may well have saved *Mike* from failure.

It was fired on 1 November 1952 at 7.15 am (local time).[68] A huge fire-ball developed, expanding into a mushroom cloud more than 100 miles wide. The coral island was vaporized leaving a circular crater 200 feet deep. Fourteen miles away trees and brush were scorched; sick sea birds were grounded, many with scorched feathers. The yield was 10.4 megatons. More than 75 per cent came from the big uranium-238 tamper, fissioned by very fast (14 Mev) neutrons. It was perhaps less a thermonuclear bomb than a very big and dirty boosted fission bomb, but the principles of the new Super had been proved.

The ideas conceived by Ulam, improved by Teller and de Hoffman, and brought to reality by Carson Mark and Marshall Holloway and their teams, had become a landmark in history.

The second shot in the *Ivy* series, *King*,[69] was a pure fission bomb with a yield in the megaton range, 500 kilotons. A fallback device in case of the thermonuclear design failed, it seems odd that it was fired after the success of *Mike*. True, the huge and cumbersome *Mike*, with all its cryogenic apparatus, was a scientific experiment rather than a practicable bomb; nevertheless it was weaponized and taken into service as an emergency weapon for a short period.

The *Castle* test series

In October 1952 preparations began at Bikini Atoll for the next American thermonuclear weapon tests, the *Castle* shots, beginning in March 1954.[70] This series was intended to develop deliverable weapons besides furnishing important scientific information. Seven shots were planned but actually six were fired, between 1 March and 13 May. All were two-stage devices using solid thermonuclear fuel, lithium deuteride, and all were practicable weapon designs. Two (*Bravo* and *Koon*) were surface bursts, and four (*Romeo*, *Union*, *Yankee* and *Nectar*) were fired on barges. *Koon* was a failure, yielding only 110 kilotons. The others were all big, ranging from 1.69 megatons to 15 megatons; the first, *Bravo*, was the largest and it was very important politically.

The *Castle* series was a challenge for the weathermen.[71] The scientists intended that debris from the *Castle* shots should move in a north-east direction, avoiding Eniwetok to the west or the Marshall Islands to the east, but emergency evacuation plans were drawn up and a large exclusion zone or danger area was defined. The *Bravo* device – the *Shrimp*[72] – was a cylinder weighing 23,500 pounds, much smaller than the 62-ton *Mike*. It was mounted horizontally, 17 feet above sea level, on a reef at the atoll's north-west perimeter. The expected yield was 5 to 6 megatons. On 27 February the weather conditions were near perfect and deteriorated only slightly by dawn on 1 March.[73] It was decided to fire on schedule and countdown began at 6.45 am. The fireball rose to about 45,000 feet in one minute, sucking up pulverised coral from the crater into the huge cloud, whose top reached almost 114,000 feet in about four minutes.

It was obvious at once that the yield was much greater than predicted – actually 15 megatons, the biggest test explosion that the Americans ever carried out.[74] The reason for the miscalculation was that the weaponeers at Los Alamos had considered only the lithium-6 content and ignored an important fusion reaction in the lithium-7 which makes up 60 per cent of the total lithium. They sent a last minute warning when they realised the error, but it reached the trials staff at Eniwetok too late. The fall-out was severe. Very high radiation levels were recorded, and the maximum permissible exposure standards had to be relaxed for key personnel such as helicopter pilots, flight deck staff and boat pool operators. The widespread devastation and heavy fall- out made Bikini all but uninhabitable. People were affected by fall-out well outside the expected limits and 'horrible white stuff' rained for several hours on a task force ship 30 miles away.

By 8.00 am sailors on board the task force ships noticed ash falling from the sky. All hands were ordered below decks and pre-arranged washing down procedures began. Fall-out was heavy too on the Marshall Islands, Rongerik, Rongelap, Ailinginae and Utirik. Twenty-eight American personnel were evacuated from a weather station at Rongerik on 2 March but the 64 native islanders could not be rescued until the day after. By 5 March American ships had picked up 236 natives from these islands and taken them to hospitals in Kwajalein; they had incurred exposures of 14 to 175 r, and nearly all suffered from radiation burns, hair loss and lowered blood counts, but none died.[75] The servicemen had received much lower doses, and after medical examinations at the army hospital in Honolulu they returned to duty.

The *Lucky Dragon*

More unfortunate was the crew of a Japanese boat, the *Lucky Dragon*.[76] It was fishing about 85 miles east of Bikini, outside the declared danger zone – of which the captain was fully aware – and outside the predicted fall-out pattern. A fisherman on deck was startled to see a dazzling light in the west; his shipmates feared it was a 'pika-don' – an atomic explosion. Within a few minutes they felt the shock wave, but saw no mushroom cloud. Then about two hours later a light rain began to fall, and silvery flakes of ash which they brushed off. Their tuna catch was disappointing and at the end of the day they hosed down the ship and turned home, unaware of the radiation exposures they had received.

The AEC issued a brief announcement about the detonation of an atomic device on 1 March, but information began to leak out and it soon became impossible to keep *Bravo* secret. It was announced that 28 Americans and 236 Marshallese had been exposed to radiation during a routine atomic test but all were reported well.

When the *Lucky Dragon* reached Japan nearly all 23 of the crew were sick, with classic symptoms of radiation sickness. Their contaminated tuna catch was destroyed by the Japanese authorities. Newspapers carried huge headlines, violent anti-American protests erupted and the Japanese government demanded a formal inquiry.

The alarm quickly spread to the United States where *Bravo* and the *Lucky Dragon* became front page news. The chairman of the JCAE, Sterling Cole, announced a congressional investigation of *Bravo*, and the subject reached White House level at a press conference on 24 March. President Eisenhower promised reporters a full explanation as soon as Lewis Strauss – now AEC chairman and special adviser to the President on atomic energy matters – got back from the Pacific. He returned to Washington after the second test, *Romeo*, on 26 March, and read a reassuring statement at the President's news conference[77] on 31 March, about the Marshallese, the servicemen, and the Japanese fisherman (who, he said, would quickly recover from the effects of their alleged 'inadvertent trespass'). He emphasized the enormous military benefits of the test to the United States. Then a journalist asked him how large and powerful an H-bomb might be. He replied that 'in effect it can be made as large as you wish, as large as the military requirement demands, that is to say, an H-bomb can be made as – large enough to take out a city'. 'How big a city?' he was asked. 'Any city? New York?' 'The metropolitan area, yes', he answered. His answer had an electrifying effect.

Next day the *New York Times* headline read 'H-bomb can wipe out any city'. Fall-out, and its victims in the Pacific, disappeared from the nation's front pages, replaced by terrifying pictures of single H-bombs destroying great cities. The horrors of the hydrogen bomb were suddenly revealed, and a fierce public debate broke out. There were protests against the H-bomb, the continuation of testing, and the secrecy in which nuclear decisions were made; there were counter-arguments based on intense fears of Communism and Soviet aggression. Abroad, protests about American tests were even stronger – in Japan, India, and Europe.[78] Concern about thermonuclear weapons was powerfully voiced by Prime Minister Nehru of India; by Albert Schweitzer, the revered philosopher, doctor, and musician; and by Pope Pius XII,[79] who, in his 1954 Easter message to the world, called for efforts to banish nuclear war. The debate was especially vigorous in Britain.

The JCAE chairman, Sterling Cole, wrote to President Eisenhower on 5 April:[80] 'The American people, and more particularly people throughout the world, have been struck with terror by the horrible implications of nuclear weapon development – and I think with much justification'. However the President, in a broadcast to the nation, told his audience that hydrogen bombs were not a great threat to them. At a press conference next day, asked if the United States planned to build bigger and bigger H-bombs, he replied that he knew no military requirement for a bigger bomb than had already been produced. Whatever the USSR might do there was, he said, no advantage in building bombs beyond a certain yield.[81]

Bravo had aroused a world-wide movement[82] of public opinion that, as we shall see, was to have a powerful effect on the nuclear weapons programmes of the superpowers and Britain and would lead eventually to the test moratorium of 1958 and the Partial Test Ban Treaty of 1963.

The American programme continues

After *Bravo*, operational plans for the remaining *Castle* shots had to be extensively modified. Stringent meteorological criteria were adopted, and the exclusion zone was extended. *Romeo* and some later shots had to be postponed because of unfavourable weather conditions.[83]

With *Castle* completed, the United States had a repertoire of practical designs for thermonuclear bombs,[84] and subsequent tests in the Pacific were mainly to improve them and to obtain additional information on effects. The *Redwing*[85] series, consisting of 17 detonations between May and July 1956, included three thermonuclear shots – *Cherokee* (21 May), *Zuni* (28 May) and *Tewa* (21 July). The last two were a surface and a barge burst respectively; *Cherokee* was dropped from a B-52 bomber. This was the first American airdrop of a thermonuclear weapon, seven months after the first Soviet thermonuclear airdrop (see chapter 3). *Cherokee* was a successful shot but, disappointingly, four miles off target. The fall-out from *Zuni*, a surface explosion, was the most thoroughly documented in all the weapon tests in the Pacific from 1946 to 1962. *Tewa* was also important for fall-out documentation; the fall-out material included 410,000 pounds of steel in the structure of the barge as well as the coral reef material created by the explosion. (As the British weapon tests always – except for one 1.5 kiloton ground burst – used tower or balloon shots or airdrops to minimise fall-out, there is something strange to British eyes in these high-yield surface bursts, and especially those designed apparently as fall-out experiments for purposes of investigation.)

After *Bravo*, the Joint Chiefs of Staff, keenly aware of the global fall-out problem, had asked for a continuing study of the subject. The greatest uncertainty related not to the local fall-out of relatively large solid particles, but to the fission products in the stratospheric reservoir – their quantity and the rate and mode of their transfer to the biosphere. This led to a high-altitude sampling programme using the U-2 aircraft, capable of flying at 70,000 feet (then recently developed for intelligence-gathering flights over the Soviet Union).

The last American series containing megaton tests before the 1958–61 test moratorium was *Hardtack* I,[86] from April to August 1958. The whole series consisted of 34 shots of which eight were megaton shots.

American development of a practical thermonuclear weapon was essentially complete by the end of the *Castle* series; eight years after the 'classical Super' conference of April 1946, just over four years after the President's directive, less than three years after the Princeton meeting in June 1951, and 18 months after *Mike* in November 1952. Once the massive stumbling block of the classical Super was removed, progress had been extremely rapid.

The American H-bomb has been discussed in some detail for several reasons. It was the first in the world, and an epoch-making step into the unknown, representing a thousand-fold advance in the power of weapons of mass destruction. It showed that such weapons could be made – if by the Americans, then no doubt by other industrialized nations. The problems that they met and the solutions they found prefigured the problems that the Soviet and British weaponeers were to face and solve independently. (The information in the previous pages was not, of course, available to them – or only to a limited extent, as we shall see.)

Finally, the American H-bomb set a new international agenda. The Soviet Union was aware very early – before Hiroshima – that thermonuclear work was going on in the United States, and reacted quickly (see Chapter 3).

3
The Second Superbomb Project – the Soviet Union

Beginnings

In late 1945 the Russian physicist Y. I. Frenkel[1] wrote to Igor Kurchatov – who was in charge of Soviet atomic research – about the theoretical possibility of a thermonuclear weapon, using a fission bomb to initiate the fusion of light nuclei. But Kurchatov already knew about work on these lines being done in the United States, from huge quantities of intelligence material that began to reach the Soviet Union in 1945 and 1946. (By the end of the war thousands of pages of reports were already awaiting evaluation in Moscow.)[2]

In November 1945, when the world-renowned nuclear physicist Niels Bohr had returned from the United States to Denmark, a Soviet agent named Terletsky was sent to Copenhagen by Beria (head of the Soviet secret police and in overall charge of all Soviet atomic activities) to interview him.[3] But the agent, a competent scientist from Moscow University, who was briefed by experts, could not get any secrets from Bohr, only information that had already been published. As for the superbomb, Bohr considered it either unreal, or else possible but irrational given the huge destructive power of existing atomic bombs.

In September 1946 the first information came in[4] on a possible device on 'classical Super' lines, featuring a gun-type uranium-235 bomb, an intermediate chamber containing a mixture of deuterium and tritium, and a cylinder of liquid deuterium. The document explained the effect of adding tritium to lower the ignition temperature and gave approximate D–T cross sections. Another paper described another device; a double bomb, not using thermonuclear materials, in which the explosion of a fission primary would implode and detonate a secondary sphere of plutonium. (Chapter 2 mentions this idea, never actually used by the Americans but highly significant because of the part it was to play in Ulam's thinking about a two-stage thermonuclear design in 1951.)

Though the A-bomb had to be given a high priority, news of American thermonuclear thinking prompted the Soviet Union to action. In late 1946 Kurchatov directed four scientists – Gurevich, Khariton, Pomeranchuk and Zel'dovich – to study the possibility of releasing energy from the fusion of light elements. They produced a report by December 1946[5] on 'Utilization of the nuclear energy of light elements'. It proposed deuterium as the thermonuclear fuel and noted that the reaction would proceed 'only at very high temperatures of the entire mass'. A small group was set up under Zel'dovich at the Institute of Chemical Physics in Moscow to continue this work and to check on the relevant intelligence material arriving from the West. Some came from Klaus Fuchs, but he was not the only source. One Russian source says that at least ten British spies – apart from the American spies – supplied the Soviet Union with nuclear secrets,[6] most presumably related to atomic, not thermonuclear, bombs. (In 1949, after the first Soviet test, the supply dried up.)

What Fuchs told the Russians about the H-bomb – some American scientists argued after his arrest – cannot have helped them because, up to the time he left Los Alamos in June 1946, 'every important part of the American thermonuclear program had been wrong. If the Russians started a thermonuclear program on the basis of the information received from Fuchs, it must have led to the same failure.'[7] Teller, on the other hand, argued that Fuchs' information might have given the Soviet Union a head start, especially as he feared that he might have disclosed the central principle of radiation implosion. (He had done so, though he did not admit it to the FBI in 1950.) Teller said later[8] that it was a miracle, not that the Americans solved the H-bomb problem in 1951 but rather that – given the ideas already available in 1946 – they had failed to solve it sooner, so his fear that the Russian scientists might be ahead was understandable.

However, though initial Soviet interest in thermonuclear weapons was triggered by intelligence information from the West, Fuchs' reports on the early American ideas did not lead the Soviet scientists to a workable design. Nevertheless they were valuable. Back in England and heading the theoretical physics division at Harwell, he met Feklisov, a Soviet intelligence agent, on two occasions, in September 1947 and March 1948. On 28 September Fuchs gave oral information about the classical Super studies in the United States, the characteristics and operating principles of the Super and the use of deuterium and tritium. He did not know if any practical work on its construction had begun, but said that Fermi and Teller had proved the 'workability' of such a bomb. The following month an intelligence report from the United States mentioned the use of lithium as a thermonuclear fuel; the Zel'dovich group reported shortly after on the possibility of achieving a detonation in deuterium using lithium-7 deuteride.[9]

Fuchs met Feklisov again on 13 March 1948, 'an event ... that played an exceptional role in the subsequent course of the Soviet thermonuclear program', in the judgement of German Goncharov, who has worked at Arzamas–16 since the 1950s and now heads the theoretical department there.[10] Fuchs

> handed over materials of paramount importance. Included in the documents was new theoretical information pertinent to the superbomb ... a detailed description of the classical Super project with the new initiation system developed since the 1945 project – the two-stage configuration operating on the radiation implosion principle ... A gun-type ^{235}U bomb with a beryllium oxide tamper was used as the primary atomic bomb. The secondary unit of the initiation was a heavy liquid D–T mixture with a high concentration of T. A heavy jacket of opaque radiation-impervious material confined radiation within the cylindrical chamber containing the primary and secondary units. This initiator was joined to a long cylinder containing liquid D for most of its length but with a liquid D–T mixture (with a small concentration of T) in its first section ... The document presented experimental and theoretical data substantiating the project's workability ... [and] included the D–T and ^{3}He-D reaction cross sections.

The information was probably consistent, by and large, with information set forth in the Fuchs–von Neumann patent of 1946. On 20 April 1948 a Russian translation of this material was forwarded to Beria, Molotov and Stalin himself.

This is the view expressed by an expert weapon scientist with unrivalled access to super-secret archives. In the last four or five years, as more information has been released in the former Soviet Union, a war of words has broken out over the role of intelligence in the development of nuclear, including thermonuclear, weapons.[11] Some of the scientists thought that self-justifying members of the secret services were spreading 'myths and legends', exaggerating the part played by the intelligence community. On the other hand it was argued that the scientists wanted to minimise the intelligence contribution because it seemed to detract from the brilliance and originality of their own independent achievements, of which they were justifiably so proud. In the battle of the two elites Goncharov does not take sides. Scientists who took part in the early Soviet programme may say in all honesty that they did not benefit from foreign intelligence, but they may have done so unknowingly. Intelligence material was very closely controlled, and would be distributed to only one or two people, 'who then appeared as geniuses to their subordinates, because they always made the right guesses'.[12] If Fuchs' information was of such value to Soviet scientists, how much did he also give to the British and how important was it?

The Soviet programme is launched

Translations given to Stalin, Molotov and Beria in April 1948 were direct evidence of possible major advances by the Americans, which demanded decisive action. Vannikov,[13] Kurchatov and Khariton were asked to make recommendations and the Council of Ministers of the USSR approved their proposals in June 1948. Kurchatov's laboratory Arzamas-16 at Sarov, 400 kilometres east of Moscow, was to do theoretical and experimental work on advanced atomic bombs and a hydrogen bomb (code-named RDS 6). Khariton was in charge of the RDS 6 group. Only one scientist there, Zel'dovich, was allowed access to the 1948 intelligence material; only Zel'dovich and one other could see even the 1945 material.[14]

A special theoretical group was also set up at the Physics Institute in Moscow under Igor Tamm, an internationally famous scientist and 1958 Nobel laureate. He recruited several young physicists including Andrei Sakharov, Vitalii Ginzburg and Yuri Romanov. Sakharov had previously declined to join the atomic project, but now joined Tamm's group, because he thought the work so interesting and because he had 'no doubts as to the vital importance of creating a Soviet superweapon for [the] country and for the balance of power throughout the world'.[15]

The first and second ideas

In September and October 1948 Sakharov was studying calculations by the Zel'dovich group on liquid deuterium, possibly mixed with tritium, as the thermonuclear explosive. Sakharov thought of an alternative (his 'First Idea') which he called a 'layer cake'.[16] The idea was to place alternate layers of thermonuclear material – deuterium, tritium and their chemical compounds – and uranium-238 inside a fission bomb, in between the fissile core and the high explosive charge. It was very like Teller's *Alarm Clock* – an independent reinvention of it. Its great virtue was that there was no doubt it would work, only just how well it would work. Then in November 1948 Ginzburg suggested the 'Second Idea'[17] – using lithium deuteride in the fusion layer, instead of deuterium and tritium. This, as we have already seen, would have great advantages. The inspiration may have come from the United States; a recent book on atomic espionage[18] attributes it to the American agent Theodore Hall.

The Soviet scientists, unlike their American counterparts at this time, now had a feasible design for a thermonuclear device. It was not a two-stage bomb, nor was it a bomb of virtually unlimited potential, such as Teller dreamed of. But it was a practical device which Sakharov estimated might well yield a megaton. About 15–20% of its yield would come from thermonuclear reactions alone, and about 90% from the thermonuclear reactions plus the fission caused by the fast neutrons they generated.

Tamm's group, including Sakharov but without Ginzburg, then moved to Arzamas-16 to join Kurchatov and Khariton. 'We were all encouraged', Sakharov remembered, 'to throw ourselves into our work by the fierce concentration of a single goal, and perhaps also by the proximity of the labour camp and strict regimentation. ... The rest of the world was far, far away, somewhere beyond two barbed wire fences.'[19]

Arzamas-16 was the main centre but other institutes took part, including the Moscow Institute of Applied Mathematics, the Moscow Institute of Physical Problems (which designed the deuterium production process) and the Leningrad Physicotechnical Institute (which designed methods of lithium-6 separation).[20]

The GAC had feared that the Soviet scientists might gain useful information from the *Mike* shot in November 1952. But they did not as they had no facilities in the Pacific for sampling radioactive debris.[21] As for fall-out collected in central USSR, the most significant fission products, beryllium-7 and uranium-237, would have decayed to an undetectable level. In any case the Soviet scientists did not then have the capacity for the radiochemical analysis involved.

Joe 4: The first thermonuclear test – August 1953

Stalin died in March 1953 and so did not live to see the first Soviet thermonuclear test. The Semipalatinsk site was made ready for the test of a 'layer cake' device in the summer of 1953.[22] It was to be detonated on a 30-metre tower, with an observation post 20–25 kilometres away. At a late stage in the preparations, the scientists realized that radioactive contamination might endanger people living locally. After consulting the unclassified Los Alamos manual on nuclear weapons effects, they were able to calculate the fall-out and to decide which areas to evacuate before the test. People were removed to safety from houses hundreds of kilometres from ground zero, thanks to American information on radiological hazards.

The test device used kilogram quantities of thermonuclear fuel and contained alternating layers of light elements and heavy elements, including uranium-238. It incorporated Ginzburg's idea – 'the Second Idea' – of using solid lithium deuteride (LiD, which he nicknamed 'Liddy') instead of tritium and liquid deuterium. Fast neutrons generated by the thermonuclear reactions would fission the normally non-fissile uranium-238, thus producing a fission–fusion–fission bomb of greatly enhanced yield. The design, like Teller's

Alarm Clock, used HE (high explosive) implosion, not radiation implosion; it had intrinsic limitations but was thought to have a potential yield of 1 megaton.

Joe 4 exploded at six o'clock on the morning of 12 August 1953. The top of the mushroom cloud reached a height of 12 kilometres and the yield was estimated at 400 kilotons – 20 times more powerful than the first atomic bomb, though only one twenty-fifth the power of *Mike*. The explosion made an awesome impression on all those who witnessed it; as one said, the effects of the first Russian atomic explosion had not inspired such flesh-creeping terror.

It was announced as a test of 'one of the types of hydrogen bomb'.[23] In the United States Hans Bethe, who chaired a scientific intelligence panel to analyse the results of foreign tests, denied that it was a true hydrogen bomb because it was not based on the principles discovered by Teller and Ulam. Lewis Strauss, the AEC chairman, keen to emphasize the urgency of the American H-bomb programme, argued that *Joe 4* was a true hydrogen bomb (and moreover deliverable) though not of the Teller–Ulam type and not having its multi-megaton potential. The detection of beryllium-7 in the atmospheric debris from *Joe 4* did, however, indicate that lithium-6 deuteride had been used – a very advanced feature of the design.

Khariton later disagreed strongly with the opinion of Bethe and other American physicists that *Joe 4* was not a 'real' hydrogen bomb.[24] He wrote:

> The effectiveness of a thermonuclear design is, to a significant degree', determined by the degree of compression of the thermonuclear fuel that is provided by the initial explosion of the atomic device. Admittedly, the two Soviet hydrogen bombs tested in 1953 and 1955 were indeed different. But the yield of the bomb tested in 1953 was 20 times greater than that of the bomb dropped on Hiroshima, yet it had the same dimensions and weight. For that reason alone, the tested charge was a major step in the development of nuclear weapons. Moreover the design of the device would have made it possible to create a hydrogen bomb of the order of 1 megaton. The 'thermonuclearity' of the charge – the contribution of thermonuclear reactions to the total value of the yield – was an important indicator. This indicator was in the area of 15 to 20 per cent.

It was quite different from the *Mike* device, he argued, in using lithium deuteride – not employed in American devices until 1954 – to produce tritium in the explosion and to create the 'three step' fission–fusion–fission effect essential to modern nuclear weapons.

Certainly by the end of 1953 the United States had the capacity to build multi-megaton, radiation-imploded, 'wet' bombs (and were even weaponizing the unwieldy *Mike*), while the USSR did not. But the USSR had a thermonuclear 'dry' bomb (whether or not called a 'true' hydrogen bomb), that was compact, practical for air delivery and as powerful as seemed necessary. Some of the American scientists quite understandably feared that the Russians were catching up, and in some respects might even be ahead; they were well advanced in rocketry and at the time of the *Joe 4* test were already beginning construction of a missile that could carry it. But, as we saw, 1954 marked an enormous advance for the American weaponeers.

The 'third idea' and *Joe 19* – November 1955

In the early spring of 1954 Sakharov, Zel'dovich and colleagues produced the 'Third Idea'.[25] (The first and second had been the 'layer cake', and then Ginzburg's 'Liddy'.) The 'Third Idea' was similar to Teller's and Ulam's 1951 breakthrough. After this, progress was very rapid and all the scientific, technical and technological problems were soon solved, including techniques for the first-ever parachute airdrop of an H-bomb.

The politicians wanted Arzamas-16 to concentrate on the 'layer cake' and not to risk an untried new idea, but they did not succeed in persuading Kurchatov, Khariton, Sakharov and Zel'dovich to change their minds about the excellent promise of the 'Third Idea'.[26] The two-stage weapon, *Joe 19*, was ready for testing at the Semipalatinsk test site by November 1955. The first shot, however, on 6 November, was of a back-up device (an improved layer cake), in case the two-stage design should fail. According to an American source, it was an air-burst of a boosted fission weapon with a uranium-235 core, yielding approximately 215 kilotons. It was probably a weaponised version of the 1953 boosted device, *Joe 4*, reduced to a more deliverable size.

The test of the two-stage weapon was planned for 20 November 1955. It was to be dropped from a bomber and detonated in the air to minimize fallout. (The first American airdrop, it may be remembered, was *Redwing Cherokee* in 1956.)

This test was an historic achievement, even more so because the aircraft had succeeded in landing safely with the test bomb on board after the drop was delayed. The aircraft, a Tu-16 bomber, had already taken off when low cloud suddenly covered the test site; the bomb crew could not see the ground zero marker, and the optical instruments would be unable to monitor the explosion. So the aircraft landed at the airfield near Semipalatinsk. A crash could have been devastating but Sakharov and Zel'dovich advised Kurchatov that the risk was very small.[27] The drop took place successfully two days later.

Sakharov described it in his memoirs:

> I saw a blinding yellow-white sphere swiftly expand, turn orange in a fraction of a second, then turn bright red and touch the horizon, flattening out

at its base. Soon everything was obscured by rising dust which formed an enormous swirling, gray-blue cloud, its surface streaked with fiery crimson flashes. Between the cloud and the swirling dust grew a mushroom stem, even thicker than the one that had formed during the first thermonuclear test. Shock waves criss-crossed the sky, emitting sporadic milky- white cones and adding to the mushroom image. I felt heat like that from an open furnace on my face – and this was in freezing weather, tens of miles from ground zero. The whole magical spectacle unfolded in complete silence. Several minutes passed, and then all of a sudden the shock wave was coming at us, approaching swiftly, flattening the feather-grass.[28]

The device, *Joe 19*, had been designed to yield 3 megatons but for the test this was reduced by half. The result was estimated at 1.6 megatons. The problem of creating high-performance thermonuclear weapons for the Soviet Union was solved. There were two fatalities. A young soldier was killed in a trench which fell in 'dozens of kilometres' from ground zero. The other was a two-year- old girl, in a village some distance from the test site, who died in a bomb shelter which collapsed. Sakharov never forgot the horror that he and many others felt.[29]

Hans Bethe considered that *Joe 19* was a true hydrogen bomb. He believed at one time that the 'Third Idea' had been stimulated by analysing the debris from the *Mike* test in 1952, but later concluded that this was not so and that Sakharov had probably developed the idea independently. There is no evidence to suggest that analysis of debris from the 1954 *Castle* tests in the Pacific provided any clues. But exactly how the 'Third Idea' originated remains unclear.[30]

Further development and further tests would follow, including the notorious 58-megaton test at Novaya Zemlya in October 1961. But the initial period of Soviet development of thermonuclear weapons was completed with *Joe 19* in November 1955.

Time-scales

In comparing the time-scales of the superpowers' programmes – from the first fission bomb test to the first H-bomb test – what should one compare? If one accepts Khariton's contention that *Joe 4* was a real H-bomb but *Mike* was not, the time-scales are:

    United States *Trinity to Bravo*   103 months
    Soviet Union *Joe 1 to Joe 4*   48 months

But if, like Bethe, one accepts *Mike*, but not *Joe 4*, the time-scales are:

    United States *Trinity to Mike*   87 months
    Soviet Union *Joe 1 to Joe 19*   63 months

However, if one takes the first two-stage, solid-fuelled, radiation implosion test devices as the end points, the time-scales then become:

United States *Trinity to Bravo*   103 months
Soviet Union *Joe 1 to Joe 19*   75 months

There are other possible parameters. Whichever one chooses it is clear that the Soviet Union made extraordinary advances and caught up with the United States very rapidly. It was a brilliant achievement, even if there is some scope for further discussion of the part played by espionage.

Postscript

The world strategic situation had been revolutionized in the early 1950s. In this new context Britain had to decide her own nuclear future. Less than a month after her first atomic bomb in October 1952, the United States conducted the first thermonuclear test, the 10-megaton *Mike*. *Joe 4* followed nine months later. What did the British know about thermonuclear weapons, and about what the two superpowers were doing? What was Britain to do?

Part II
Britain and the Thermonuclear Question

4
What Must Britain Do?

Triumph and disappointment – October 1952

Hurricane, Britain's first atomic bomb test, on 3 October 1952 off the north-west coast of Australia, was almost universally acclaimed as a triumph – a great scientific and technical success and a proof of Britain's status as a major power though not a super power. It promised greater military security and would surely win increased respect from the United States.[1] Britain desperately wanted to restore the atomic partnership so abruptly ended by the 1946 US Atomic Energy Act – the McMahon Act – which made it a criminal offence, subject to the gravest penalties including death, to transmit any restricted atomic information to another country.[2] This had left Britain on its own in the atomic weapons business, obliged to be independent or to opt out. But for its security an effective deterrent was needed. The Soviet Union soon had an atomic capability, as demonstrated by its August 1949 test, and the presence of American bomber bases here made Britain especially vulnerable.

The bases had an important bearing on British defence policy.[3] After the US Strategic Air Command was created in 1946, its new commanding general, the forceful and bellicose Curtis LeMay, in 1948 ordered the formation of a mobile operational force capable of delivering at least 80% of the atomic stockpile by 1 January 1949.[4] During the spring and summer of 1948 the Cold War intensified, with the Communist coup in Czechoslovakia and then the blockade of West Berlin. The United States wanted to consolidate the informal strategic partnership with Britain and to establish air bases here, and in June 1948 three B-29 bomber groups were stationed in East Anglia.[5] Britain was in the front line of a war that, it seemed, could break out at any moment. But the Chiefs of Staff had no access to American strategic plans.

Arguments against air bases were strong. As a forward base for American strategic bombing this country was likely to become a, or the, primary target for any Soviet attack. The public might not be happy about the bases.

Communist propaganda might suggest that Britain had become an occupied territory. Problems of jurisdiction might arise. But the government found the opposing arguments conclusive. The primary aim of British foreign policy must be to keep the United States firmly committed in Europe; this island was strategically well placed as an advance base and must accept that role.[6]

Acceptance of the American bombers in 1948 was based on a 'gentleman's agreement' but when, next year, the United States government requested more bases in Oxfordshire Foreign Secretary Bevin argued for further safeguards. His anxieties were shared by the Chief of the Air Staff, Sir John Slessor,[7] who was concerned that United States policy, while explicitly rejecting preventive war, left open the possibility of seizing 'the military advantage of landing the first blow' and 'striking with our full weight as soon as we are attacked and, if possible, before the Soviet blow is actually delivered.[8] We could not risk a situation', said Slessor, 'in which the Americans had decided to use the atomic bomb while we were still arguing about whether it should be used.'[9]

As a result, an informal agreement was reached with the United States in 1950, the so-called Ambassador's Agreement,[10] but it still did not deal with two questions: would the Americans agree to prior consultation about the use of bomber aircraft based in Britain, and would the President consult the Prime Minister before launching a nuclear war in general? These questions were raised by Attlee when he visited Washington in December 1950, by Bevin in January 1951, and again in September 1951 by the then Foreign Secretary Herbert Morrison. It was intolerable, Morrison told Secretary of State Dean Acheson, that Britain, as a priority target, should 'risk annihilatory retaliation without being first informed or consulted'.[11] Acheson personally thought consultation would take place but, constitutionally, there could be no restraint or veto on the President's power to launch nuclear forces to safeguard American interests. Eventually the 'Attlee–Truman understandings' were agreed, and became the legal basis for the United States military presence in Britain. They were later re-affirmed as the 'Churchill-Truman understandings'. But the lack of precision was to be a continuing source of embarrassment for governments.

Britain was in a peculiarly vulnerable position *vis-à-vis* both superpowers. In the event of war she was likely, the Chiefs of Staff thought, to be the Soviet Union's first and principal target, but she could not be sure of prior consultation by the United States. Nor could she rely on the American air force to deal with Soviet targets that were not of direct American interest. So Britain needed to be able, if necessary, to attack Soviet forces directly threatening this country; it was hoped that this would be in the context of a combined strategy but the British had no information on the American air plan. Another anxiety – since the prevention of war was of supreme importance to Britain – was that the United States might act rashly in a crisis and might be provoked by some comparatively minor injury into precipitating war. A British contribution to the Western deterrent was essential in order to influence and restrain the United States, as well as to ensure that Britain's vital interests were protected in the event of war. To have no share in what was the main deterrent in the Cold War (and what was also recognized as the only allied offensive weapon in world war) would seriously weaken British influence on American policy and planning in the Cold War, and would mean that, in the event of war, Britain could claim no share in the policy or planning of the offensive.[12]

Churchill succeeded Attlee in October 1951, with exaggerated hopes of restoring the Anglo-American partnership, and he regarded the forthcoming *Hurricane* trial as a trump card. But British hopes that it would impress the Americans were to be disappointed. Indeed, immediately after the success of *Hurricane* the American press generally favoured co-operation with Britain. But interest soon died down as, barely a month later, the Americans tested *Mike*, their first thermonuclear device (see chapter 2). Congress did not favour co-operation and one Congressman commented[13] that it would be 'trading a horse for a rabbit' Britain had to do much more to prove her worth as a partner.

Taking counsel

In February 1953 Churchill asked Cherwell, his ministerial adviser on atomic policy, to report on the possibility, and cost, of producing British hydrogen bombs. Cherwell was already consulting Penney, the head of the atomic weapons group, and Cockcroft, the director of Harwell, to whom the subject was by no means a new one. Indeed, an excellent article on the principles of the H-bomb had appeared in *The Times* in January 1950. Cherwell reported to the Prime Minister in mid-April. The size and power of the H-bomb, he told Churchill, was limited only by what the aircraft could carry; but it might be found that an H-bomb of 'reasonable power' could not be carried by any of Britain's proposed medium bombers. The radius of heavy damage would be about five miles, and the lethal heat flash would have a considerably greater range. The knowledge that each of a country's principal cities could be wiped out by a single bomb would certainly be a powerful deterrent against aggression.

'We think we know how to make an H-bomb', he concluded confidently, 'but at this stage we can only make very rough estimates of various materials required.' An H-bomb could only be detonated by a special kind of atomic bomb, and there would be an 'intermediate detonator'; the most vital and expensive substance needed, he said, would probably be 'super-heavy hydrogen called tritium'. The other costly ingredient would be uranium-235, required to set off the tritium, and to make three or four H-bombs a year would take nine-tenths of the country's annual production. Expensive additional plant would be needed. However, new discoveries and production methods might alter the figures completely in the next five years.

Cherwell added a warning postscript. As Fuchs – who had been arrested for atomic espionage in February 1950 – had told the Russians all he knew about the superbomb, no one should be surprised if they detonated one within a year or two. (As we saw, they detonated their first 'thermonuclear' bomb – a boosted device – in August 1953 and their first 'true' H-bomb in November 1955.)

The subject was not high on the political agenda. What were the British scientists' early ideas of a superbomb? Two British scientists had attended the 'Conference on the Super' in April 1946 at Los Alamos where they had been members of the wartime British team. They were the Swiss-born Egon Bretscher and the German-born Klaus Fuchs. Their chief, Sir James Chadwick – head of the British mission to the Manhattan Project,[14] discoverer of the neutron and a Nobel laureate – wrote a concise and secret report on 'The Super Bomb' in May 1946. It outlined the perceived problems in making a thermonuclear weapon, included a schematic drawing, and explained the function of each component. A gun assembly weapon, which Chadwick called 'detonator', and a 'primer' containing deuterium and tritium, were enclosed in a heavy cylindrical radiation shield. Radiation from the detonator would heat and compress the primer, causing thermonuclear reactions. These would produce fast neutrons, which would 'ignite' a 'booster' of tritiated deuterium; this charge could be of a size to produce any desired yield. (It is unclear how close this model was to that of the April 1946 conference and whether it incorporated new ideas or modifications by Bretscher, Fuchs or Chadwick himself.)

The top copy of Chadwick's report (only three copies were made) was handed to Sir John Anderson,[15] scientist-politician and chairman of the Whitehall Advisory Committee on Atomic Energy. He signed his copy in June 1947 and gave it to Lord Portal who – as Controller of Production (Atomic Energy) in the Ministry of Supply – was the top official in Britain's post-war atomic organization.[16] Subsequently the document found its way to AERE, the Ministry's atomic energy research establishment at Harwell near Oxford. We do not know when it reached the Aldermaston weapons laboratory – perhaps in March 1950, when Cockcroft, the director of AERE, arranged a meeting with Penney to 'go over a number of subjects, including the first Soviet A-bomb test, the 'Super', and papers belonging to Klaus Fuchs[17] (who, after returning from Los Alamos, was head of theoretical physics at Harwell until his arrest). As for Chadwick's superbomb report, we do not know which if any of the weapon scientists at Aldermaston ever saw or used it.

Even before *Hurricane*, Penney's staff were thinking about improved designs. The New Weapons Committee first met at Aldermaston on 15 October 1951 to consider major modifications in design to produce a much lighter and more efficient atomic weapon. The mathematical physicist John Corner even suggested a megaton bomb – not a thermonuclear bomb but one employing fission only, with a yield 'in the megaton range' (that is, upwards of 500 kilotons). He said it would be large and costly, requiring some 20 times the amount of plutonium used in the Nagasaki bomb, but it would have a much greater yield proportionately. This idea was not pursued at the time but it led to an operational requirement some years later. Penney was attracted to very large fission weapons by their cost effectiveness; comparing blast damage per square mile from a 1-megaton bomb and a 10-kiloton bomb, he calculated that the former would cost half as much. He thought megaton bombs would become a 'must' when the military realised their value. But the RAF at this stage wanted more bombs for more targets, not bigger – and fewer – bombs.

In spite of Cherwell's belief that 'we know how to make an H-bomb' in 1953 the scientists at Aldermaston clearly did not know how. Penney did not fully understand what the American devices tested in November 1952 (*Mike* and *King*) really were. The first, as we saw in Chapter 2, was an experimental multi- megaton staged thermonuclear device, and the second a high-yield, pure fission weapon (about 500 kilotons), but in July 1953 Penney thought they were megaton-boosted bombs.

Nevertheless in December 1953 Cherwell – writing to Churchill urging a new approach to the United States on atomic co-operation – was still confident:

> Discussions with Penney, Cockcroft and Hinton[18] have shown that the exchange of information with the United States on the production of fissile material and the design of bombs is no longer of great importance to us. Six or eight years ago it could have saved us a great deal of money and effort. But today we are convinced that we know practically as much as the Americans do. Whilst we should, of course, like our scientists and engineers to be able to talk to theirs freely on matters of joint interest, we are convinced that it would not be worthwhile making any sacrifices to achieve this.

(Only Hinton, head of the atomic production group, would have had some small justification for thinking any such thing.)

For politicians, officials and scientists, early 1954 was a period of intense thinking and discussion that led up to the government's H-bomb decision of June 1954. Home defence problems provided the first impetus to a very serious consideration of H-bombs. A Home Defence Committee had been set up in February 1953 to ensure consistency in military and civil planning for the defence of the United Kingdom in a future war. It was chaired by the omni-competent Sir Norman Brook, the secretary to the Cabinet from 1947 to 1962, an immensely influential figure under four Prime Ministers,[19] who was to play a crucial role in the formation of nuclear defence policy. In January 1954 Brook sent Sir Edwin Plowden, chairman-designate of the United Kingdom Atomic Energy Authority, the committee's appreciation of a probable atomic attack on Britain assuming that the enemy could drop 200 atomic bombs in the first stage of the war. A variation in the number of bombs – say 300 instead of 200 – would not be important, Brook wrote, but it would be very different if it were known that the enemy could drop on London a bomb 'very much greater in size than those we assumed'. He wanted to discuss this with Plowden and Penney.

What was Penney thinking? A long paper which he probably wrote about this time describes various high-yield nuclear bombs. 'Hybrids', it said, were fission bombs enhanced by incorporating 'relatively cheap thermonuclear material'; perhaps increasing the yield two-fold. A 2-megaton hybrid weapon could be made and it was important to test it. To make five or six such weapons every two years, uranium-235 production capacity at Hinton's Capenhurst plant would have to be increased by 50%; ministers were considering this. Hydrogen bombs would be even more powerful than 'hybrids'. The hydrogen bomb as he conceived it consisted of three components. The first was a powerful fission explosion (comparable to a large hybrid). This would set off a thermonuclear reaction (about which, he confessed, 'our ideas ... are still hazy'). This would set off another thermonuclear reaction, in about 300 pounds of liquid deuterium – the main explosive in a hydrogen bomb. The liquid deuterium would have to be held in a large vacuum flask, and it would gradually boil away, so that this would not be any normal bomb; the explosive would have to be poured in only a few hours before detonating the weapon. Such a system, he believed, could be successfully developed in the United Kingdom, but nothing had yet been attempted.

By the end of January 1954 Penney's opinions were changing somewhat. 'I thought I knew the main features of the recent American and Russian thermonuclear explosions', he wrote, 'but it now seems that a vital part is missing.' The explosions he had in mind were *Mike* in November 1952, and the Soviet Union's test of Sakharov's 'layer cake' in August 1953. The thermonuclear fuel of the former, as we saw in Chapter 2, was liquid deuterium but the latter used a solid fuel, a compound of lithium, deuterium and tritium.

Summing up the position about this time Penney said that some work on thermonuclear weapons had been done in the British atomic energy establishments, beginning with the incomplete knowledge available to the British scientists who were at Los Alamos. (Corner remembered later that in 1948–49 he and his friend and colleague Herbert Pike had worked for six months on the 'classical Super', and had concluded that it was not a practicable design and would be too expensive for Britain to try to develop.) It seemed that an enormous scientific, as well as production, effort would be needed to achieve a successful weapon. However in the last two years, Penney said, the Americans had given 'certain snippets of information' to the British scientists so that they could jointly evaluate the bomb debris collected from Soviet test explosions. (This exchange was permissible under a 1948 agreement, known as the *modus vivendi*,[20] which provided for limited co-operation in some research areas including 'detection of a distant nuclear explosion'.) This information, though limited, had stimulated the British scientists to the point where they began to have much clearer ideas about thermonuclear weapons; some of the conclusions Penney described as sensational and revolutionary and of such far-reaching importance that the Chiefs of Staff should be made aware of them.

Two forms of hydrogen bombs, he went on, were now known. One, the easier to make, used a comparatively cheap thermonuclear material to supplement a fission weapon; this type, a hybrid of fission and hydrogen bomb, probably had a maximum yield of 1 or 2 megatons. *Joe 4*, the Soviet thermonuclear bomb test announced by Malenkov in August 1953, was probably of this type. The second type – a true hydrogen bomb – derived most of its explosive power from thermonuclear reactions in heavy hydrogen; it needed a fission warhead to start the reaction, as well as a 'booster'. Its yield would be limited only by the maximum container size and aircraft capacity. No estimate of the cost could yet be made but there would be substantial research and development costs. However, Penney believed his atomic engineering department could make a true hydrogen bomb within five or six years. If a small annual production were then required some difficult policy questions would have to be settled. Enriched uranium (U-235) would be required from the uranium isotope separation plant at Capenhurst, as it would be much better than plutonium for the fission unit; however this demand would compete with the A-bomb programme. Heavy water supplies would be needed for deuterium production and this would mean investing in a plant in New Zealand. Extra high-grade scientific staff would be needed for the task at Aldermaston, and perhaps Canada, Australia and New Zealand might help.

There were certainly some misconceptions in Penney's picture, but ideas were now beginning to develop and events quickly gathered pace in the next few weeks. In February 1954 came a startling revelation from the United States, in a public statement by the chairman of the Joint Committee on Atomic Energy, Sterling Cole. It was promptly and fully reported next day in the *Manchester Guardian* of 18 February. It suggested that the United

States now had a hydrogen bomb even more powerful than *Mike*, the experimental device which, in November 1952, had torn a crater one mile wide and 175 feet deep in the floor of the Pacific Ocean. In a modern city, that explosion would have caused absolute destruction within a three-mile radius, severe damage within seven miles and light damage up to ten miles – a total area of some 300 square miles. On 29 February, the *Castle* test series began and the new weapon was exploded at Eniwetok, in the notorious *Bravo shot* (see Chapter 2).

Penney was visiting Washington during the month, and on 1 March he wrote a memorandum on his return – 'Trip to Washington February 1954' – containing much speculation about Soviet bombs and the Americans' 'true' hydrogen bombs. He was still convinced that a true hydrogen bomb contained small amounts of fissile material – plutonium and uranium – and tritium, and 'a lot of deuterium' in a large vacuum flask. The neck of this flask, he thought, fitted conically into a space in the explosive lenses; some surviving drawings at Aldermaston show some such device. It had been suggested to him in Washington that the British could produce hydrogen bombs by sacrificing a small part of Windscale's plutonium production to make tritium in the piles. Penney seems to have placed all his reliance on such ideas as he was able to pick up from the United States; the Aldermaston theoretical physicists at this stage do not seem to have been involved much in these exploratory ideas, which appear to have been discussed between Penney, Cockcroft and Dolphin, the chief engineer at Aldermaston (see Chapters 5 and 6).

Sterling Cole's statement and then the huge *Bravo* explosion prompted Brook to urgent action. The devastation that the new weapon could create would revolutionize Britain's civil defence ideas; the Home Defence Committee's conclusions were based on the effects of 200 Soviet A-bombs of the Nagasaki type. The pattern of active defence might also be substantially affected. On 5 March, Brook sent the Chiefs of Staff the Sterling Cole statement and invited them to a meeting with Plowden, Penney and Cockcroft on 12 March to discuss the implications. Penney had, he said, previously given him detailed information which had been confirmed during his February visit to the United States. Brook also wrote to Plowden asking for a talk with him, Penney and Cockcroft immediately before the meeting. 'The Prime Minister', he wrote, 'has all this very much in the forefront of his mind and we should hasten to put ourselves in a position to submit some advice to him.'

Brook analysed the situation and outlined a plan of action. In the light of new information there was a need to reassess (i) the likelihood of war; (ii) the form war was most likely to take if it came; (iii) the changes that would have to be made in defence policy to meet the most likely contingency; (iv) the extent of the insurance possible against the chance that war might take some other form than the one that now seemed likely; (v) the current British atomic weapon programme. The Prime Minister, he thought, would want to appoint a small ministerial committee to review these questions. Work on the first four subjects, he suggested, should be apportioned to the Chiefs of Staff, the Foreign Office and the Defence Committee. The fifth, the weapons programme, would be for the Ministry of Defence, the Atomic Energy Authority and the Ministry of Supply: after a reassessment of the fundamental issues of foreign policy and strategy.

At the meeting (GEN 465) on 12 March[21] Penney gave the latest information on United States and Soviet development of the H-bomb. He described the 10-megaton *Mike* explosion, of which Sterling Cole had given details. He explained the two forms of H-bomb as he conceived them – the 'hybrid' (a fission bomb boosted with a light material, lithium deuteride) and the 'true' H-bomb. The Russians, he said, had developed a 'hybrid' in 1953. The true H-bomb was a new departure, involving a series of chain reactions; in theory there was no limit to the yield, and it was very economical in fissile material. He described the effects of a 5-megaton 'true' H-bomb dropped on London; it would produce a fire-ball two miles across and a crater three-quarters of a mile wide and 150 feet deep. The Admiralty Citadel (Whitehall's emergency nerve centre) would be crushed at a distance of one mile; houses would be wrecked three miles away and badly damaged at seven miles; within a radius of two miles all habitations would catch fire.

He then gave details of the American hydrogen bomb as he understood it. It was 6 feet in diameter, 10–30 feet long and weighed 7–8 tons, and could be carried on B-29 or B-36 bombers, or the B-52s just coming into production. It was fuelled by liquid deuterium and there were now several plants in the United States where bomber aircraft carrying H-bombs could pick up deuterium to arm the bombs. (Deuterium has to be cryogenically stored to be kept in the liquid state.) Clearly Penney realized that the Americans were weaponizing the *Mike* device but did not seem to know that, in the recent *Castle* series, they had moved on decisively from 'wet' bombs to 'dry' H-bombs using solid thermonuclear fuel.

Writing that day to Plowden and the other Atomic Energy Authority board members Penney speculated on the outcome. He guessed that the Authority would be ordered to produce H-bombs, A-bombs, and boosted A-bombs of moderate size, but *not* megaton, boosted, fission bombs. 'Of course', he wrote – surely Cherwell would have been surprised – 'we do not know how to make any form of hydrogen bomb. Our expectation is that it will be based on a large spherical implosion with a tamper weighing about 1 ton of either natural uranium or preferably thorium ... Inside the tamper is a large vacuum flask full of liquid deuterium.' (He did not seem to have a staged design in mind.)

He had shown some such scheme to three of his Aldermaston staff a few days earlier and they had been puzzled. John Corner, the brilliant head of the theoretical division, sent him a note on 10 March: 'In the spherical scheme which you showed to Pike, Woodcock and I yesterday, most of the energy comes from fissions. This seems to disagree with the statement you heard that in really large weapons most of the energy release comes from the thermonuclear reaction rather than from high energy fissions in uranium.'

Brook's next GEN 465 meeting – with the Chiefs of Staff, senior Foreign Office and Ministry of Defence officials, Plowden and Penney – was a week later, on 19 March. Penney was asked more about the information he had acquired, officially or unofficially, in the United States, and how many bombs the United States and the Soviet Union possessed. The latest American explosion, he said, had been much larger than earlier ones. The bombs they were making required liquid hydrogen (or, rather, deuterium), with limited life and requiring special plant, but if liquid hydrogen could be dispensed with it would be possible to stockpile H-bombs. The Russians had not yet detonated a bomb of the kind the Americans exploded in November 1952 (*Mike*) but were expected to do so in 1954. (In fact the Russians bypassed the liquid deuterium model and went straight from a boosted device to a dry H-bomb using lithium deuteride – Chapter 3.)

There had been brief, low-key reports in the British press of the *Castle Bravo* test of 1 March 1954, the first on 2 March in the ever alert *Manchester Guardian*. The official American reports were extremely terse. But information began to leak out after a letter from a serviceman with the *Castle* task force was published in a Cincinnati newspaper on 11th.[22] By 12 March accounts began to appear of a 'mishap' in which 264 people had been 'caught in atom radiation'. Then came a second dramatic announcement by Sterling Cole on 16 March; the United States possessed a deliverable H-bomb and had plans to take it to any target in the world.[23] He also announced plans for a Congressional enquiry into what had gone wrong at Bravo.[24]

Panic and anger broke out in Japan[25] when the *Lucky Dragon* returned to port on 14 March with nearly all her crew suffering from the symptoms of radiation sickness. The first country to suffer from atomic bombs had been stricken again. (Little attention was paid at the time to the contamination of the Marshall Islands and fall-out that had rained down on some of the islanders.) Japanese papers carried huge headlines, anti-Americanism flared up, and the Japanese government demanded a formal United States government enquiry. Alarm spread to the United States, where there was extensive press coverage.

Cherwell and Brook both wrote to Churchill about the H-bomb. Cherwell said two H-bombs had been exploded to date, both in the Eniwetok area. (He omitted the Soviet test of November 1953.) The first *Mike*, had been described in the *Manchester Guardian* of 18 February, which Churchill had read. The second (*Bravo*), according to newspaper reports, was three or four times as powerful as expected and 600 times more powerful than the Hiroshima bomb. That would make it equivalent to about 12 million tons of TNT. Japanese fishermen some 90 miles away had sustained damage from the radioactive dust which had rained on them. As Churchill had mentioned in a previous speech, if the Russians realized the power of this weapon they might be induced to seek means of living in peace with the West.

Brook sent Churchill a full account of the meeting with the Chiefs of Staff on 19 March. A new strategic appreciation must distinguish between period 1 (when the Russians might have developed the H-bomb but not the means of delivering it against North America) and period 2 (when they would be able to do so). During period 1 the United Kingdom would be in range and would be especially vulnerable. After that date a state of equilibrium might conceivably be reached in which neither of the main protagonists would think it worthwhile to start a major atomic war. American H-bombs in their present form had to be activated with liquid hydrogen and became ineffective after 27 hours; so long as this was so, they would be carried by intercontinental bombers based in the United States, not from United Kingdom bases. The Chiefs of Staff and Ivone Kirkpatrick of the Foreign Office, Brook continued, would assess the likelihood of major war. Penney and Cockcroft would report on the probable development of the Russian strategic bomber force and estimate when Russia would be able to drop a significant number of H-bombs on North American targets. The Lord President would submit tentative plans to improve Britain's capacity to manufacture H-bombs (if it were decided to do so) by obtaining heavy water from New Zealand and thorium from South Africa. Thorium, Penney then believed, was a desirable or even essential ingredient. These various studies, Brook said, would provide the basis for the small ministerial committee which he had already proposed to the Prime Minister. Churchill agreed.

There was a Cabinet discussion the same day, 22 March 1954, and on 23 March Churchill was to answer questions in the House, giving assurance that the United States government would not use atomic weapons without consulting the United Kingdom, especially in circumstances which might provoke retaliatory attack on this country. He was advised to reply that he was satisfied with the existing arrangements for consultation but, after the recent American revelations about the H-bomb, he doubted whether that would satisfy Parliament. The Cabinet felt that, despite these disclosures, there had not yet been much public anxiety.

There soon would be. The press was full of reports and comments on the *Lucky Dragon* and the contamination of Pacific fishing grounds, as reports came in of more Japanese fishing vessels found to be contaminated on arrival in port. There were headlines about the 'stupendous problem' of the H-bomb, the unknown risks of nuclear tests, and the dangers to the whole human race, and calls for international action and for a ban on all H-bomb tests. In late March the Labour Party introduced a resolution in Parliament asking the government to seek a summit meeting on the suspension of all testing. The United States government had in hand a worldwide survey of nuclear test fall-out, and Cockcroft suggested that the British should also start work on the possible biological effects.

On 1 April the *New York Times* headline read 'H-bomb can wipe out any city'. Suddenly public anxiety in the United States was diverted from preoccupation with *Bravo* and its effects, and from fear of nuclear tests and fall-out, to fear of nuclear war itself and the threat to the American population.

Meanwhile the British scientists and officials were going on steadily with the tasks defined by Brook and approved by Churchill. Cockcroft and Penney were trying to assess the Soviet H-bomb potential. American analysis of the Soviet *Joe 4* explosion of August 1953 indicated a yield of 0.3 to 1.5 megatons, examination of radioactive dust by the United States, the United Kingdom and Canada revealed the presence of beryllium-7, showing that lithium deuteride had been used to boost the bomb and that the resultant high energy neutrons had caused fission in the natural uranium (not normally fissile), thus enhancing the yield. It appeared to be a bomb of the 'intermediate' type (which Penney had previously called a 'hybrid'). Penney and Cockcroft now redefined the types of weapons in four classes, making a distinction between 'hydrogen' and 'thermonuclear' as follows:

I Straight fission weapons

II Boosted fission 'intermediate' weapons – yielding up to 2 megatons; they would be boosted with lithium-6 deuteride but would be expensive in fissile material (that is plutonium-239 or uranium-235).

III Hydrogen weapons – physically large, weighing about 8 tons and yielding 5 to 20 megatons, they would require difficult-to-handle deuterium and some tritium but would be cheap in terms of fissile material and would be boosted with lithium deuteride.

IV Thermonuclear weapons – weighing 4 to 10 tons and yielding 5 to 20 megatons, they would use comparatively little fissile material, a little tritium (in a lithium compound), a large amount of lithium deuteride, and a heavy tamper of natural uranium or thorium.

Both Penney and Cockcroft were obviously still thinking of hydrogen bombs as essentially liquid deuterium bombs. It was not known if a class IV weapon could be made, the scientists wrote. (Nevertheless they thought it would be 'comparatively cheap and easy to make'.) If it could, then class

III – liquid deuterium – weapons were obsolete. A note added to their draft in Cockcroft's handwriting says, 'We now believe that the United States have successfully tested such a weapon in their recent series of tests.' (Indeed they had.)

The Russians, their draft continued, must be assumed to have effective class I weapons; they had already tested class II, not always successfully, and more such trials were to be expected. The major uncertainty was whether they would try, and succeed, with class III or go straight to class IV, which would be a natural development from class II. Given a success with class IV they would at once be level with the Americans. No bottle-necks in key materials for their programme seemed likely, especially as much less tritium was needed than had been thought earlier. The American and British scientists would be able to detect any Soviet tests of weapons in the megaton range, but would not be able to distinguish between class III and class IV explosions. Estimates of the size of the Soviet nuclear arsenal, on the basis of intelligence estimates of their fissile material production, would depend on the alternative assumptions about the types of weapons chosen.[26]

Of course Britain so far had only class I (fission) weapons. There was, as yet, no government decision on whether or not to develop H-bombs, and – for all Cherwell's confident assurance – the British scientists did not yet know how. They had, in Penney's words, 'about 20 different schemes for hydrogen weapons' containing deuterium, but no very clear ideas.

Public relations

Amid growing press clamour for an end to tests, one Sunday paper, under the headline 'The big decision – NO H-BOMBS'[27] announced that 'although we have the know-how and the means ... the Cabinet has decided against the "ultimate" weapon'. Wrong on both counts, it purported to reveal Britain's technical prowess *and* her moral superiority.

On 30 March 1954 the Prime Minster made a statement to the House of Commons about the latest H- bomb test.[28] It had been detected by the British scientists' instruments, but their knowledge of these tests was necessarily limited, he explained, since the United States government was prevented by law from divulging secret information about them. He assured the House that there was no foundation for the suggestion that the tests could be out of control – or that those making the tests could not set limits to the explosive power or calculate the results. The injuries suffered by people outside the prohibited area were, he said, 'neither serious or lasting'. As for the idea that further tests should be the subject of international consultation or control, United States law would make this impracticable; even if it were not so, he would not himself be ready to propose it. He rejected suggestions that he should try to persuade the United States government to abandon their current tests. Britain had no power to stop them, and it would not be right or wise for us to ask; no one had suggested representations to the Soviet government about their tests. No satisfactory arrangements to limit atomic weapons could be made except as part of a general disarmament agreement. The American Pacific tests were an essential part of the defence policy of a friendly power without whose massive strength and generous help Britain would be in mortal peril.

Mr Attlee, the Labour Party leader, urged a full Parliamentary debate before Easter, 'in view of the public disturbance of mind on this matter', but the Prime Minister thought it impossible until after Easter. He was unwilling to press the Americans for more information. The most cogent comment came from the former Labour War Minister, John Strachey; Britain, he said, had the right to the fullest consultation since 'it is from British airfields that hydrogen bombers might take off, thus possibly endangering the lives of every man, woman and child in this country'.

Churchill bowed to the storm[29] and the following day, 31 March, he promised the House a full-scale debate within a week. Newspapers next morning were full of Lewis Strauss' press conference in Washington and, a day later, carried startling front page photographs – just released by the United States government – of the 1952 *Mike* shot, showing the gigantic fireball and cloud. British viewers were shown a short version of the film released in the United States, and Chapman Pincher, a hardened press correspondent, was 'chilled with fear'.[30] In a *Daily Mirror* opinion poll on 5 April, 14,035 people took part and 92% voted for a Big Three conference and a suspension of test explosions; less than 2% voted to the contrary.

There was uproar in the House during the debate on 5 April.[31] When the Prime Minister rejected Attlee's motion calling for an immediate government initiative to seek a three-power meeting on the H-bomb, Churchill revealed the secret wartime Quebec agreement,[32] and blamed the Labour government for its supine acceptance of the 1946 McMahon Act.[33] He told the House that President Eisenhower was seeking for some latitude in the application of the Act and that nothing should be said or done to arouse 'needless antagonism' in Congress or throughout the United States.

'A common level of ignorance'

What was happening at Aldermaston all this time? Most of the staff there were busily engaged on the design and production of atomic bombs for the stockpile, while Penney and a few others were thinking about superbombs. One of them was the chief engineer, John Dolphin; he had come from industry, with no expertise in physics or weapons technology, but was clever and inventive and highly valued by Penney. During April 1954 he produced a plan for 'A Thermonuclear Device'.[34] Briefly it consisted of a conventional implosion system round a fissile core into which was inserted the conical end of an otherwise spherical vessel containing the hydrogen isotopes deuterium and tritium. The whole was surrounded by a massive case of uranium, weighing three or four tons. We do not know what the Aldermaston physicists thought of this device, if they ever saw the drawing.

At this time the theoretical physics division under John Corner was being prepared for 'Super work'. A group – initially only four or five – was to set up within the division, to work exclusively on Super problems as personnel became available. They would 'start on a common level of ignorance'. Corner, always orderly and methodical, began to plan the work. First of all he and Herbert Pike would collect all the information on 'the 1946 position', and then the group would survey the work 'in super-abundant detail'. Then Aldermaston could have its own 'Super conference', perhaps in the autumn of 1954. Topics for study could be identified and allocated and the real work could begin. The original small group, called 'the Astrophysics Committee',[35] first met under Corner's chairmanship on 13 April 1954. At last the investigation of the Super problem was being put on a systematic basis, and Corner told the group that he expected that almost everyone in the theoretical physics division would be working on it by mid-1955 as a matter of top priority. But Corner knew that there was more information on the 1946 Super Conference that Aldermaston lacked; physicists at Harwell apparently still had some of the papers. At his prompting, Penney asked Cockcroft if he would see what they had so that Corner could see, or possibly borrow, them.

The government had, as yet, taken no decision on a British H-bomb, and Aldermaston was far from knowing how to design one but, if the option was to be kept open, some procurement action could not wait. Supplies of thorium for making tampers had been ordered from the Anglo-American Corporation, lest large United States orders should take up all its capacity for several years. As for heavy water to produce deuterium, earlier plans to build a heavy water plant in New Zealand for civil power purposes had been abandoned but might be revived for an H-bomb programme. If so, the New Zealand government needed a firm decision in little over a week's time.

The first ministerial meeting on the H-bomb took place in Churchill's room in the House of Commons on 13 April 1954[36] and endorsed the 'wise and prudent' action on thorium and heavy water. Then the Foreign Secretary told them of a new development that could jeopardise any proposal to make H-bombs in the United Kingdom. A tentative suggestion had just been put to him by Secretary of State Dulles that the United States government might call for international agreement on a moratorium for H-bomb experiments. This was an advantageous moment for the United States, which had just completed its *Castle* series, whereas the Russians had not yet tested an H-bomb, only a boosted fission bomb.

The moratorium idea is discussed elsewhere, in chapter 9, and we return here to the development of the 1954 British H-bomb decision. Penney was becoming convinced of the need for the H-bomb, and he thought it possible that in ten years' time it would put Britain in a military position equivalent to that of the superpowers. By the end of April he thought it likely that hydrogen weapons or even more 'advanced' types of weapon could be made at very little extra cost. It would be rash, Penney thought, to agree to anything that prevented Britain from having hydrogen weapons if the United States and the Soviet Union had them. 'Are we prepared to stand aside when a little further effort will give us at least the bargaining power that comes from being able, if necessary, to strike back?' Cockcroft echoed this view: 'Thermonuclear weapons are undoubtedly simpler to make than scientists thought ... we believe the US have successfully tested such a weapon in their recent series of tests. The weapon is comparatively cheap and easy to make.'

More news from the United States

An eventful April ended with another important speech by Sterling Cole, reported in the *Manchester Guardian* on 1 May 1954. A single plane on a single mission, he had said, could carry more destructive cargo than the total carried by the combined air forces of all the Allies and all the Axis nations through all the years of World War II. Penney prepared a note for Churchill about the speech, which Plowden sent to the Lord President. It said that a superbomb of the kind recently tested by the United States made as big an explosion as 10 million tons of high explosive. Carried by a single aircraft it could destroy a city; houses would be torn to pieces at four miles and damaged beyond repair at eight miles; at least a million people would be killed and many more injured. Damage and casualties from fire would undoubtedly be on the same scale as direct blast damage. The Russians by this time probably had at least 50 superbombs, perhaps a hundred. If not as powerful as those recently tested by the Americans they were certainly capable of 'destroying the heart of New York, Chicago or Washington'. (Penney does not comment on whether the Soviet Union had the delivery capacity.) Cherwell also sent comments to the Prime Minister, making two tremendously important points. First, multi-megaton bombs were much less effective than the equivalent number of 1-megaton bombs; therefore the Chiefs of Staff doubted the value of developing them. Secondly, one unhappy consequence of the enormous power of the H-bomb was the supreme advantage it gave to the country that got its blow in first. He and the Prime Minister had a discussion with Penney at Chequers, and Cherwell asked Penney some searching questions on H-bombs and bomb tests, especially on Penney's idea of the possibility of small- scale tests.

Cherwell was understandably anxious about this problem of the first blow, and the fearful possibility that the United States might – as a Joint Chiefs of Staff study group suggested in May 1954 – consider 'deliberately precipitating war with the USSR in the near future' before Soviet thermonuclear capability became a 'real menace'. However, the Army Chief of Staff denounced this idea as 'contrary to every principle on which our nation had been founded' and 'abhorrent to the great mass of American people',[37] and a security policy paper later in 1954 stated firmly that 'the United States and its allies must reject the concept of preventive war or acts intended to provoke war'.[38]

The military point of view

In May 1954 the British Chiefs of Staff also reviewed United Kingdom strategy against the broad background of problems facing the Free World. They considered that both sides in the Cold War were so anxious to avoid war that even unintentional war was unlikely. The fear of nuclear war was the chief deterrent to war. However, in the event of war the United Kingdom was extremely vulnerable – in the next few years the number one target on the Soviet list – and unrestricted nuclear war would be likely to destroy the country. The United States, the most powerful nation in the Free World, could launch a nuclear attack on the Soviet Union without fear of effective retaliation. But it was less experienced than Britain – a cherished British notion – and it was important to retain and strengthen influence over its policy; essential, too, to maintain Britain's influence as a world power, and leader of the Commonwealth, with a position to maintain in world affairs. If its influence declined it would be virtually impossible to regain its rightful place as a world power. So it was essential to be able to produce the H-bomb ('as cheaply as possible').

But Aldermaston scientists were certainly not yet ready with definite ideas despite Penney's and Cockcroft's confident presentations in Whitehall. The Astrophysics Committee was still collecting information about superbombs. By mid-May 1954 it had not yet got all the Los Alamos information from Harwell; Bretscher was still sorting out his notes, but Fuchs' notes had been received.[39] During May Penney made a rare appearance at the Astrophysics Committee and surveyed the probable course of nuclear weapons development. He had apparently changed his mind very recently about hydrogen bombs, for he told the Committee that 'wet' bombs (that is, using liquid deuterium) were now obsolete. (There had, in fact, been an astonishingly well-informed article in *Time* magazine in April 1954 about 'dry' hydrogen bombs using solid thermonuclear fuel.)

Penney was under pressure from the Chiefs of Staff for information. Brundrett, the Ministry of Defence scientific adviser, asked him urgently on 25 May for a paper on superbombs to be considered by the OAW[40] (a working party on operational use of atomic weapons) on 31 May and by a Chiefs of Staff meeting on 2 June. Penney thought his draft should first be approved by the Atomic Energy Executive but the time was so short that it had to be agreed by Plowden, Cockcroft and himself. (That left out Hinton, who was in charge of the crucial materials production programme.)

The OAW, in reporting to the Chiefs of Staff, identified three main areas of difficulty – supplies of raw and processed materials, scientific and technical staff, and proving trials. The only materials problem was likely to be tritium; steps had been taken at Windscale to produce enough for two hydrogen weapons in 1958, but for further weapon production a new reactor would have to be built. Recruiting additional scientists and engineers for the project would be much more difficult; Aldermaston was already below strength in all grades (see Chapter 6). A major trial, both to prove the weapon and to demonstrate Britain's possession of this awesome power, would be necessary, and the bomb would have to be fired high in the air, probably over remote sea areas, to avoid large-scale contamination. The report observed that, biologically, there was a limit to the cumulative quantity of certain products of nuclear explosions that could be tolerated without endangering the health of human and animal populations of the world. The production requirement was for a small number of weapons in the 5 to 10 megaton range designed to put Russian airfields out of action in a first attack. Beyond a certain limited number, increased H-bomb stocks would not confer corresponding military advantage. There was to be no capacity for overkill. If the programme was begun at once it appeared possible to test two hydrogen weapons in 1958 and begin producing weapons of 5 to 10 megaton yield soon afterwards. The practical and political problems of testing should be addressed immediately.

In conclusion the report posed a choice of policies:

1. to continue the existing atomic bomb programme and leave the manufacture of hydrogen bombs to the United States;
2. to take special steps to increase staff at AWRE, start work on the hydrogen bombs, and aim to test it in 1958 and then produce the weapons;
3. to continue the present programme with existing resources, adding H-bomb development to it, and accepting considerable delays.

The first option was hardly, if at all, considered.

A decision is imminent

The Chiefs of Staff submitted their general strategic assessment to the Defence Policy Committee on 1 June 1954. It reviewed defence policy in the light of political and military changes in the previous two years, paying special attention both to the significance of nuclear weapons and to the pressing need for expenditure cuts. It emphasised that, more than ever, the aim of United Kingdom policy must be to prevent war; 'To this end we must maintain and strengthen our position as a world power so that Her Majesty's Government can exercise a powerful influence in the counsels of the world.' The world situation, it continued, had been completely altered by recent progress in the development of nuclear weapons and the latest techniques; the United Kingdom would be the primary military target for initial nuclear attack in any future war, and ten bombs of 2 to 20 megatons on the United Kingdom might kill 5 to 12 million people. Britain's scientific skill and technological capacity to produce the H-bomb put within its grasp the ability to be on terms with the United States and the Soviet Union, and this should not be beyond her financial capabilities.

Linked to this assessment, the Chiefs of Staff presented a long and detailed paper on H-bomb research and production in the United Kingdom, appending Penney's OAW report prepared under such pressure at the end of May. The Chiefs of Staff recommended that

(a) immediate approval [should] be given to the putting in hand of a programme for the production of ten hydrogen bombs a year for five years starting not later than 1959, subject to review. ... If a programme were started at once and sufficient staff were recruited a test of two weapons in 1958 should be possible;

(b) the present programme for the production of other types of nuclear weapons should proceed as planned, certainly until 1957 ... subject to review;

(c) the existing research and development programme for the improvement of the Mark I bomb ... should proceed as planned in addition to work on the H-bomb;

(d) special steps should be taken ... to increase the staff at AWRE to enable such a programme to be achieved.

The OAW paper attached gave estimated costs and forecasts of future weapon stocks, and emphasized the three problem areas – materials, recruitment of staff, and facilities for major trials. The H-bombs it foresaw would be in the 5 to 10 megaton class, but the type was not specified and the remarks on materials are not informative. Were the bombs to be what Penney and

Cockcroft had called class III (liquid deuterium) or class IV (with solid thermonuclear fuel)? Presumably they were to be class IV, which Penney and Cockcroft had earlier called 'thermonuclear'. High-yield, boosted, fission weapons were not mentioned at all.

The Defence Policy Committee discussed both papers on 16 June 1954. Members were much concerned with public reactions. The policy could not be sustained unless the British public was prepared to accept the risks it involved, and public opinion must be carefully prepared. It could not be concealed from the people that during the coming four or five years the main risk was of a 'forestalling' war initiated by the United States, and that if it occurred it would bring down on Britain a weight of air attack against which no defence or protection was in sight. The Home Secretary believed that there was still a role for civil defence but Coventry City Council, for example, was already abandoning civil defence preparations as useless. This line of reasoning might lead to a demand for the withdrawal of American strategic forces from United Kingdom bases.

Ministers then discussed the cost of the H-bomb (which they wanted concealed as far as possible). They noted that production could be started soon if tritium could be obtained from Canada, and agreed that the Prime Minister should take soundings during his forthcoming visit to North America with the Minister of Defence. They agreed to keep open the possibility of a larger H-bomb programme, and they decided that no official statement of government policy should be made, at any rate for the moment. The Lord President and the Minister of Supply were authorised to initiate the programme for hydrogen bomb production set out in the Chiefs of Staff paper, and the Lord President was to take steps to recruit the scientific staff needed. Finally, the committee asked the Lord President and the Commonwealth Secretary to consider asking Canada for free tritium supplies.

So it was that Churchill, during his visit to North America, told Canadian ministers that the British government had decided to make the hydrogen bomb. The occasion was an official dinner party[41] at the Château Laurier in Ottawa on 29 June 1954. This decision, he said, was not known to the Cabinet as a whole, only to selected ministers, and it was therefore a matter of the utmost secrecy. The reasons that he gave for the decision were, firstly, that it was necessary in order to belong 'to the club' and, secondly, that possessing effective deterrents was the only sure way of preventing war. Moreover, if we had it, the Americans would respect our intervention in world affairs far more than if we did not. Then he came to the point. Britain needed tritium for the bomb and understood that the Canadians could produce it in their reactor at Chalk River, Ontario. If so, this would save a year. Would they provide tritium as part of a Commonwealth defence effort, or on a commercial basis? Payment could perhaps be made with 'finished articles' St Laurent said

Canada did not want H-bombs, but tritium supply could be discussed next day by Cherwell, Plowden and the Canadian authorities. It was, but in the end there was no deal.

The Cabinet has something to say

The final decision was still uncertain, however. On 7 July 1954 Churchill told the Cabinet that the Defence Policy Committee had approved a proposal to produce hydrogen bombs, and his recent discussions in Washington and Ottawa had, somewhat prematurely, been conducted on that basis. We could not, he argued, expect to maintain our influence as a world power unless we possessed the most up-to-date weapons. The primary aim of our policy was to prevent major war, and the possession of these weapons was now the main deterrent to a potential aggressor.

The Defence Policy Committee, chaired by the Prime Minister, had included the most senior Cabinet ministers, and Churchill had, mistakenly, taken Cabinet agreement for granted. But the Cabinet was indignant at not being given the opportunity to participate in the decision. The Lord Privy Seal (H Crookshank) complained that the Cabinet had received no notice of this question and he hoped that it would not have to make a decision without more time to consider it. The discussion continued the next day and dealt with five major questions – costs; the moral issue; the need for influence and standing in world affairs; concern that other European nations, particularly Germany, might also want to produce thermonuclear weapons; and the need to justify production of thermonuclear weapons to public opinion.

Cost was discussed first. The initial capital cost of adjusting the weapons programme to include hydrogen weapons should not exceed £10 million, it was considered. (This unrealistic figure did not reflect the greater expenditure needed as the work progressed.) The moral issue, raised for the first time, was dealt with simply. There was no difference in kind, it was argued, between atomic and thermonuclear weapons and so far as any moral principle was involved it had already been breached by the Labour government's decision to make the atomic bomb. The moral argument would not arise so much on the decision to make hydrogen bombs as on a decision to use them.

The next consideration prompted the most serious discussion. It was argued that no country without the most up-to-date weapons could claim to be a leading military power and unless Britain possessed thermonuclear weapons it would lose its influence and standing in world affairs. Strength in these weapons would henceforward be the most powerful deterrent to a potential aggressor. But deterrence took second place; first and foremost, the government wanted thermonuclear weapons to provide influence. At present some people thought that the greatest risk was that the United States might plunge the world into war, either through misjudged intervention in Asia or in order to forestall an attack by the Soviet Union. Britain's best chance of preventing it was to maintain its influence with the American government, which would certainly respect its views more if it continued to play an effective part in building up the strength necessary to deter aggression and did not leave it entirely to the United States to match and counter the Soviet strength in thermonuclear weapons.

The decision is made

Again the Cabinet deferred a decision. On 27 July, though there was no mention of it on the agenda, the Cabinet secretary had arranged for the Lord President to raise it, and the Prime Minister had been so informed. Plowden, briefing the Lord President for the meeting, emphasised the need for a definite decision to make H-bombs – if that was the Cabinet's wish – as recommended by the Chiefs of Staff and the Defence Policy Committee. The main implications of this decision for the Atomic Energy Authority were certain requirements for materials – probably thorium, heavy water and tritium – and the need to strengthen the scientific staff at Aldermaston. Steps had already been taken to obtain materials; if not required they could be disposed of without difficulty. And – a very important development – the Lord President had persuaded the First Sea Lord to release William Cook from the Royal Naval Scientific Service to act as deputy to the overloaded William Penney, who had repeatedly asked for his help (see Chapter 6). The Cabinet meeting on 27 July briefly discussed the arguments rehearsed previously and then agreed to authorize the Lord President 'to proceed with his plans for the production of thermonuclear bombs in this country'.

It had been a fraught five months since the Sterling Cole speech and the *Bravo* shot in February. Norman Brook, at the centre of Whitehall, had initiated a quick and effective response and had guided the decision-making process with a firm hand. Penney and Cockcroft had given their scientific opinions, the Chiefs of Staff and their experts had supplied wide-ranging military advice, ministers had considered the questions and a momentous decision had been reached.

Soon after President Truman's historic directive on the American Super in January 1950, the Los Alamos scientists had had to admit that the Super would not work and that they did not know what would. The British situation in 1954 was not dissimilar. A Cabinet decision had been taken but, as the Lord President wrote two days later: 'While we are confident of our ability to carry through the necessary research and development, we do not yet know how to make a hydrogen bomb, or exactly how long it will take, nor do we know what route of research and development we shall need to follow to find out how to make one.'

For Westminster and Whitehall, the next stage would be a test of their political, administrative and presentational skills; for Aldermaston, it would be a search for scientific and engineering answers to some extremely difficult questions.

5
A General Instruction from the Government

The Cabinet in authorising the Lord President 'to proceed with his plans for the production of thermonuclear bombs in this country'[1] did not specify what it understood by thermonuclear. Writing to Duncan Sandys, the Minster of Supply, on 29 July the Lord President said that the Atomic Energy Authority needed a 'general instruction', not a restrictive commitment to produce a thermonuclear explosion in a particular way, using particular materials, by any specified date. In some official papers at this time one finds the words 'hydrogen bomb' crossed out and replaced by 'higher powered bombs', or 'higher powered bombs employing thermonuclear techniques.'

An official in the Ministry of Supply summed up the prevailing state of ignorance:

> It has already become clear that we must in the first instance strive to arrive at some definition of the general term 'hydrogen bomb'. Any such definition should seemingly include two main elements connected with (a) power and (b) technique. ... What the RAF need is a weapon of very high power that is capable of production in reasonable quantity, that can be reasonably easily handled and maintained and that can be accurately delivered ... I do not believe it matters to the RAF by what scientific means the effects they desire are obtained. ... It thus seems that there are two objects ... the first being the provision of powerful weapons for the RAF, and the second, which may be quite independent of the first in practice, the staging of what one may term a propaganda operation which shall be, from the political point of view, the equivalent of the present American and Russian trials.

A 'general instruction' was certainly what Aldermaston needed. A month after the Cabinet decision, they produced a 20-page 'survey of nuclear reactions for multi-megaton weapons – a collection of what we know or suspect, to see whether we are missing some big possibility'.

The Cabinet decision of July 1954 was still secret, and the government now had to consider when and how to tell the country, as unobtrusively as possible. The scientists for their part had to answer two basic questions – what *is* a hydrogen, or thermonuclear, bomb? How can it be made? The government announcement was made seven months later, in February 1955, but it took much longer to answer the scientific questions. In September 1954 William Cook, released by the Royal Naval Scientific Service specifically on account of the H-bomb programme, arrived at Aldermaston and – as deputy director to Penney – took charge of the H-bomb project. A transformation began at the site, as we see in the next chapter. In October, Corner described the aims and possible methods of the programme to Cook in a lengthy note on 'how to get a major thermonuclear bomb.' Aldermaston, he wrote, was undertaking to make a 5-megaton test weapon. But since, in *Mike*, the Americans had achieved 17 megatons – it was actually 10.4 –. Aldermaston ought to aim at producing, by some means, a reasonably cheap weapon design that could yield 20 megatons if need be. Though not aware that this had been explicitly stated, Corner said it was clearly in Penney's mind. (If so, had Penney not told Cook? And what military need can the scientists have been thinking of?) A big fission bomb using uranium-235 could be developed to give a few megatons. Boosting would multiply the yield by an unknown factor, which Harwell was investigating, and it might double the yield or might even achieve 20 megatons. Other schemes were being discussed, but the use of liquid deuterium, as in the classical Super, was not being explored. Evidence at the Oppenheimer hearings[2] clearly showed that the classical Super had never been tried; it would be costly in tritium, and the Americans apparently had a much better solution. Earlier, Corner wrote, we had thought there were three thermonuclear schemes – the classical Super, the lithium-6 deuteride booster, and another unknown American scheme. It now seemed possible that the third did not exist and that Teller's bright idea related to a high achievable boosting factor. This would be splendid. Almost no tritium, plenty of energy from natural uranium fissions, guaranteed to work! If Aldermaston went for a booster design, it would be no disgrace and no one should feel that they had dodged their job, they would only be trying to get 20 megatons in an economical way. They had been aware of boosting for a year but had not realised how extremely effective it could be. More staff would be needed to develop it – but hard-working types rather than ultra-brilliant. (Corner was over-optimistic about boosting, which the British had not yet tested at all, and he had not yet understood the American tests – about which hardly any information was available to him.)

At about this time Penney was giving some news to Plowden, Cockcroft and Hinton.

> Some important information [not specified] has come to me by various routes; and for the first time I have a feeling that we now have enough knowledge to start designing the H-bomb with some degree of certainty, and that we can say how much of various materials are required. The information I have received is not as definite as I would like and I have asked for check backs on certain items. ... The information I now have, if reliable, is startling.

This new information, Penney said, made present plans for lithium supplies hopelessly inadequate.

The Astrophysics Committee continued its work steadily, its members pursuing the lines of investigation mapped out by Corner. In late October Fraser and Scriven were working on comparative rates of travel in lithium deuteride of hydrodynamic shock waves and radiation shock waves; they thought the latter might even be the faster. But the full potential of this idea was not to be realised for another year. In November the nucleonics specialist, Woodcock, was puzzling over United States thermonuclear weapon development and the nature of Teller's invention. Was a separate cylinder of lithium-6 deuteride used to implode a secondary fission bomb? He was sure the classical Super had not been fired and he rightly linked the 1951 *Greenhouse George* shot with Teller's invention and with *Ivy Mike*. But he was puzzled by the sequence of events. Soon afterwards Herbert Pike suggested, correctly, that there was some fundamental difference between *Mike* and the *Castle* devices.

Elsewhere at Aldermaston, a 'project committee' was chaired by the inventive chief engineer, John Dolphin, who admitted his complete ignorance of physics but produced elegant drawings of strange 'thermonuclear' devices – perhaps his own ingenious ideas or perhaps based on discussions with Penney, to whom he was close.

All this time, most of the Aldermaston staff were very busily engaged in the fission weapon programme – improving the kiloton designs, and starting to build up a modest stockpile. But as for the H-bomb, at the end of 1954 the Aldermaston theoreticians were plainly baffled. If this state of bafflement was realized at the highest government levels there was little sign of it, even among those best informed. For instance, Cherwell, commenting on American delays over starting discussions on Soviet nuclear weapons, thought that the Americans seemed afraid that they might conceivably give some hints about their hydrogen bombs to the British. 'But', he wrote to Churchill, 'we are really not interested in this for we already know how to make hydrogen bombs.' The scientists, he said, were only waiting for 'the new ingredients' before doing the tests.

True, the Lord President and the Minister of Supply were clearly aware that policy was running far ahead of policy execution. But there seemed to be a wide gap between perceptions in London and the realities at Aldermaston. Was it perhaps because Britain had nothing comparable to the General Advisory Committee in the United States, to advise and inform the policy makers and the government? Were the channels of scientific communication adequate? Whitehall officials and committees, and Westminster politicians, got their scientific information and advice exclusively from Penney and Cockcroft, whose apparent confidence did not seem to be borne out by the work of the Aldermaston weaponeers. Penney must have been relying heavily on his intuitive scientific ability, his unique Los Alamos experience, and the 'snippets of information' (his words) that he acquired officially or unofficially from the United States. He was – understandably – so impressed by the galaxy of nuclear talent, wealth of experience, and industrial and engineering strength in the United States that he doubted the ability of his small establishment and modest staff to achieve much without American information. One of his scientists said later that Penney thought he could deduce the answers from hints picked up on visits to the United States, but he did not get enough detail and sometimes misinterpreted what he heard. He was also chary of passing on information to his staff, perhaps for reasons of secrecy, and he may have thought it best simply to give them his own conclusions rather than the data. Useful knowledge that the Aldermaston staff lacked included results of monitoring of weapon tests; the analysis of radioactive debris was the responsibility of Harwell chemists, and the data were available to Cockcroft and Penney, but the Aldermaston scientists apparently did not have them until 1955 or even early 1956 when Cook managed to obtain them. Penney, it seems, was originally sceptical about their value but was later converted.

By the beginning of 1955 there was a complete change of direction in weapons development policy. The Chiefs of Staff had agreed only in November 1954 that, of two types of 'thermonuclear' bomb – Type A, a boosted fission bomb and Type B, an H-bomb – the latter should be chosen for development. The programme was to be aimed at a 5-megaton bomb, with the first tests in late 1958 – admittedly 'an immensely difficult undertaking'. But then Penney had doubts about this weapon. The bomb would be very heavy; very large quantities of lithium would be required, and it would be scarcely possible to get enough for a test in 1958. Large-scale production of lithium-6 by known methods would be extremely costly. In January 1955 he told the Atomic Energy Executive that he now inclined to a different approach. The first thermonuclear weapons should be smaller and lighter, and there should be two trials of smaller bombs (one about a megaton, another half a megaton) in 1957. Meanwhile work on methods of separating lithium-6 should continue with a view to testing a 5 to 10-megaton bomb in 1959. Hinton thought this more within the Atomic Energy Authority's production capacity, and it was agreed that Penney should put the new plan to the Chiefs of Staff.

Penney's report for the Chiefs of Staff, sent to Brundrett, explained the supply position and said that, assuming the 1957 tests were successful, the supply to the RAF of 1-megaton, free-falling, boosted bombs (Type A) should begin by mid-1959. Then, if Type B H-bomb tests were successful in 1960 it might be possible to begin production in 1961/62. (The H-bomb test had already slipped from 1959.) The whole programme depended on sufficient staff, Penney stressed; Aldermaston was seriously under strength. There were, he declared, positive advantages in the revised programme. Type A weapons would be available sooner and in larger numbers. The 1-megaton weapon would be more adaptable, as a powered guided bomb or in a ballistic missile, and would have safety advantages in use as a free-falling bomb. Developing Type A before Type B was, he now argued, the natural approach and technically sound; it was the route followed by the Americans, and probably the Russians too. But Penney feared that, if sufficient amounts of lithium-6 were not ready in good time for Type A trials in 1957, they might slip to 1958. Lithium technology was indeed full of problems (admirably solved later by the Aldermaston chemical engineers, led by P. A. F. White),[3] but difficulties in the supply of materials were masking a more basic problem – that Penney, and Aldermaston, did not yet know how to design the bombs. Brundrett's terse annotation on the paper was 'Volte-face No. N!'

General Sir Frederick Morgan, the Controller of Atomic Weapons at the Ministry of Supply, was highly critical of the paper, with its vagueness on costs and quantities, the slippage of trials dates and the unwarranted assumptions about what the service users really wanted. The 5-megaton yield, for example, had, he said, been given only a very cursory examination by the Chiefs of Staff in May, and had been a technical suggestion made without regard to the users' requirements or the performance of definite military tasks.

However, the weapons programme was, of course, revised as suggested. Corner told the Astrophysics Committee in February 1955 that, owing to a change of policy, 'cylindrical bombs' might not be made before 1959, and heavily boosted spherical bombs had become much more important. The committee's discussions of cylindrical bombs suggest that, by this time, the physicists had a fair idea of the components and characteristics of staged bombs, but exactly how a hydrogen bomb could be made to work, and how a primary bomb would detonate a secondary, still eluded them.

Announcing the H-bomb decision

While the scientists were engaged in the technical problems of thermonuclear weapons, ministers and officials were studying how and when to publish the secret H-bomb decision and how to deal with the inevitable public controversy. Ever since the news of *Bravo* and the *Lucky Dragon* had revealed something of the nature of the H-bomb, its destructive power and the hazards of fall-out, there had been worldwide debate and protest, more in Britain than perhaps any country other than Japan.

There would be no special announcement of the government's H-bomb decision of July 1954. It was revealed in February 1955 in the annual Defence White Paper:[4]

> Overshadowing all else in 1954 [it began] has been the emergence of thermonuclear bombs. This has had, and will continue to have, far-reaching effects on the policy of the United Kingdom. ... We have to prepare against the risk of a world war and so prevent it; it is on the nature of these preparations that the existence of thermonuclear weapons has it main effect. At the same time we must contrive to play our part in the defence of the interests of the free world as a whole, and particularly of the Commonwealth and Empire, in the 'cold war'; and we must meet the many other peacetime commitments arising from our position as a great power with world-wide responsibilities. ... The United States government has announced that it is proceeding with full-scale production of thermonuclear weapons. The Soviet government is clearly following the same policy; although we cannot tell when they will have thermonuclear weapons available for operational use. The United Kingdom also has the ability to produce such weapons. After fully considering all the implications of this step the government has thought it their duty to proceed with their development and production.

The ultimate aim, the White Paper said, was a practical scheme of disarmament and 'the abolition of the use, possession and manufacture not only of all nuclear weapons but also of other weapons of mass destruction, together with reductions of conventional armaments and armed forces to agreed levels which would redress the present Communist superiority'. Meanwhile Britain must build up 'the most powerful deterrent we can achieve', must work for peace through strength, and so would develop and test hydrogen weapons. The power of these weapons, the White Paper explained, meant that accuracy of aim assumed less importance, so that attacks could be delivered by aircraft flying at great speed and altitude; this would greatly increase the difficulty of the defence, making the Soviet Union more vulnerable to a hypothetical

British attack and enhancing Britain's deterrent capability. The existence of thermonuclear weapons, it was argued, 'had considerably reduced the risk of war on a major scale ... The knowledge that aggression will be met by overwhelming nuclear retaliation is the surest guarantee that it will not take place'.

What if the deterrent failed? The White Paper addressed the possibility:

> Until the Soviet Union agrees to participate in a secure system of disarmament, the free nations must base their plans and preparations on the assumption that if a major war were precipitated by an attack on them they would have to use all the weapons at their disposal in their defence. The consciences of civilised nations must naturally recoil from the prospect. ... Nevertheless, in the last resort, most of us must feel that determination to face the threat of physical devastation, even on the immense scale that must now be foreseen, is manifestly preferable to ... subservience to militant Communism. ... Moreover, such a show of weakness or hesitation to use all the means of defence at our disposal would not reduce the risk. All history proves the contrary.

(It was not manifestly preferable to everyone in the country, as the rise of the protest movements and peace campaigns was to prove.)

The White Paper emphasized the Soviet danger; understandably it did not mention the fear of American initiation of a 'forestalling war', and the consequent need to be in a strong position to influence the United States, which had featured so prominently in British defence discussions during 1954.[5] Nor did it mention the possibly reduced credibility of United States protection after the United States itself became vulnerable to Soviet attack, perhaps in a very few years' time.

The Defence Debate in the House of Commons took place on 1 and 2 March 1955 and Churchill made a momentous speech, lighting up the rather colourless official words of the White Paper.[6] He compared the limited terrors of the atomic bomb, awful as they were, with the unprecedented horrors of the hydrogen bomb. With it 'the entire foundation of human affairs was revolutionised, and mankind placed in a situation both measureless and laden with doom'. A small amount of plutonium would suffice to produce weapons which would give indisputable world domination to any great power which was the only one to have it. There was no absolute defence against the hydrogen bomb, and no method in sight by which any nation could be completely guaranteed against the devastating injury which even a score of them might inflict on wide regions. 'I find it poignant', he said, 'to look at youth in all its activity and ardour and, most of all, to watch little children playing their merry games, and wonder what would lie before them if God wearied of mankind.'

After speaking of the problems of disarmament, he explained the evolution of strategic ideas of deterrence and the political thinking behind British policy. It was widely believed that, but for American nuclear superiority, Europe would already have been reduced to Soviet satellite status, but Britain needed to make its own contribution, both to reinforce the free world's deterrent power and to strengthen its influence within the free world. He did not think that Britain would have much influence over United States policy and actions while largely dependent on their protection. Without a British deterrent force:

> we cannot be sure that in an emergency the resources of other powers would be planned exactly as we wished, or that the targets which threaten us most would be given what we consider the necessary priority. The targets might be of such cardinal importance that it might ... really be a matter of life and death for us. ... Then it may well be that we shall by a process of sublime irony have reached a state in this story where safety will be the sturdy child of terror, and survival the twin brother of annihilation.

Harold Macmillan, Minister of Defence, echoed Churchill's views. The idea that since the main deterrent was American, there should not be a British contribution, was dangerous. Politically it would surrender Britain's power to influence American policy. Strategically and tactically would equally deprive Britain of any influence over the selection of targets and use of its vital striking forces. He mentioned especially the possibilities of tactical use of nuclear weapons in the Middle East and Far East.

There was little or no dissent in the House of Commons. Clement Attlee, Leader of the Opposition, agreed that Britain's influence in the world must be maintained. 'That influence', he said, 'does not depend solely on the possession of weapons, although I have found, in practical conversations, that the fact that we do possess these weapons does have an effect upon the rulers of other countries. It is quite an illusion to think that it does not have an effect.'[7]

The press, including those papers most often critical of the government, also supported the government's policy.[8] The *Manchester Guardian* thought the decision sound, and believed that the government was right to build up a powerful deterrent, especially in the absence of a close partnership with the United States. The paper did, however, criticize the government for relying on developing bombers rather than missiles to carry the weapons. The *Daily Telegraph* and *The Economist* both supported the policy of developing the hydrogen bomb.

The aged Churchill's rhetoric was deeply felt; it was his last statement on a subject which profoundly concerned him. He appeared an unequivocal supporter of deterrence, but shortly before his speech, his mind was 'full of foreboding, his mood dark and sombre'. His doctor, Lord Moran, wrote of him, 'It is his belief – and this he holds with a fierce, almost religious intensity – that he and he alone can save the world from a frightful war which will be the end of everything in the civilised globe that man had known and valued.' It was this fearful anxiety that 'robbed him of all peace of mind' and kept him hanging on in office so long,[9] but he was soon to hand over the burden of responsibility to his successor, Anthony Eden.

Only a few miles from Westminster but far from Churchill's 'tortured vision of the future'[10] the Aldermaston scientists were struggling with the problems of thermonuclear weapons, Types A and B. (Type A was thermonuclear only in using thermonuclear reactions to boost large fission bombs.) No one reading the 1955 Defence White Paper would have realized that neither type was yet well understood. Proposals for a Type A megaton design, *Green Bamboo*, were discussed by the Astrophysics Committee in March, and its feasibility was thought to be far from certain. Meanwhile work on Type B, called *Green Granite*, was given a low priority. Work on *Green Bamboo* continued and in May it was hoped that it might be fired in April 1957 'on some uninhabited island'. This would depend on two 1956 atomic trials in Australia. In April 1956, one or two bombs containing a little lithium deuteride would be fired in the Monte Bello Islands, off the north-west coast of Australia, to investigate the boosting factor. (This operation was later code-named *Mosaic*.) Then in October 1956 another trial (later called *Buffalo*) would be carried out at the Maralinga test site in South Australia, and would include up to three 'thermonuclear' weapons (depending on the *Mosaic* results). By the term 'thermonuclear' the scientists must still have meant 'boosted' (for there was absolutely no question of testing H-bombs in Australia, and it was difficult enough to explain even the *Mosaic* shots so as to gain the Australian government's approval).[11]

The Aldermaston scientists do not yet appear to have discussed an idea suggested by the Polish-born Professor Josef Rotblat[12] in London. He had been a member of the British wartime mission at Los Alamos, but had left when the war in Europe ended, as he believed the mission's purpose – to forestall any possible Nazi atomic bomb – had been fulfilled. After reading United States press reports and official statements about the *Bravo* shot, and studying Japanese analyses of materials which fell on the *Lucky Dragon*, he calculated that the fall-out contained 40 times more fission radioactivity than could have come just from the core of the fission bomb primary. The fission radioactivity appeared instead to be related to the total explosive power of *Bravo* and he concluded that fission, not fusion, accounted for most of the energy released in the explosion. He deduced that if a hydrogen bomb was surrounded with a natural uranium shell, the fast neutrons released in the thermonuclear reactions would be sufficiently energetic to cause abundant fissions in the natural uranium (which is not normally fissile). If so, Rotblat argued, the so-called hydrogen bomb was really a fission-fusion-fission bomb. He visualized it as a fission core probably containing plutonium, surrounded by a mass of lithium deuteride, surrounded in turn by a uranium shell which would also act as a tamper. This would result in high yields – he mentioned 20 megatons as a possibility – but much fall-out since fission, unlike fusion, creates fall-out. Rotblat had identified one important feature of *Bravo*, but not, apparently, that it was a staged device and not an integral one.

The small group which had come together in the first Astrophysics Committee meeting had now grown, as recruitment at Aldermaston went ahead and the numbers of theoreticians increased. New members appeared from time to time and in the summer of 1955 some key figures in the British H-bomb story made their first appearance.[13] The group was still trying to work out, from the scanty information it had, how the American programme had developed, and to chart all the relevant facts and dates so far as they were known. The scientists continued with various lines of theoretical work on thermonuclear reactions and radiation hydrodynamics, and on practical aspects of weapon design, as we shall see in Chapter 7.

Part III
Britain's Response

6
Aldermaston and the Weaponeers

Aldermaston and the Atomic Energy Authority

Whose task was it to produce the H-bomb? The government's 'general instruction' was given, as we saw, to the Atomic Energy Authority (AEA), newly set up in July 1954. The Atomic Energy Authority Act removed atomic energy from the Ministry of Supply and placed the project – research, production and weapons R&D – in a novel body outside the civil service. Its governing board was chaired by a chief executive, Sir Edwin Plowden, a senior civil servant – 'the chief of planners'[1] – from the Treasury and Cabinet Office. Cockcroft, Hinton and Penney were board members, while continuing to manage their respective groups. Cockcroft's group at Harwell would still provide research assistance to Penney's group, and Hinton's factories would go on producing the fissile and other special materials for it. But the main weapons task would fall on Aldermaston[2] and Penney.

Penney, and the origins of Aldermaston

Some of the scientists who faced the H-bomb challenge had been with Penney for seven or eight years. Some were later recruits and there was an influx of new men into Aldermaston after mid-1954. Aldermaston had grown from the Ministry of Supply's wartime Armament Research Department (ARD) and its main establishment (ARDE) at Fort Halstead in Kent. ARDE was a big and successful R&D organization, staffed largely by scientists recruited before the war when jobs were scarce and the scientific civil service could pick and choose from men with first class honours degrees.

Dr William Penney, newly returned from Los Alamos, had been appointed as the Ministry's Chief Superintendent, Armament Research, and head of ARDE, in 1946, in charge of all types of weapons R&D. Penney was a youthful and unconventional CSAR (or 'Caesar') – a big, athletic, handsome young man in his mid-30s with an engaging personality, who seemed as much at home on the football field as in the laboratory. From a modest (military) family background, he had had a brilliant academic career as a mathematical physicist of great power and versatility, a professor at Imperial College at the age of only 27. Directed into war work in 1940,[3] in 1944 he was sent to Los Alamos with the British mission. There he won golden opinions and gained the especial confidence of General Groves, the formidable and somewhat Anglophobic chief of the Manhattan Project.

Penney's ambition had been to return to academic life when the war ended. But Chadwick, the head of the British mission to the Manhattan Project, had already recommended him to London as the best man to lead a post-war British atomic bomb project. Lord Cherwell called him 'our chief – indeed our only – real expert on the construction of the bomb'. (There were others but he was the only one of the Los Alamos team who joined the British bomb project.) 'The Americans admit frankly', Cherwell wrote, 'that they would give a great deal to get him back. But on an appeal to his patriotism he gave up the offer of a very attractive professorship.'[4] Though he made his choice reluctantly, Penney was motivated not only by patriotism but also by a fervent hope that nuclear deterrence could mean the end of appallingly destructive world wars such as he had seen twice in his lifetime.

Penney's assets

In 1947 Penney was officially directed to create a super-secret atomic enclave inside Fort Halstead (code-named HER, short for 'high explosives research'). No one else in the Fort had any nuclear background, but there was a wealth of other expertise, especially on electronics, the testing and operation of high explosives, and the observation and measurement of phenomena of very short duration measured in fractions of milli-seconds. He hand-picked 34 ARDE staff, all experienced conventional weapons scientists, some division heads in their 50s, and they began work on Britain's first A-bomb, to be tested in the autumn of 1952. HER was to be the nucleus of the future Atomic Weapons Research Establishment (AWRE) and some of the original staff played important parts in the H-bomb programme.

Among the younger HER scientists were four specialists in electronics and instrumentation, Charles Adams, John Challens, L. C. Tyte and Ieuan Maddock; the mathematician John Corner and the physicist Herbert Pike; Graham Hopkin, metallurgist; David Lewis, chemist; Ernie Mott and Bill Moyce, both explosives specialists; and Roy Pilgrim, an expert on blast. Most of them went on to life-long careers in nuclear weapons.

Penney considered Corner to be the cleverest member of his staff.[5] A creative scientist with a quick, wide-ranging and endlessly enquiring mind, he was also a meticulous and well-organized worker. An exacting and somewhat authoritarian division head, his slight, austere figure was regarded with awe by some of his staff. He could be quick-tempered but was witty, courteous, fair, and especially kindly towards young colleagues and had a surprising sense of fun. His close friend, Herbert Pike, though slightly senior to him, was happy to act as his deputy. Pike, a gentle, thoughtful man whom no one could imagine losing his temper, was an experienced weapons scientist with a penetrating intelligence.

His second cleverest scientist, Penney thought, was the Welsh chemist, David Lewis, a teacher before the war. He was later known as 'Dai Trit' because of his expertise in tritides. Penney said of him; 'He works harder and faster than any other chemist in the establishment, and his staff are inspired by his example.'

Another Welshman, Graham Hopkin, had worked in ARDE, with distinction, since 1930. In HER he was faced with an entirely new range of metallurgical problems and new materials, beginning with the unknown plutonium and going on to many more exotic and equally unpleasant substances. He and his staff were to be among the heroes of the British H-bomb story.

Outstanding was another Welshman, Ieuan Maddock who, after a successful career at Aldermaston, achieved distinction in Whitehall and in the academic and business worlds. Then there was John Challens, patrician in manner, who had worked during the war at the rocket research establishment at Aberporth on the Welsh coast. Towards the end of the war he had been sent to Germany to study V1 and V2 establishments, and then to the United States to help with rocket research – work for which he later received the American Medal of Freedom. In his mid-30s, already a leading rocketry expert and a young man of outstanding drive and leadership,[6] he became one of HER's and Aldermaston's most notable figures (and a future director of AWRE).

An invaluable addition to HER in 1949 was a lively young scientist named P. A. F. (Percy) White, who made some crucial contributions to the weapons programme and especially to the H-bomb. Like many of his colleagues – and Penney himself – he was a 'scholarship boy' from a modest family background. Penney described him as an excellent colleague and 'an extremely able chemical engineer who has the ability to express himself with extraordinary clarity ... self-confident, energetic, and [with] an enquiring mind'.

Another very able young scientist, who joined Penney three years later, was W. H. B. (Bill) Lord, who had been given an award for the wartime invention of the radio-proximity fuse. He became Graham Hopkin's deputy and later Aldermaston's chief metallurgist, and subsequently had a successful career in the Ministry of Defence.

Penney greatly appreciated his chief engineer, John Dolphin, whom he described as 'quite the most inventive man on my staff'. He was most anxious to keep him but feared that he would not stay long at Aldermaston 'at a salary so far below that which he [was] being offered regularly by industry' (£5,000 in 1953).[7] Dolphin combined self-confidence and a flamboyant personality with a capacity for getting things done, as rapid construction work at Aldermaston showed. He spent boldly and would confidently put up new buildings and order plant to anticipate possible future needs; sometimes saving precious time and sometimes wasting resources. Though a prolific inventor, his enthusiasm for inventing nuclear weapons, as he admitted, was not backed up by a knowledge of physics. For all his talents, he was not universally admired at Aldermaston.

A key member of the senior staff was the experienced 'Shack' (J. Shackleton), a much respected figure at the Institution of Mechanical Engineers. As head of Aldermaston's weapons design division, he was the design authority, with the onerous responsibility for the translation of the physicists' conceptual designs into practical engineering drawings.

Many other members of Penney's early staff should no doubt have been mentioned in this brief account and it may be hoped that some will appear in a future history of Aldermaston.

Without ARDE, and the scientific civil service, Penney could never have built up a nuclear weapons team so quickly. There was an acute post-war shortage of scientific and technical manpower, and competition was severe. The civil service could no longer pick and choose as in pre-war days but it did provide Penney with a nucleus of staff and a channel of recruitment. Even so, it was hard for HER/Aldermaston to attract its share of candidates who were often averse to weapons work and discouraged by secrecy. Harwell was a honey-pot for those who wanted to work in the atomic field.

Lost assets

The most obvious source of talented and uniquely experienced scientists to work in the post-war atomic weapons project was the British mission to wartime Los Alamos. But of the 30 men, only Penney did so (and his experience was in weapon effects rather than in weapon design). Some of them felt, after the war, that weapons development was not a satisfactory field of work in peacetime.[8] Some wanted to resume their academic careers. A few chose to work abroad.[9] Others joined Harwell which, besides its many attractions, had the advantage of an earlier start.

What might have been the effect on the weapons project – and especially on the H-bomb – if it had had at its command the talents and experience[10] of, say, Tuck, Rotblat, Fuchs and Bretscher (who had worked on the Super), Titterton and, pre-eminently, Peierls and Frisch?

However it would be a mistake to assume[11] that Tuck, Fuchs, Bretscher, and other Harwell scientists had no contact with the weapons programme. Fuchs and Penney corresponded at length about the A-bomb and there were quite numerous exchange visits between Harwell and HER and, later, a liaison committee.

After Fuchs' arrest at the end of January 1950 some of his scientific papers were passed to HER though, as we saw (Chapter 4), as late as April 1954 Corner was urging Penney to try to extract more Super papers from Harwell. We now know (Chapter 3) that Fuchs probably gave the Soviet Union more useful information about H-bomb possibilities than was formerly thought. We do not know what information, if any, he gave the British weaponeers about the Super (including his May 1946 patent) and whether his own thermonuclear ideas developed further after leaving Los Alamos in June 1946. Unfortunately no evidence seems to have survived, an unfortunate gap in our scientific history.[12]

Aldermaston – a new site and a new organization

Long before the AEA was set up in 1954, the growing HER needed to disengage from ARDE and find a new site. In 1950 Penney's responsibilities were redefined to exclude non-nuclear armaments and he became CSHER instead of CSAR. An airfield at Aldermaston in Berkshire was taken over in April 1950 and the building of laboratories, workshops and offices began. HER staff moved gradually from Fort Halstead to Aldermaston over four years. Working at two locations – one resembling a huge construction site – must have been difficult and Percy White said that Aldermaston looked like a Romany camp. In these conditions the *Hurricane* weapon was designed and produced. It was an unsettling time, especially while it was uncertain which staff would remain on ARD strength and which would transfer to Aldermaston.

Then, in 1953–54, came even more uncertainty and disruption as AEA was set up, and the atomic project was taken out of the civil service. Existing staff had the option of transferring to the new AEA, or quitting atomic work in order to remain in the scientific civil service (which had some decided advantages). They were given two years to make up their minds and for a difficult two years the Aldermaston management never knew just where it was; at one point Penney feared that he might lose 18 out of 40 men in one group. All this exacerbated a chronic staff shortage for, though staff numbers had increased, they were always seriously under strength, particularly in some disciplines and skills; and wastage was worrying.

Whether the setting up of AEA at this stage was a wise, if difficult, measure to meet new circumstances and needs, or an untimely disruption at a critical period, is an interesting subject for discussion (but not here).

Aldermaston in crisis

The *Hurricane* programme, and then the rush to mount the two-shot *Totem* trial in Australia in 1953 just a year later,[13] had been a heavy strain. Everyone had been seriously overworked for two or three years. Now the immediate task was to weaponize and improve the *Hurricane* test device and to build up a stockpile (for Aldermaston was a factory, responsible for warhead production as well as for R&D).

When Penney returned from Australia in November 1953, after *Totem*, there were no plans for British H-bombs. In his view they were too expensive and too intricate for the British to contemplate making them. Aldermaston only needed to work on 'orthodox' A-bombs. On these, Penney felt that he had taught his staff all the principles, and what remained was largely a matter of application. His prime task accomplished, he hoped to resume an academic career and return to Imperial College as professor of mathematics, perhaps assisting Aldermaston as a consultant. But, as he said, things did not work out like this. The Russians had made great progress and the Americans had developed and tested the H-bomb. Even on atomic weapons, immense possibilities had opened up. The British were behind in what might be a race for their lives. 'I have therefore', Penney wrote, 'without hesitation, but with a heavy heart, decided that I must stay in my present job, at least for the initial five-year period.'

Yet the A-bomb programme alone was going to be very difficult to carry out. In May 1954, before the H-bomb decision, Penney again emphasized Aldermaston's staffing problems. Morale had steadily declined since *Totem*. His staff feared an unknown future, and possibly worsened conditions, in the new AEA. The popular anti-nuclear outcry after *Castle Bravo* in March 1954 created a feeling of impermanence; they were worried that a possible change in government policy might mean redundancies. Recruitment was getting even more difficult, since most potential recruits thought AEA's future unreliable. New intake hardly kept pace with wastage, and organisation charts showed many gaps at all levels.[14] All these problems faced Aldermaston just as its 'already crushing programme' was being hugely increased.

By this time (Corner said) the establishment was displaying classic symptoms of an approaching nervous breakdown. There was no long-term research, and little co-ordination; decisions were deferred, or quickly made and then reversed. Penney, desperately overloaded, was frequently absent on other urgent government business, and there was no one to mind the shop. If Aldermaston was to have a long-term future, big changes were needed urgently.

Until 1953 Penney had not wanted nuclear physicists, believing that the Manhattan Project data would be enough, but that in any case Harwell would provide nuclear data. However the new thermonuclear demands, and disappointment with Harwell's contributions, convinced him that Aldermaston must have its own nuclear physicists to achieve fundamental and continued advances in weapons.

He wanted physicists who were both project-minded and capable of original work in the nuclear field. So he began to create a nuclear physics group and build up a school of nuclear physics at Aldermaston, headed by Dr K. W. Allen. Allen was to be one of Aldermaston's most talented and creative scientists and to make important contributions to nuclear physics and to H-bomb research.

Despair

In the weeks before the H-bomb decision, Penney confessed to being 'terribly depressed'. He had just failed to persuade two men whom he especially wanted to join him.[15] He wrote in May 1954:

> The plain fact is that weapons work is unpopular and nobody wants to do it. If I have to run with just the same people that I have had for the last year or two we are going to make a mess. Even the programme which is now definite is somewhat above the present capacity of the establishment to bear and with the possible new requirements I am sure that we shall steadily fall behind and not meet our dates. ... A large number of my electronics staff are trying to get other jobs.

He urgently needed a strong scientific deputy to share his intolerable work-load. After failing to obtain the distinguished metallurgist, Dr Vivian Bowden; he had made enquiries about the possibility of Dr Henry Hulme, whom he called 'a theoretical physicist of considerable distinction'; and he had more than once asked for W. R. J. Cook, Chief of the Royal Naval Scientific Service (CRNSS).[16] 'Very great pressure would have to be put on the Admiralty to get their consent to his release', Penney told Perrott (a senior AEA administrator), 'and I do not know if he would be willing to come'.

The Cabinet's H-bomb decision made a decisive difference. The Lord President took a hand, and pressure was brought to bear on the Admiralty to release Cook (as we saw in Chapter 5). He arrived at Aldermaston on 1 September 1954, to Penney's immense relief. He had been perfectly right when he identified Cook as the man who was wanted; it was an inspired appointment. Cook came very willingly because he thought the post would be exceptionally interesting and because he was convinced that deterrence would be the surest way to peace.[17]

The two leaders

Penney and Cook, both mathematicians, were alike in their quiet and unassuming manners, equable temperaments, unfailing courtesy – Cook the more formal – and dedication to public duty. Otherwise, they were very dissimilar, and they complemented each other admirably.

Penney, who was held in great affection, was an inspiring leader – the experienced Sam Curran said he had not known a better[18] – but not an organizer. A brilliant and intuitive scientist, he was, at heart, an academic, a young professor caught up into government service with all the 'wartime irregulars'[19] who had transformed Whitehall – and beyond – in World War II. With some reluctance he remained in government service for over 20 years until he returned to Imperial College as its Rector in 1967. He had a gift for communication and for building trust and confidence. But behind his frank, simple and unpretentious exterior he was a reserved and private man and a complex personality. A strong believer in nuclear deterrence, his view of nuclear weapons was ambivalent, and he worked indefatigably for a test ban treaty in the late 1950s and early 1960s.

Cook was a superb organizer, and a decisive project manager, with a powerful grasp of detail and an infallible eye for essentials. He was tremendously admired and respected, rather than loved, at Aldermaston. A scientific civil servant from 1928 until he retired in 1970, he was the complete professional and, in Penney's words, 'at heart a "defence" man'. He was familiar with the workings of Whitehall and knew the defence scene intimately. But at Aldermaston his first concern was to 'mind the shop' while Penney dealt with the wider world. He deprecated his own scientific talents – 'Sam, I'm not a real scientist', he said to the chief scientist, Sam Curran[20] – but in Curran's opinion he richly deserved the FRS he was awarded. Corner too considered him an extremely able scientist, as he needed to be in order to understand and evaluate such a wide range of advanced scientific ideas and data, to make decisions and to give firm direction to the immensely difficult H-bomb programme.

It was characteristic of Cook to take a logical step-by-step approach to a problem, with instructions to 'keep it simple, stupid!' (In this he rather resembled Hinton, the great project engineer who ran the AEA's industrial group, who always sought simplicity and would remind his engineers that they were paid to achieve results, not to be clever.) Cook would always give his full attention to any question that required it; unlike Penney who was said to be wonderful on problems that interested him but whose eyes would 'glaze over' if he was bored.

As deputy director, Cook's responsibilities covered the full range of Aldermaston's work, but the H-bomb programme was especially assigned to him. When he first arrived, in September 1954, he knew nothing about nuclear physics – much less thermonuclear weapons – and he had to learn fast. But his capacity for work seemed boundless. Unsparing of others, he was even more so of himself. He was beginning what must have been the four hardest years of his life and (Corner observed) was never the same man afterwards.[21]

Under the Penney–Cook duumvirate Aldermaston was soon remarkably transformed. The two men, so different, worked closely and well together. They would talk together at length two or three times a week, exchanging information on what each was doing and thinking, and in a broader context would 'try to understand whether nuclear war could happen'.[22] They had the highest regard for each other. Cook said of Penney 'I don't suppose the H-bomb would have been done but for him.'[23] Curran too considered Penney to be 'undoubtedly the man who led us to the H-bomb'.[24] Certainly the Aldermaston scientists were convinced that it could not have been achieved without Cook. Just after his arrival, Cook asked to be briefed in detail by all the division heads, and he discussed the current situation with each one. He was, as he told Corner years later, 'shattered'.[25] But he was heartened by the outstanding quality of such staff as Corner, Pike, Hopkin and Challens. The first priorities were to build up the staff, in particular to create a strong nuclear physics division, and to tighten up the organization. A vigorous recruitment campaign brought in a new wave of talent.

The new men

Among the older men who joined the project in late 1954 and 1955 were Henry Hulme and Sam Curran. Hulme was a distinguished mathematician and astronomer, recently returned to England after his wife's tragic death in New Zealand. Too senior to be placed under Corner in the theoretical physics division, he was attached to the director in an independent post with special responsibilities for what became known as the *Granite* (that is, the double bomb) project. Urbane, witty, companionable, and an excellent scientist – and famous for a fund of very funny, often improper stories, and for his vintage car emblazoned with his initials, HRH – he was greatly liked and admired. A good listener, an excellent co-ordinator and a lucid writer, his *Granite* papers are models of clarity; but it is impossible to tell how far they embody his own original ideas or are syntheses of ideas under current discussion. It has been suggested to us that his individual scientific input in key areas may have been considerable. Cook talked to him a good deal.

Curran was the clever son of a working class Scottish family,[26] who had won scholarships to Glasgow and Cambridge universities and studied in Rutherford's Cavendish Laboratory. During the war he had worked on radar and on the proximity fuse, and then in the Manhattan Project (at Berkeley) where he invented a scintillation counter. He returned to Glasgow University and then in 1954 – aged 42 and already an FRS – he joined Aldermaston in charge of the radiation measurements division.[27] He became very close to both Penney and Cook. His division included nuclear physics, headed by Ken Allen, radiochemistry under Frank Morgan, radiation physics under J. T. Dawson, and health physics under D. E. Barnes.

Ken Allen, from Liverpool University, who had been at the Anglo-Canadian-French research establishment at Chalk River, Ontario, for four years, joined Aldermaston in September 1954 to create the nuclear physics team that Penney wanted because the nuclear data provided by Harwell was inadequate for H-bomb studies.[28] Allen had shrewdly stipulated before joining that his group should be free to spend half its time on publishable research. He was one of the most lively and creative minds at Aldermaston, sometimes at odds with the theoreticians with whose mathematical labours he had limited patience. He did first-class work on nuclear cross-sections, and made important contributions to H-bomb thinking and especially to *Grapple Y*. Aldermaston was very strong in radiochemical analysis, under Frank Morgan, another original and creative scientist whom Penney and Curran valued very highly; and Henry Wilson did outstanding work in mass spectrometry.[29]

There were several very clever younger recruits in 1955 including Peter Chadwick, a geophysicist; Peter Roberts, a quantum physicist; Keith Roberts and Bryan Taylor, whom Corner (and others) considered to be the British counterparts of Teller and Ulam; and John Ward (whom Sakharov lists with Feynman, Freeman Dyson and others among the 'titans' of electrodynamics[30] (see also Appendix 5).

A new style

A characteristic of work at Aldermaston was 'compartmentalization', and the strict control of information on a 'need to know' basis. Compartmentalization was not based on wartime Los Alamos experience since there Oppenheimer had encouraged discussion and the exchange of ideas inside the wire. But after the atom spy cases (Nunn May, Fuchs and Maclean) and the defection of Pontecorvo, the British were intensely anxious about American distrust of British security.

The geography of the site at Aldermaston – where some of the divisions were far apart – reinforced compartmentalization. Cars were not common on the site in the 1950s and talking to someone in another division might well mean a long walk or a cycle ride in bad weather. So divisions were rather cut off from each other. Then the theoretical and nuclear physicists complained of a lack of information from the top; especially that Penney did not pass on information which could have been useful to them, including data on weapons debris analysis, kept locked in his safe either because he thought them too secret to share or because he did not realize their value to them.[31]

If division heads complained, so did some of their own staff, who wished their superiors would explain more how their tasks fitted into a wider context. Corner, for instance, kept a tight hold on the allocation of work and the flow of information in his division, but also encouraged the production of hundreds of scientific papers (Theoretical Physics Notes or TPNs) for internal distribution.

Penney disliked committees and preferred talking to people individually or in small informal groups; many ad hoc meetings took place, but were not recorded. Cook recalled[32] that Penney 'used to run, fairly spasmodically, a series of meetings with the senior people, perhaps a dozen, batting ideas to and fro'. The most systematic forum for exchange of ideas was Corner's Astrophysics Committee which consisted at first of half a dozen members of his own division and was gradually enlarged to include others. Another committee run by Corner was the Psi Committee, which provided a forum for discussion of thermonuclear problems with a few Harwell scientists.

Cook soon transformed the organization and working methods. Keith Roberts' memory of Aldermaston was that 'the establishment ran like clockwork under Cook; everything was well-documented; there was a lot of open discussion; and everything operated on a very short time-scale'.[33] One of Cook's management tools was the Weapon Development Policy Committee which he set up in April 1956. It met weekly, or more often if necessary; it directed the entire range of Aldermaston's weapon development – fission bombs, boosted bombs and H-bombs. It covered all aspects of development – conceptual design, materials, engineering, fabrication and testing. Systematic, thorough and decisive, it dealt expeditiously with major decisions and a huge amount of detail. No one who witnessed Cook's WDPC in operation ever forgot such an educative experience.

About the time the WDPC was created, the Astrophysics Committee closed, having (Corner said) completed what it had been set up to do. Some people regretted the loss of this forum for free scientific exchange but perhaps the time had come to stop 'batting ideas to and fro' and to concentrate on the most promising ones and the requirements of the approaching *Grapple* trial. Cook also set up the useful intelligence (I) committee which studied the results of monitoring weapons debris and liaised with a United States panel chaired by Hans Bethe.

A committee that was wound up when the WDPC began was a 'project committee' chaired by the chief engineer, Dolphin. (Later, Dolphin transferred from Aldermaston to Harwell but left there quite soon for a senior post in industry.) Cook thought it unsatisfactory to have a chief engineer with overall responsibility both for weapons engineering and for construction and site engineering services, since the two requirements were so divergent; the two functions were split into warhead development and engineering services.[34]

There were various other changes in organization in the next five years. Early in 1955 apparently Cook proposed to Penney a radical reorganization of AWRE on a project basis but the suggestion came to nothing. Then in 1958–59 very considerable changes resulted from the impact of the 1958 bilateral agreement, as we shall see in Chapter 14.

Motivation and morale

What motivated the Aldermaston men? For many it was the challenge of unique and difficult scientific work. For many, perhaps most, it was the sense that they shared with Penney and Cook of making an essential contribution to national defence and to world peace. Some certainly felt that an American–Soviet nuclear duopoly was unacceptable. For some young men it provided an attractive alternative to National Service. To some it was no doubt simply a job.

For family men it offered the added advantage of a house, at a time when housing was scarce. There was a lively social life, with varied activities and sports, and Penney and his warm-hearted and practical wife did their best to make Aldermaston a family-friendly place. The overpowering secrecy of the work, its heavy demands, and (for some) long absences on weapon trials over-seas, often made life difficult or lonely for Aldermaston wives and families.

Whatever the varied motives, morale seems to have been almost universally high after the 1953 nadir. There was a sense of urgency, common effort and absolute commitment. Just before the 1957 trials (*Antler* in Australia and *Grapple X* in the Pacific) sick staff carried on working through an epidemic of Asian flu. To avoid spreading infection they hung notices on their doors warning people not to come in but to telephone instead. It is said that when Keith Roberts was in hospital for an operation he came round from the anaes-thetic to find Henry Hulme bending over him waiting for some urgently needed information.

No one at Aldermaston appears to have considered nuclear weapons, above all H-bombs, as weapons for waging war. They were for deterrent and diplo-matic purposes. One weaponeer remarked that Aldermaston seemed to him more like an agency of the Foreign Office than the Ministry of Defence. Others said that they firmly believed Britain had to have the H-bomb in order to influence the United States. None of them talked about national prestige, and Aldermaston was not a natural home for chauvinists, warmongers or Dr Strangeloves.

In this sketch of the men and the organization we have mentioned only a few people and other names will occur in other chapters, but we are sorry for any culpable omissions. The next chapter returns to the subject of the 'general instruction' given to Aldermaston, and the struggle to carry it out.

7

The Megaton Mission

1955 began with the Defence White Paper that announced the Government's decision about the H-bomb. Aldermaston was then charged with developing megaton bombs (not necessarily the same thing – chapter 5). The first priority was a 1-megaton device of the boosted Type A, which was the simpler solution. The more powerful and more difficult Type B – an H-bomb, whatever that might be – was a deferred possibility. A test of Type A was expected in 1957; of Type B, in 1958 or later, perhaps even 1960. These priorities were open to review if the difficulties of Type B could be resolved.[1]

Apart from all the unknowns facing the theoreticians, Type B presented crucial materials problems. It would require massive amounts of lithium compounds,[2] and lithium technology was unexplored territory. No one in this country had ever produced lithium metal in more than fractions of a gram, much less separated the isotopes (lithium-6 and lithium-7) in quantity, or made lithium compounds and used them to fabricate components.

The months following the White Paper of February 1955 were an anxious time for the Aldermaston theoreticians as they groped for solutions, and for the chemists, metallurgists and chemical engineers as they studied how to meet probable demands for strange and problematical materials. For the historian it is a somewhat impenetrable period. Then, early in 1956, Corner commented enigmatically, 'the light was switched on'; prospects for the H-bomb (Type B) looked much more promising, it was given a new priority, and test plans went ahead (see Chapter 10). Here we look at some landmarks in the uncertain months between summer 1955 and spring 1956.

A summer meeting – August 1955

In the summer of 1955, soon after John Ward arrived at Aldermaston,[3] there was a meeting at which, he remembered, three projects were discussed – *Green Granite*,[4] which, he said, was assigned to him; *Orange Herald*, which was to be

Bryan Taylor's responsibility;[5] and a pure fission weapon. Then Ward was 'privy to a super secret meeting' with Penney, Cook and Keith Roberts, and went to Penney's office where the latter revealed what he thought he knew so far – that the H-bomb had a primary and a secondary, that the secondary was in two pieces, and that shielding was required. He also knew how much plutonium was used in the primary, and that the Americans were making lithium hydride [sic]. On the basis of this information, Ward recalls, he was asked to 'come up with something'.[6]

Tom, Dick and Harry – September 1955

One Monday morning in September, Penney called together a small meeting.[7] Those invited were Sam Curran, John Corner, Herbert Pike, Ken Allen and Keith Roberts. Cook and Hulme were not there, nor was Ward. Corner recalled that Penney told them for the first time that in the spring of 1954 he had arranged for Foulness to make microbarograph readings of the American *Castle* shots, and had found that they fell into two groups – one batch around 1 megaton and another batch of 7 to 10 megatons. These he interpreted as two-stagers, giving near 1 megaton, and three-stagers, giving 6 to 9 megatons. Since the British requirement was only 1 megaton it would suffice, he said, to construct a two-stager.

Ken Allen remembered this occasion[8] as the 'Tom, Dick and Harry meeting', at which Penney told the five scientists how they were going to make an H-bomb. One type, Penney said, would have three basic parts mounted, and fired, in a closed cylinder. The primary stage, Tom, would be a fission bomb which would provide the flux of radiation needed to initiate the implosion of a second, possibly boosted, fission device; this he called Dick, and immediately forestalled any ribald comments on the name. Between them, Tom and Dick would supply enough energy to ignite the third component which he called Harry. However, he thought the combination of Tom and Dick would be sufficient for the yield the Chiefs of Staff wanted, and Harry would not be needed. Can Penney have meant that a double *fission* bomb was the answer? According to Pike, 'The names Tom, Dick and Harry originated when it was thought that a simple fission device was inadequate for compressing thermonuclear fuel but could be used to implode a much more powerful U235 device. This idea was soon dropped but the names remained.'[9] One thing is certain – that staged bombs were envisaged; the names Tom and Dick stuck, and were generally used for the primary and secondary in the British designs.

This important meeting raises other puzzling questions. The *Castle* series had been completed in May 1954; why were these deductions only emerging after 16 months? Why had the scientists at the heart of the thermonuclear project not heard earlier about the microbarograph scheme and the Foulness readings? In fact, microbarographic readings were unreliable over intercontinental distances, being highly dependent on weather conditions, as Corner confirmed in discussions with American colleagues in 1958. So Penney, Corner said, had got the right answer but from the wrong data. The results of analysing atmospheric debris from the *Castle* tests, which Penney had been given, would have been valuable, but were not available to the Aldermaston staff. They did indeed prove useful when at last Cook succeeded in getting access to them. The analyses of the *Mike* debris were not given to the members of the I (Intelligence) Committee until August 1956, nearly four years after the shot.

A note on blue paper – September 1955

A mysterious piece of blue foolscap paper next appears. It is dated 20 September – was it written before or after the Tom, Dick and Harry meeting? It is in Penney's handwriting, but is unsigned; it appears to be a cryptic personal working note about a two-stage device. After some brief calculations he appeared to have satisfied himself that the implosion of the second stage would be completed before the shock wave from the first stage arrived; 'Looks just about O.K.' he wrote. The key ideas were therefore in place – two separate stages and radiation transfer to operate the second stage – and Penney apparently had specific ideas about the dimensions and geometry of the device. Rather strangely, nothing was said about this striking concept at the Astrophysics Committee meeting on 28 September, even though it was central to the work the committee had been expressly set up to do. Nor, it seems, was the Tom, Dick and Harry meeting mentioned there.

By late September 1955 sufficient confidence prevailed for Dolphin to order the plant needed to manufacture large uranium cylinders 'such as may be necessary for *Green Granite*'. Work at Aldermaston on big bombs gathered pace as the scientists pursued two separate routes to the megaton objective – single-stage and two-stage designs. Though the latter (Type B) was looking more promising than formerly, Aldermaston could not afford to neglect the easier and more certain alternative (Type A), and some of the theoreticians were convinced that the big single-stage device was still the right one to go for. Three who disagreed strongly were Allen, Roberts and Taylor.

Thoughts on single-stage bombs – October 1955

Two different types of boosting were possible, Keith Roberts wrote in October 1955 – core boosting and tamper boosting. The former, suitable for smaller weapons, would best be effected by placing lithium deutero tritide (LiDT) at the centre of the core. Tamper boosting, he thought, would be more suitable for large weapons, using a layer of lithium deuteride placed between the fissile core and a thick uranium tamper; the aim would be 'to catch neutrons as they come out of the core, convert them into 14 Mev neutrons, and burn up the tamper'.

By December the dimensions of two core-boosted fission devices – *Orange Herald (Large)* and *Orange Herald (Small)* – had been handed over to Dolphin for illustrative sketch-making. The difference between the two lay only in the size and power of the HE supercharge. The object of the first, *Orange Herald (L)*, was to demonstrate a yield of about 1 megaton with the greatest certainty; that of *Orange Herald (S)* was to determine whether a yield of about 1 megaton could be obtained from a warhead weighing only about 2000 pounds. Only one *Orange Herald* would be fired at the *Grapple* trial, the choice depending on the success or failure of *Green Granite*, the two-stage device, and *Green Bamboo*, a spherical thermonuclear device.

Green Bamboo, though a single-stager, was not a boosted device in the same sense as *Orange Herald* or the two designs tested at *Grapple Z* in 1958. In a boosted device the purpose of adding a *small* quantity of thermonuclear fuel is to enhance the yield of the fission explosion by increasing the burn-up of fissile material. But a *large* quantity of thermonuclear fuel may be used in a single-stage bomb (as Keith Roberts described); then the thermonuclear yield, plus the burn-up of uranium-238 in the tamper by fast neutrons, should provide a significant proportion of the total yield. This latter type, similar to the Soviet 'layer cake' device detonated as *Joe 4* in August 1953, was sometimes regarded in the early days as one kind of H-bomb. The Russians considered *Joe 4* to be an H-bomb and, though Bethe denied it, Khariton maintained his view (see Chapter 3). In *Green Bamboo* Aldermaston produced a similar thermonuclear device, a single-stage layer cake. It was included in the plans for the first *Grapple* trial, but was not in fact fired and never became a weapon (see Chapter 10).

A blackboard bomb – December 1955

On 2 December a progress meeting was held with Penney and Cook at which, among several others, Corner, Pike and Ward were present.[10] According to Ward it stopped almost as soon as it started 'because there wasn't any progress'. After a silence Cook said, 'Well, does anybody know how it's done?'. There was an embarrassed silence for two or three minutes, and then Ward drew a staged device, including a primary – of which he had already given a drawing to Pike – on the blackboard. Pike left the room and came back with a detailed drawing of this primary which Ward had not, he said, seen himself.

There was another stage, which he described. Cook asked about the shielding. Ward had not had time to calculate the shielding. Another deadly silence: then Penney said, 'Well, this is too much like a piece of clockwork. If this were wartime we might consider something along these lines.' The drawing was rubbed off the blackboard and that, apparently, was the end of the meeting (see Appendix 5).

Soon after, Keith Roberts told him, there was another meeting to which Ward was not invited. A week later, when his re-entry permit was due to expire, he told Cook he was leaving and returned to the United States.

Ward had already been talking to Pike and Roberts about radiation implosion, and had suggested to the latter a calculation that it would be useful to do – a 'trivial calculation', he said, but which had never been done. Roberts did it in a few days, remarkably rapidly, and wrote a paper which he showed to Ward, who was 'quite impressed'. He complained that he did not receive a copy but this is perhaps not surprising as he was about to leave Aldermaston and go to the United States. (His departure caused considerable consternation in Whitehall because it meant a loss of talent, but perhaps also for reasons of secrecy.)

Radiation implosion was not, in itself, a new idea; it had been around at least since the 1946 Fuchs-von Neumann patent, but there is a great difference between thinking of the possibilities of using radiation implosion and knowing how to make it work.[11] However, its practicality certainly seems to be implied by Penney's 'note on blue paper' of 20 September 1955.

A change of emphasis – December 1955

By the end of the year confidence in the double bomb idea was sufficiently strong for Cook to write to E. S. Jackson (Director-General of Atomic Weapons – DGAW – in the Ministry of Supply) on 3 December:

> We have now come to the conclusion that there is a strong incentive to test at *Grapple* a variation of *Green Granite* sufficiently light to be capable of adaptation, if necessary, to *Yellow Sun* and the powered guided bomb. The weight, excluding electronics, would be about 2 tons. We can have such a weapon ready by 26 June 1957 for air transport to Christmas Island. ... If it succeeds we should have made a big stride forward in development for service of these economical true thermonuclear weapons.

It was time to make a submission to the Ministry of Defence and the Chiefs of Staff about the changing picture. The inclusion of *Green Granite* in *Grapple* plans was of great importance, especially if, as it now appeared, an early ban on megaton tests was more likely than ever.

The scientific position was described in a report to the Chiefs of Staff:

Our scientific knowledge of megaton warhead design is, at the present time, entirely unsupported by experimental evidence. ... Although there are certain design difficulties the most certain way we know of producing a trial megaton explosion in 1957 and thus achieving our initial aim is to use a large pure fission assembly in a Mk I case with enough fissile material to ensure a megaton yield. Such a device will be big, heavy and extravagant in fissile material and its military application could only be as a free-falling bomb.

In our present state of knowledge we cannot be certain that we know how to achieve explosions of several megatons involving large-scale thermonuclear reactions. On the other hand we should be able to prepare an experimental assembly involving the only economical way of achieving multi-megaton warheads (*Green Granite*) by 1957. Such an experiment would be essential as a basis for future development.

Between these two methods lie megaton boosted fission assemblies. This principle is intended for use in the free-falling bomb and the powered guided bomb (*Green Bamboo*). Certain preliminary experiments in boosting techniques will be carried out in 1956.[12] The essential basis of the long range ballistic missile programme ... is the development of a small light-weight megaton warhead (*Orange Herald*). This will have to be a pure fission assembly. Because of the limitation in size it would not have the same chance of success at the first trial as the pure fission assembly in the Mk I case. ... In all of the above experiments, if they are carried out in 1957, there is a risk of failure. Since our initial aim is the successful demonstration of our ability to achieve a megaton explosion, we must have an assembly based on the most certain method we know. ... There will be no need to fire this [pure fission] assembly if *Green Bamboo* is fired successfully.

Clearly, the British had to make the most of the trials planned for 1957 as it seemed increasingly possible that no further opportunities would occur. The Chiefs of Staff agreed Type B was no longer to be a deferred possibility; Types A and B were both to be developed, and tested in 1957. As 1955 ended, prospects for the H-bomb seemed promising, but the Aldermaston scientists still did not know exactly how to design one and there were important unsolved difficulties.

On 21 December, when Cook sent Dolphin a hand-written note with details and dimensions of *Orange Herald (S)* and *Orange Herald (L)* for illustrative sketch-making, he added 'Penney is running out a diagrammatic sketch of *Green Granite* for you. PS he has just brought it in and I attach it. I have added some explanation. He wanted it diagrammatic only.'

'An elementary theory' – December 1955

At the end of December Keith Roberts circulated a substantial TPN entitled 'An elementary theory of detonations I'.[13] The introduction announces it as the first in a series of notes to be issued, giving the results of work by Keith Roberts and John Ward on the design of 'Harry'. This was the first and last note in the promised series, as at the turn of the year Ward left Aldermaston. The TPN does not deal with Tom or Dick, and it is not clear exactly what Harry was; presumably it was part of a three-stage device, though we saw that, in September, Penney had ruled out three-stage devices. The TPN referred to 'the U_{235} rod' and described 'a mechanism that will give a yield of the order of 1 megaton of which not more than 10 per cent comes from the fission of U_{235} or plutonium', so that it was necessary to consider extra sources of energy, and a list of possible reactions was given.

Harry would be a cylinder about one metre long, 'initiated at one end'. Roberts and Ward had started by investigating the propagation of thermonuclear reaction waves, which they called 'detonation' waves because the reaction always involved a pressure increase. The problem was difficult because the propagation mechanism was not known *a priori*. A thermonuclear reaction, Roberts wrote, produced a pressure and temperature pulse ' ... which could not in general initiate the reaction by itself, and it was necessary for neutrons to diffuse ahead quickly enough to keep up with the pressure pulse if the wave was to be maintained ...'. It appeared that one of the main problems would be to design a thermonuclear diffusion wave capable of travelling with the rather large velocity predetermined by hydrodynamics. In most cases, Roberts thought, a thermonuclear detonation wave was probably not initiated by shock; some type of diffusion process (radiation or neutrons) seemed more likely. They would have to go back to the same starting point as John von Neumann, when in 1942 he enunciated the physical mechanism of a detonation wave.

This TPN was the basis for a colloquium in the theoretical physics division at the end of January.[14] Though the paper is full of ideas it is difficult or impossible to see in it the outlines of an H-bomb and, if John Ward had given his Aldermaston colleagues the 'secret' of radiation implosion, no clear understanding of it is reflected here.

Two stages, three stages, or only one? – January/February 1956

Alan Fraser and his radiation hydrodynamics group in the theoretical physics division continued their work on 'radiative diffusion'. Meanwhile more notes, and more sketches for *Green Granite*, were emerging from the Director's office. One described as 'D/AWRE's latest', dated 13 January, appears in one of

Dolphin's files. It is of a cylindrical case with a *Red Beard* fission bomb at one end, but otherwise does not bear any resemblance to later *Granite designs*.

At the same time new inspiration was coming from a different quarter, from the radiochemists and nuclear physicists. From 1949 on, the evolution of the Soviet weapon programme had been followed by analysing debris from Soviet atmospheric weapon tests, and also by geophysical techniques. Then arrangements were made with the United States which permitted the British to collect samples from the 1954 *Castle* tests, but there was some considerable delay in the data becoming accessible to the Aldermaston scientists. However, at some time apparently in late-1955 Cook obtained them, and passed them to the physicists and radiochemists, with immediate and interesting results.

The *Castle* series confirmed ideas that were slowly evolving at Aldermaston. There was abundant evidence from the presence of beryllium-7 in the debris that lithium-6 was involved and that uranium-238 was being burned in some way. The same was true of *Joe 4*, the Soviet detonation of August 1953. Then came the big Soviet test of November 1955, *Joe 19*. The British radiochemists, who were very good, were able to calculate the approximate masses of lithium-6 deuteride and uranium-238, but the Harwell-designed mass spectrometer at Aldermaston was apparently too insensitive for satisfactory observation of the long-lived isotopes of uranium,[15] which would have been extremely helpful at this stage.

Joe 18 and *19* were discussed with American scientists in November 1955, and again in January 1956. The American representatives, aware of special British interest in mass spectrometry, quoted their own observations. A vital point was the amount of residual uranium-233 – much too large to be accounted for by fast neutron reactions on uranium-235. The most probable explanation the British representatives could advance was that the Soviet weaponeers had used uranium-233 to differentiate between the behaviour of uranium components in two separate parts of the test device. This interpretation clarified British ideas on the mechanism of a two-stage device. *Joe 19* was a successful demonstration of a staged weapon which achieved a high degree of compression of the secondary. It did not give the British scientists new ideas that they had not yet been thinking about, but it confirmed one direction of their thinking and reinforced their confidence in it.

Yet at the end of January 1956 a paper by Henry Hulme summarizing current ideas on *Green Granite* began: 'We are confident ... that the bomb is a three-stage one in which the first bomb is imploded by ordinary explosive and the second by energy from the first bomb. The thermonuclear material which constitutes the third stage is ignited by energy and neutrons from the second bomb. We shall refer to the three components as Tom, Dick and Harry ...'. Thus, his paper suggests that Tom and Dick were fission bombs in sequence and that only the third, Harry, contained thermonuclear material.

The reference to unspecified 'energy' and neutrons suggests that he did not understand radiation implosion at all. 'We are not certain of the method of implosion of Dick', he wrote, 'but at present we cannot see how it can be done by radiation.' After discussing the problems of Tom and Dick, he came to Harry, the thermonuclear component, which he envisaged as a relatively small mass of a mixture of lithium-6 deuteride and uranium-238, possibly with some uranium-235 added. The energy from Dick, about 200 kilotons, would ignite Harry, producing tritium which would then react with deuterium to produce fast (14 Mev) neutrons, and they would then react with uranium-238 to give further fission neutrons. Pre- compression of Harry would be very important. Hulme's paper concludes with two alternatives: in one the thermonuclear fuel (possibly in the form of a rod) is separated from Tom and Dick; in the other, the thermonuclear fuel is placed all round the core of Dick (so in effect reducing the stages from three to two).

Two weeks later Ken Allen, in a fresh and lucid paper,[16] described his rather different concept. He explained the nuclear physics of the lithium-6/uranium cycle in the light of the most recent nuclear data obtained in the laboratory and from the analysis of bomb debris from American explosions. He believed that five points were established with some certainty: (1) in large thermonuclear weapons, almost all of the energy was obtained from the destruction of natural uranium in the Li6/U cycle; (2) it was not necessary to get the D-D reaction going though it might be possible in the final stages of a large weapon; (3) the main thermonuclear burning was very efficient; (4) high efficiency could only be obtained through high compression of the main charge by the atom bomb trigger; and (5) the efficiency of burning uranium-235 in *Green Bamboo* devices was about 5–10 times less than in the double-bomb variety.

After some discussion of the sanitised transcripts of the 1954 Oppenheimer hearings,[17] which he and Corner and some other Aldermaston scientists had been studying assiduously without much result, he suggested that the 'new line' adopted by the Americans in 1951 was to compress a mixture of lithium-6 deuteride and uranium surrounding a fissile core using energy from an A-bomb trigger. In the few weeks since Roberts' 'elementary theory of detonations' and Hulme's *Green Granite* paper, Allen's note marks rapid progress towards solving the main problems of the H-bomb.

At the same time, the ever-inventive Dolphin sent Penney, Cook and Hulme some notes on his 'new system for obtaining thermonuclear explosions'. 'It should be made quite clear', he wrote, 'that I have no knowledge of physics'. He describes a cylinder containing an atomic bomb, Tom, at one end, which detonates a secondary bomb, Dick, at the other. Dick is detonated, he says, by 'compression from neutron heating' but admits that no method of achieving this result has been found to date. Nevertheless he suggests that his 'new scheme solves the Teller secret'. His notes were accompanied by drawings which do not appear to resemble any likely model for *Granite*.

Penney, still working on *Green Granite*, sent Dolphin revised dimensions and modifications for Dick and Harry and asked for drawings. Killingback, one of Dolphin's staff, distributed them on 15 March 1956 when Penney held a meeting to discuss the redesign of a three-stage *Green Granite*. The decisions at the meeting were recorded by Cook himself. The details of Tom were agreed, and the design of the steel cylinder, the number of shells and the weights of uranium and lithium deuteride in the Dick were settled; Roberts was to redesign Harry.

Modifications and drawings went back and forth throughout March until, at the end of the month, Penney declared that the engineering designs must now proceed with no further modification by the scientists, and that as soon as possible RAE Farnborough must be given the data they needed in order to proceed.

Nevertheless, the basic design was still far from settled. By 4 April new drawings were produced, now showing a two-stage, not a three-stage, *Granite*. Early in April R. A. Scriven, of the theoretical physics division, circulated a paper describing a *Green Granite* in which Dick would be a simple assembly of thick spherical shells encased in a reflector.[18]

But by 27 April 1956 an authoritative engineering drawing (called a Drawing Office Sketch, or DOSK) for *Green Granite* was in existence. It shows a two-stage device and is recognisably an ancestor of the later *Granite* devices. The basic features of H-bomb design – Tom, the fission primary; Dick, the secondary with its solid thermonuclear fuel; radiation implosion; and the exploitation of the lithium-6/uranium cycle – all seem to have fallen into place by mid-April. But exactly how, in that crucial week or two, is far from clear.

Up to then perhaps the most cogent exposition had been Ken Allen's paper of 14 February, but it was not immediately followed up. The very difficult question of Dick remained: its shape; exactly what to put in it; the number, thicknesses, and arrangement of the layers.

Though hopes for the *Granite* double bomb device were now so greatly improved, the alternatives remained important, and the weaponeers pressed on with developing very large pure fission bombs, core boosted bombs in the megaton range, and also *Green Bamboo*, the thermonuclear layer cake analogous to *Joe 4*.

Progress towards the H-bomb was both incremental and uncertain, sometimes advancing and sometimes retreating. Penney, the main architect of *Green Granite*, produced a series of ideas and frequently changing sketches. But where the essential ideas came from, how they were brought together, and how the design really evolved is something of a mystery. Later accounts by participants focus on the answers to problems, rather than the tortuous search. (The development would no doubt be much easier to trace if Penney's and Cook's files still existed.)

Certainly between February and March 1956 there were some decisive steps forward, and it seems probable that the study of foreign weapon test debris, especially from the *Castle* series and *Joe 19*, was very influential. It apparently helped to clarify and confirm ideas which the British scientists were already exploring rather than to provide new ideas, and this was important. Would the Aldermaston scientists have made quicker and more direct progress if they had had such data sooner, immediately after the *Castle* series?

From April 1956, the evolution becomes more logical and easier to follow, as Cook's famous WDPC (see Chapter 6) moves into action and takes charge of weapon development and test planning. There would still be new ideas and changes of programme right up to D-Day, as we shall see in the account of the first *Grapple* trial (Chapter 10). But, first, a new test range had to be found and the test operation planned (Chapter 8), urgently, for intense political pressures for a test ban were building up in the world outside Aldermaston (Chapter 9).

8
Captain Cook's Coral Island

Full-scale thermonuclear trials were implicit in the decision to build a British hydrogen bomb for two reasons. First, the scientists had to be sure their ideas would work, and secondly, for propaganda purposes, the politicians wanted a very big bang. Since there was a 50-kiloton limit on tests in Australia, and an embargo on thermonuclear weapons as a type, it would not be possible to fire a test shot there. So, as the scientists at Aldermaston began working on a hydrogen bomb, and even before the July 1954 Cabinet decision, the search began for a suitable location.

Penney was always concerned about safety and he decided that a site for the new range should be assessed first from a scientific and safety viewpoint, even before military or feasibility considerations. After the *Castle Bravo* incident he wrote to the Director of the Meteorological Office seeking information about wind structure in the southern hemisphere, particularly towards the polar regions – information essential for reliable prediction of fall-out patterns. Aldermaston estimated that 500 miles was the minimum safe distance from inhabited land, or from shipping, for a near-surface explosion of a high yield weapon; for an airburst the safe distance would be 300 miles. To ensure the safety of trials personnel the safe distance would be 50 to 100 miles. Much depended on the type of trial but, at this stage, ideas of how it would be carried out were still very open because ideas about the weapons themselves were so rapidly changing.

Penney summed up current thinking in December 1954. Choice of both site and type of test presented great difficulty. There were various options. The bomb could be tested in an unmanned radio-controlled aircraft; on a ship moored in a 'safe' place at sea, a method favoured by Aldermaston; or in a 'V-2 type rocket' at high altitude – but this would entail much effort to develop a launch vehicle. Possible locations considered included various remote islands or the icy wilderness of Antarctica. An airburst from an unmanned aircraft would need a base for the unmanned aircraft and the 'mother' aircraft, perhaps (Penney thought) in territory belonging to Australia, New Zealand or South Africa. He discussed the matter with Vice-Admiral Clifford, the Deputy Chief of Naval Staff. The Navy favoured the Antipodes Islands, some 500 miles south-east of New Zealand. *Green Bamboo* – the single-stage, spherical, thermonuclear design then favoured for the megaton bomb – might, it was thought, be detonated in a ship anchored close to the selected island (as at *Hurricane* in 1952).

About this time the chairman of the United States Atomic Energy Commission, Admiral Lewis Strauss, spoke informally to the British Ambassador in Washington about possible British use of the American base at Eniwetok and, rather surprisingly, indicated that Britain would not have to pay for it. However, the British government did not favour the suggestion, because ideas on the conduct of the tests were not yet sufficiently advanced for them to put forward any firm proposals, and the search for a new range continued. In early May 1955 the Foreign Secretary, Selwyn Lloyd, after con-sulting departments, concluded that the Kermadec Islands in the South Pacific, 600 miles north-east of New Zealand, would be suitable. As the islands were New Zealand territory, he advised the Prime Minister, Anthony Eden, to ask Sydney Holland, the New Zealand Prime Minister, personally for his help. Holland refused, despite detailed assurances about the safety precautions, and much emphasis on the importance of the tests for Britain and the defence of the Commonwealth. Holland feared an unfavourable public reaction if such a decision became known in the run-up to New Zealand's 1957 general elec-tion. But for the next few months he and his colleagues were under much pressure from the British government to change their minds.

Doubts of success in persuading Holland prompted Eden to ask the Foreign Office about alternatives. The department replied that the Kermadec Islands were only the first of four possibilities; the others were Malden Island (in the mid-Pacific Line Group); McKean Island (in the Phoenix Group), and the old favourite, a ship in mid-ocean. Alternatively, an American test site was still on offer. Action on these options began at once, and an outline of the require-ments for an island site was sent to the Acting High Commissioner in the West Pacific who was asked for an urgent report. Eden sent a somewhat stern letter to the New Zealand Prime Minister but Holland would not budge from his position.

On 18 August Eden's private secretary, Philip de Zulueta, received a full account of the search. Malden Island was now the favourite; it would be linked to other islands for ancillary activities, particularly for the aircraft taking part in the operation. A preliminary photographic reconnaissance of the area would be carried out by two Shackleton bombers of RAF Coastal Command and a detailed ground survey would follow. The air survey would be based on Canton Island in the Phoenix Group (then under joint United

Kingdom and United States administration because of a dormant sovereignty dispute). It was decided to tell the Americans about the mission in the strictest confidence; especially as they would certainly be able to work it out for themselves. However – to minimize any local trouble or panic arising from speculation about possible nuclear tests – a cover plan was desirable, and the Air Ministry suggested saying that, as information on many British Islands in the Pacific was unreliable or out of date, the opportunity was being taken to combine a photographic reconnaissance with a navigational training exercise. If the Central Pacific area proved unsuitable, then the government would return to the charge with Mr Holland and, meanwhile, he would be told that the British did not regard his refusal as final. For the present, he would be asked whether the New Zealand Navy's survey ship *Lachlan* could make a detailed survey if the results of the preliminary air reconnaissance were satisfactory. He would also be asked for information on Penrhyn Island (600 miles south-west of Malden Island) which New Zealand controlled.

Eden was not altogether happy about all this. Telling the Americans about British thermonuclear test plans might lead to a leak, and the use of Canton Island as a base for the Shackletons would be dangerous from a security point of view. Was there not, he asked, another island in which the Americans were not concerned, or could not an aircraft carrier be used? The cover story was, he thought, too thin to deceive anyone. The Ministry of Defence sent him concerted Whitehall views on the plans on 25 August. Using an aircraft carrier was not practicable; the presence of such a large naval vessel was likely to cause undue speculation and anyway Shackletons were too big to land on an aircraft carrier. Canton Island was the only realistic choice, because no other islands within range of Malden Island had active landing strips. There would be considerable difficulties with the Americans if they were not told the complete truth; as they would certainly work out for themselves what was happening. A good deal of help would be required from them and the Secretary of State, the chairman of the Atomic Energy Commission and the Joint Chiefs of Staff should all be informed as a matter of course. Though still apprehensive that preliminary preparations for the forthcoming nuclear tests might lead 'to our interests becoming known', Eden was satisfied there was no alternative and he agreed to send a personal message to President Eisenhower about the real purpose of the preliminary reconnaissance.

The air reconnaissance was discussed in detail at a meeting of the Atomic Weapons Trials Executive on 1 September. The chairman, General Sir Frederick Morgan, Controller of Atomic Weapons (CAW) in the Ministry of Supply, explained the operational need for a megaton weapon. The rising tide of public opinion against atmospheric trials meant that an international agreement to halt testing might develop quite rapidly, ending any hope of developing and demonstrating a British hydrogen bomb, so it must be tested as early as possible. A trial had therefore been provisionally scheduled for April/May 1957. Scientifically and logistically this allowed little time. For planning purposes it was to be assumed that Christmas and Malden Islands would ultimately be chosen for the new range. Pending the appointment of a Task Force Commander, a small working party was set up to study the requirements of the trial, chaired by Roy Pilgrim (head of Aldermaston's trials division). Assuming that the trial would involve an airdrop from a manned aircraft, a suitable airstrip was required as a main base. It would have to be within 500 miles of ground zero (GZ), and GZ itself would be five miles from an island where cameras and diagnostic equipment could be mounted. Malden Island had already been selected as a possible site for the instrumentation, and a reconnaissance should be made of the airstrips known to exist on Christmas, Penrhyn and Palmyra Islands. Group Captain Menaul, for the Air Ministry, said it would need fourteen days' notice and would then take about four weeks – an accurate estimate as it turned out. On 17 September, three overloaded Shackletons from 240 Squadron, RAF Ballykelly, staggered into the air and began the long journey to the Pacific – first to a temporary base on Canton Island, and then on to Christmas, Penrhyn and Malden Islands.

Meanwhile Eden had written again to Holland expressing displeasure over his refusal of the Kermadec Islands. He was much disappointed that Holland did not feel able to help; other less suitable sites in the Central Pacific were, he said, being considered but the practical difficulties were likely to be serious. However, would Holland help by allowing the air reconnaissance of Penrhyn and the use of the survey ship *Lachlan*? Holland was not encouraging even when Eden pointed out that the Americans had given full co-operation. However, negotiations continued and finally, on 17 September, after assurances that the reconnaissance would not go near New Zealand itself, Holland agreed to the use of the *Lachlan*.

Pilgrim's working party considered the results of the air reconnaissance (known as the 'Cook's Tour') and the requirements of the megaton weapon trial, and affirmed that Christmas and Malden Islands should be used. At last, on 27 October 1955, the site for the new range had been chosen. Land and hydrographic surveys of the islands now had to be carried out; Eden wrote to remind Holland about the *Lachlan*, and received a favourable reply on 8 December (from the appropriately named Thomas Lachlan Macdonald, the minister in charge of defence, external affairs and island responsibilities). The survey was to begin on 20 January 1956.

In October 1955 the *Grapple* Working Party had produced a statement of Aldermaston's requirements for the trial, the tasks for the three services, and the facilities needed on Christmas and Malden Islands, with a tentative timetable of events from January 1956 to the weapon drops in May and June 1957. An airbase would have to be built at Christmas Island, capable of handling the aircraft that would drop the bomb – a four engine 'V-class' jet bomber called the Valiant, then about to enter squadron service with the RAF. The aircraft would have to drop the test devices about two miles offshore at Malden Island, where instrumentation would be set up to measure certain characteristics of the explosions.

The idea was simple, but the logistics were daunting. It was a formidable undertaking to construct an airbase large enough to handle and service all the aircraft likely to be involved, with all the facilities for weapon assembly and testing, and accommodation for several thousand people, on a small tropical island with no fresh water, no food except coconuts and fish, and a difficult climate. Much heavy equipment, and immense quantities of building materials, would have to come by sea from the United Kingdom. A big shipping operation would be needed to set up the base and then provision it, keeping it adequately supplied with vehicles, equipment such as generators and water distillation plant, and vast quantities of aircraft fuel. A regular airlift from the United Kingdom would also be essential for urgently needed items – spare parts, weapon components, fresh food and mail. To complete the initial construction work in time would call for heroic efforts from the Army's Royal Engineers.

There were also diplomatic and political problems. One concerned SPAL, the American-owned South Pacific Air Line. It was about to begin a regular service, using British-built flying boats, from the lagoon at the north-west end of Christmas Island. SPAL had been given the necessary permits by American and British authorities who were unaware of secret plans for the island. Patrick Dean at the Foreign Office consulted the ambassador in Washington, Sir Roger Makins. Withdrawing permission already given to operate the service might cause difficulty because of another dormant sovereignty dispute with the United States over the two islands, but Dean suggested discreet enquiries in Washington to see if any leverage was possible.

The Prime Minister had made a statement in the House of Commons in December 1955 about Britain's determination to manufacture the hydrogen bomb and in January, just before leaving on a visit to Washington, he gave a radio broadcast about it. 'You cannot prove a bomb until it has exploded', he said. 'Nobody can know whether it is effective or not until it has been tested.' But he would not say where or when such a test would take place.

It was time for a task force commander to be appointed to take overall charge of the operation. Rear Admiral Kaye Edden, Commandant of the Joint Services Staff College, had been sounded out for the position but he quickly saw that air operations would predominate, and suggested that an RAF officer would be more appropriate. Air Commodore Wilfrid Oulton was appointed on 6 February 1956. In his lively book, *Christmas Cracker: an Account of the Planning and Execution of Britain's First Thermonuclear Weapon Trials*, he describes how the job was given to him by Air Vice-Marshal Lees, then Assistant Chief of Air Staff for Operations, who told him he was 'to go out and drop a bomb somewhere in the Pacific, and take a picture of it with a Brownie camera'.[1]

Grapple planning now accelerated, co-ordinated overall by Grapex, as the Atomic Weapon Trials Executive was called when operating in *Grapple* mode.[2] The Aldermaston working party and a number of small ad hoc committees and groups identified and dealt quickly with innumerable problems, and Oulton quickly assembled a small central planning staff. The work was characterized by close and effective collaboration between all the parties. Many of the service officers involved had learnt and practised their planning and managerial skills 10 to 15 years earlier, in response to the extreme demands of World War II, and their experience must have been invaluable.

Oulton (now promoted to Air Vice-Marshal) realized that he had had 'a fearsome job dumped on him'. Assured of absolute authority over the trial,[3] he and his embryonic staff set to work on the detailed problems of organizing a test of four prototype megaton nuclear weapons at a remote location in the Pacific Ocean. By its nature, the task would evolve continuously, right up to the live firing phase, and he would have to control the whole process and to co-ordinate a vast complex of activities carried out by the three services and the scientific teams.

A timetable for the trials

On 21 February, a fortnight after his appointment, Oulton held a meeting of *Grapple* planning staffs at Aldermaston. His deputy, Commodore Peter Gretton RN, who would also command the naval task group, was present. Oulton outlined the plan of the operation – essentially a combined military operation in support of a scientific objective. He asked for an assurance that the scientific team would be ready by 1 April 1957 and Cook gave it. That target date established several deadlines. In particular, some of the heavy equipment for the Royal Engineers' task group would have to be on Christmas Island by 1 July 1956. Before then a small RAF party would prepare the island's existing landing strip for the Transport Command Hastings aircraft which were to fly a weekly service to and from a staging post on Canton Island, 800 miles away. Then a runway must be ready for heavily loaded aircraft by 1 November 1956. Most of the Royal Engineers would arrive during October and November and it was hoped that construction work on the airfield and elsewhere would be complete by 1 December.

Many problems were evident in this plan. There were no suitable facilities at Christmas Island for off-loading the quantity and type of construction stores required. The Engineer in Charge at the War Office, Colonel Tutton, estimated that – excluding petrol, aviation fuel and diesel oil requirements – some 18,640 tons of stores would be required for the construction plan by December 1956. A wharf had been kept usable during the war while American forces were occupying the island, but only by regularly dredging an approach channel. An alternative method would be to use a Royal Navy LST (Landing Ship Tank, with bow doors and a loading ramp) which, in theory, could be beached to unload essential stores for the advance party. But an LST could not reach Christmas Island before September. Until then, a commercial freighter, with heavy derricks, would have to unload cargo on to large pontoons equipped with outboard motors, or else on to LCMs (Landing Craft Mechanical Vehicles – like smaller LSTs), which would be run on to the beach for unloading.

Announcing *Grapple?*

Before the trial a danger zone covering a large area of international water had to be declared. The Minister of Supply wrote to the Minister of Defence and seven other ministerial colleagues in February 1956 that an announcement must be made shortly, partly because of the increasing risk of a leak – the press was already making 'intelligent guesses' – and because, to meet the target date for the test, several steps were necessary which would immediately widen the circle of those in the know. For instance, a dredger to prepare the harbour at Christmas Island would take at least a month to tow from Australia to the island. Then, as we have seen, since *Castle Bravo* international protests against testing were an ever-present political factor, and American experience showed that some local opposition to testing in the Pacific and the use of certain islands was likely. In the opinion of the Colonial Office, the more time the opposition was given to settle down after the first announcement, the better. The Australian and New Zealand Prime Ministers should of course be consulted about the form of the announcement, and other Commonwealth Prime Ministers informed in advance as a courtesy. The Resident Commissioner on Christmas Island would also have to be informed soon. Candour about the use of Christmas Island as a nuclear range might also help in the SPAL problem. All the ministers consulted concurred, as did Plowden, the AEA chairman. But Eden was not yet ready to consider making any announcement.

This continuing secrecy made an approach to SPAL advisable, and towards the end of March 1956 Makins reported from Washington that Admiral Radford (chairman of the Joint Chiefs of Staff) would help, provided the United States claim to sovereignty over Christmas Island was not prejudiced.

The installations on the island, including the airfield and the derelict port, had originally been leased by the Secretary of the United States Air Force to SPAL in 1953, but the agreement could be broken on grounds of overriding military necessity. The Americans suggested that the British should tell the airline that the operating permission was being revoked because they needed an airbase on the island, had discussed it with the United States, and would consider a claim for compensation. If SPAL approached the State Department, the latter would support the British especially if the British were willing to pay fair compensation. USAF consent was required and would be sought. The American authorities were being extremely helpful.

Then came the dreaded leak – and an accurate one – by a formidable journalist, Chapman Pincher. It appeared in the *Daily Express*, saying that a British hydrogen bomb was going to be dropped the following year near Christmas Island in the Pacific. It was widely quoted in the American press, and on 2 April the Embassy reported to London on the American reaction. The leak, Makins thought, would increase American doubts over British ability to keep anything secret at all; security had after all been a major issue in the negotiations leading to the 1955 bilateral agreement which had extended nuclear collaboration between Britain and America, as it had been in earlier talks in 1949–50. Moreover, the leak must have an important bearing on the SPAL business. However, the Embassy soon reassured the Foreign Office that the State Department believed there would be no real difficulty with the airline. Two weeks later the State Department was more concerned over SPAL's position, and urged that the airline be told what was afoot. One thing was clear: continued United States co- operation would depend on a gentlemen's agreement that their sovereignty claim was not being prejudiced.

The Lord President, Lord Salisbury, told the Prime Minister that Anglo-American relations might be severely impaired unless something was said soon. Five days later, Eden agreed that the airline should be told in strict confidence about Christmas Island intentions, but he still opposed any public announcement so far in advance. At last, on 1 May, an official letter to the president of SPAL informed him of the withdrawal of its permit to operate, explained the reasons, regretted any inconvenience to the airline and offered to consider a claim for compensation.

Pressure to make some sort of statement about *Grapple* was mounting. Towards the end of May the Minister of Defence, strongly supported by the Lord President and the Foreign Secretary, wrote to the Prime Minister that the delay was causing considerable embarrassment in Washington and creating difficulties with the American authorities on whom we were dependent for so much active assistance in the operation. The matter had become urgent.

Besides, an invitation to their next test series, in May 1957, might be withheld if Britain did not invite United States observers to *Grapple*.

A substantial reason for Eden's reluctance was that he was anxiously awaiting the findings of the Medical Research Council's 'committee on the hazards to man of nuclear and allied radiations'. This committee (the Himsworth Committee)[4] and its report are discussed in Chapter 9; here we note only its effect on the *Grapple* announcement. Ministers received the report on 28 May 1956 and found it reassuring up to a point. The Cabinet discussed the *Grapple* issue on 30 May and agreed that the Prime Minister should make the announcement in the House of Commons on 7 June, stressing that the Himsworth Committee's views had been fully taken into account. The report would be published on 12 June.

On 7 June, Eden made a short statement to the House confirming that British megaton weapons would be tested in the first half of 1957 at a remote site in the Pacific Ocean and that Christmas Island would be the main base. He emphasized the British government's willingness to discuss with the other powers concerned the possibility of regulating and limiting nuclear weapon tests.

The *Grapple* task force goes into action

Two days earlier, a party of RAF officers and men had flown to Honolulu to set up the major aircraft staging post on the routes to and from Christmas Island. Operation *Grapple* had begun to move from plan to practice. On 15 June 1956 an advance party of 14 Army officers and other ranks left London airport for Canton Island via New York and San Francisco, reaching Canton Island at dawn on 19 June. (The Treasury had decreed that – apart from two nights in a hotel in San Francisco – meals and all other expenses, even insurance cover, were the passengers' responsibility). At Canton Island they immediately transferred all baggage and equipment – including essential signals and air traffic control equipment, tool kits (and two folding bicycles) – to two RAF Coastal Command Shackleton bombers for the flight to Christmas Island. Commodore Gretton flew in the first aircraft with Wing Commander Douglas Bower AFC, the officer commanding 160 Wing, which would administer the various RAF detachments. Also in the party was Lieutenant Colonel Woollett, commanding the Royal Engineer units who would do most of the construction work for the new base. Shortly after nine o'clock in the morning, the two Shackletons touched down on Christmas Island and the advance party began turning plans into practicality.

What was Christmas Island like? It was the biggest coral atoll in the world – with an area of 248 square miles, half of it land and half lagoons. It had been named by Captain Cook, who had landed there at Christmas 1777, and he and the crew of HMS *Resolution* had stayed there for several days. He found no inhabitants, and no trace of previous human habitation.

Despite its sunshine, beaches, tropical warmth and large plantations of coconut palms, it was hardly an island paradise – unlike the idyllic Penrhyn. There was no fresh water (but torrential rain at times) and no source of food except migrant birds, fish and coconuts; it was infested with evil-smelling land-crabs and hosts of flies. Though not excessively hot, the humidity was very high. Most of the island did not rise above 15 feet, and the highest point was only about 40 feet above sea level. The main feature was a large lagoon at the northern end and a spur of land about two miles wide, extending 15 miles to the south-east. There was a village near here, occupied by transient Gilbertese islanders during the copra harvest season. Here too was the house of the local Resident, Percy Roberts, who administered local affairs on the island. During World War II the island had been an American staging post for bombers flying to the Far East, and a few of the old buildings were left, as well as roads, a wharf, and an airfield (called Casady Field in memory of a young American pilot who took off from there and disappeared in 1942).

The Polynesians called Christmas Island Abakiro – 'the far away island'. It is 1,450 miles from Tahiti and 1,335 from Honolulu; San Francisco is 3,250 miles away, Sydney 4,000. These long distances dominated the planning and logistics of operation *Grapple*.

The Joint Operational Plan for the Build-Up Phase contained a detailed Engineer (Works Services) Plan, listing the work needed to build the essential facilities on Christmas, Malden, and Penrhyn Islands. Existing airfields on the three islands would be rehabilitated or extended as required, and a new landing strip constructed on Malden Island. The Army would erect accommodation and facilities necessary for the Task Force, specialist buildings for the Aldermaston and RAF contingents, and a meteorological station at Penrhyn Island. Sea-water distillation equipment, electrical power generators and cold storage would be provided on Christmas Island. The whole programme had to run to a very tight schedule and it promised blood, sweat and toil, if not tears, for the Royal Engineers.

A major part of the work on Christmas Island was refurbishing and extending the runways at Casady Field to allow them to take the weight of modern jet bombers and heavy transport aircraft. In addition, large areas of new tarmac had to be laid down for parking the many aircraft engaged in the operation. Nearby, an extensive Technical Area was to be built, using huts and tents for workshops and storage for spare parts. Renovating as many as possible of the huts built during the war by the Americans relieved a little of the Royal Engineers' work-load. However, several new facilities were needed, the most important being the weapon assembly area, and the isolated (and, later, guarded) facility for cleaning contaminated Canberra bombers after their sampling flights through the radioactive clouds.

A few miles west of the airfield, near the shore line to take advantage of cool ocean breezes, a large tented accommodation area was set up, designated 'Main Camp'. A mile or so away, sheltered by tall palm trees, was the Joint Operations Centre (JOC) – the hutted office accommodation for the Task Force Commander and his senior Army, Navy, Air Force and AWRE staff.

Another major Christmas Island facility was built near the native village, at the extremity of the narrow strip of land forming the northern border of the great lagoon. This was 'Port London', later named 'HMS *Resolution*' after Captain Cook's ship. At Port London, too, it proved possible to rehabilitate a number of buildings built by the Americans during World War II. As for the wharf, the sea approaches had long since silted up after regular dredging had ceased. Nevertheless, during the process of building up the base, thousands of tons of cargo were unloaded here from civilian ships and Royal Fleet Auxiliary vessels. At first the vessels could not moor alongside the wharf because of the shallow water, and cargo was ferried ashore by a fleet of small boats – cutters, landing craft with drop-down bow doors, and the amphibious DUKW (an innovation of World War II). Unloading was later greatly speeded up by using large lighter pontoons equipped with outboard motors, to take the heaviest items on a short, but sometimes alarming, voyage to the shore. Each craft had a schedule of daily trips to transport items in a carefully planned order of priorities that only occasionally went awry.

Accommodation was set up at Port London in 'Port Camp'. Workshops to maintain and repair heavy equipment for the Royal Engineers and the Navy's amphibious vessels were also built in this area. A tank farm capable of storing over one million gallons of aviation fuel and diesel oil was built. Port London, the Main Camp and the airfield areas were joined by a network of primitive roads; greatly in need of upgrading and refurbishing, they suffered badly in the torrential rain that spasmodically deluged the island. The only constructional materials available on the island were coral sand and rock and lagoon mud. A big crushing plant was erected to reduce the rock to aggregate suitable for making concrete and asphalt, both needed in large quantities. A fleet of tipper trucks had to transport this material to wherever it was required, making long, slow and uncomfortable journeys by the poor roads.

Work on Malden Island began in early October 1956. The first consignment of stores and equipment was landed by HMS *Messina*, one of the two tank landing craft employed in Operation *Grapple*. A reconnaissance was made to assess pest control requirements, and to dispose of the pigs known to be running wild on the island. They were a useful addition later to the diet of the small contingent of servicemen and scientists confined to the tiny island, and soon they were using young captured pigs for breeding pork.

In December 1956, the *Messina* brought in a contingent of Royal Engineers, with more equipment and vehicles, and the work accelerated. Tented accommodation for a hundred men was erected, with a cookhouse, ablution facilities and latrines. A water distillation plant provided 15 tons of fresh water a day and generators supplied electricity to tents and office huts. Foundations for the scientific instruments were laid in a 'lane' along the coastal strip to the south-west of the island. Two other sites were established on the northern coast, 'A Site' on the north-east of the island, and 'B Site', at the north-west point. Precise instructions were given for constructing, in cement, a triangular marker painted in fluorescent 'Dayglo' and outlined in black, which would be used as the reference point for aiming the *Grapple* test weapons accurately at a precise point in space off the coast of Malden Island. Accuracy in aim was vital for the large array of diagnostic instruments to obtain the best possible measurements of weapon performance. On Christmas Island, the work on the runway at Casady Field had been completed on 31 October, just in time to receive the first of the main party charter flights, as planned, on 4 November.

Not everybody in Whitehall seems to have had a proper appreciation of so much hard work in arduous conditions. There were two complaints that would persist during the trials. The Treasury had refused to pay the usual overseas allowances to servicemen in the Christmas Island area. Despite this, Oulton reported in November, the Task Force was working very hard, although the novelty of the situation had soon faded away and there was a real need for some monetary compensation to be given. Efforts to secure it had been unsuccessful so far but would be continued. The second source of dissatisfaction was the inadequate provision of fresh vegetables, and Oulton argued that the supply should be augmented by air from Honolulu. Indeed complaints had been made that generally the food was insufficient, and small increases in the meat and sugar rations had been sought. He emphasized the importance of the welfare of personnel engaged on the Pacific project; Roy Pilgrim, the experienced head of the Aldermaston trials division, supported him, and compared their conditions with the excellent arrangements made for *Buffalo* at the Maralinga range in South Australia. There the rations were more than sufficient, and the effect on morale was profound.

By 12 December one cargo had been successfully landed on Malden Island but some landings had been difficult. A DUKW had foundered in the heavy surf; a cargo of survey equipment was lost, but fortunately the results were not worse. One hundred tons of heavy construction equipment had been unloaded from the beached *Messina* before she was forced to withdraw damaged but she was still seaworthy and could be docked in New Zealand for repairs. The Malden airstrip was making progress but rocks encountered at the eastern end would require excavation. Another DUKW had been rolled, again fortunately without casualties but with the loss of its cargo. In January 1957 the Malden airstrip was finished and a daily airlift from Christmas Island began, using a specially formed flight of Dakota aircraft.

On 12 February 1957, after a year's planning, Air Vice-Marshal Oulton held a last informal meeting at Aldermaston before leaving for the Pacific to take charge of the big, combined operation to test Britain's first megaton devices.

9
Racing Against Time

Protests and petitions

In April 1950 a hundred scientists in Britain had signed a petition to the government urging it not to follow the American example and develop a hydrogen bomb. There was no such danger then; Britain's first atomic test, of a rather primitive fission device, was still over two years distant. But even before the Cabinet's secret H-bomb decision of June 1954 launched a serious research programme, events were already in train that gravely threatened its completion.

Widespread public anxiety about nuclear weapon tests began with the successful but disastrous *Castle Bravo* shot of 1 March 1954 (see Chapter 2). The official news was scanty at first[1] but at a Presidential press conference[2] on 31 March the USAEC chairman, Lewis Strauss, newly returned from Eniwetok, revealed something of the nature of the H-bomb and its vast destructive power, though he downplayed the *Bravo* fall-out and its health effects. In the following month the White House received sackfuls of mail and the press was full of letters and articles on the subject – some approving of tests but most critical.[3]

There were growing uncertainties about the future of all nuclear weapon testing with the emergence of public fears of radioactive fall-out and, even more, of the risk of war waged with these terrible weapons of mass destruction. Public opinion worldwide began to demand an end to tests, or at least a pause for reflection.

Protests were loudest outside the United States, and especially in Asia. Speaking on 28 March and again on 2 April Mr Nehru, the prime minister of India, said that the Indian government would press for full information from the nuclear states and the United Nations on the destructive potential of these weapons, and on what was known and not known about their effects, or probable effects, on human health.[4] He called for an immediate standstill agreement by the United States and Russia to prohibit nuclear tests while the United Nations worked out a comprehensive disarmament agreement.

In Europe Pope Pius XII, in his Easter message to the world on 19 April 1954, called for nuclear war to be banished and spoke at length about the radiation hazards of the hydrogen bomb and the possibility of polluting the atmosphere, the land and the oceans. Dr Albert Schweitzer – the revered medical missionary, theologian and musician – appealed to scientists all over the world to oppose these 'horrible explosions'.[5] In Britain there were questions in Parliament about Britain's own intentions, and intense pressure on the Prime Minister to try to get agreement with the superpowers to postpone further tests. After the debate Mr Churchill promised to seek a summit conference.

The Secretary of State, John Foster Dulles, put forward proposals that he wanted to discuss with the British Foreign Secretary, Anthony Eden – that the Soviet Union be invited to join in a moratorium on H-bomb detonations and that, if a moratorium was declared, some form of international control should be set up for detecting any detonations. Such a move, he said, would coincide conveniently with talks in the newly set up United Nations Disarmament Sub-Committee.

Clearly the United States, well in the lead in thermonuclear development, had most to gain by a moratorium at this point – winning international approval and goodwill while freezing the Soviet Union into a position of inferiority. After completion of the *Castle* series (the British thought) there would surely be no great advantage to the Americans in proceeding with bigger and better explosions. But the Soviet Union, so far as the West knew, had not yet tested a 'true' H-bomb, only an intermediate – or boosted – type (*Joe 4* in August 1953), and would need a successful explosion before the Soviet scientists could be certain that they could make a hydrogen bomb.

Given the three-fold purpose of weapon testing – to help improve the power of weapons, to maximise efficiency and economy of design, and to provide data for defensive measures – what would forgoing future tests mean for Britain? The British had not yet made a hydrogen bomb and an early moratorium would prevent them from doing so. Dulles had recognised this and had mentioned that the United States would provide some nuclear information, but he had not been specific. But existing legislation – even if amended as President Eisenhower was then proposing[6] – would preclude the exchange of any information on weapon design and production.

Before responding to Dulles' suggestion, the British government had to be clear on three questions. First, was it *practicable* to devise an effective form of control and detection, and to distinguish large explosions from small ones? Secondly, was a moratorium *desirable* in terms of the strategic advantage to the United States and Britain? Thirdly, would the effect on public opinion be sufficiently advantageous?

A system of monitoring and control seemed to be scientifically practicable. A moratorium would bring the West political and strategic advantages, and the moral initiative would be most welcome. It would calm public fears of the radiation effects of testing (which might be more serious than hitherto acknowledged). It would lessen fears of nuclear war. The public had been quick to infer that the next major war, if it came, would be waged with hydrogen weapons and would obliterate whole cities. However, a moratorium would not end nuclear weapons or even all tests; Dulles had insisted that it must not debar the United States from testing 'tactical' weapons in Nevada. Nevertheless, officials thought, a moratorium on hydrogen bomb tests might help to convert British public opinion to the idea that atomic weapons, being less powerful and less indiscriminate, could properly be used by fighting forces.

Eden and Dulles, meeting in London on 12 April and again on 2 May, discussed the feasibility of an H-bomb test moratorium. Eden said that British scientists believed that two well-placed observatories would be able to detect explosions of about 50 kilotons or more, and that a moratorium on tests above that magnitude would be a good idea. If the Russians refused they would suffer in the eyes of world opinion; if they accepted, the American nuclear lead would be preserved, though the British would suffer. The Americans were at first attracted by the idea of a moratorium and the President fervently believed it was a necessary step towards a solution to the 'terrible problem' of the hydrogen bomb. But after a month's study the United States administration[7] decided not to support it, because of difficulties in setting precise limits to the size of permissible explosions and in proving infringements, as the Soviet Union might get all the information it needed from one successful megaton test and might then claim it was a miscalculation.

In fact the Soviet Union would have been unlikely to agree to a moratorium in the summer of 1954, for it was about to conduct a series of seven tests in September and October. None was apparently thermonuclear.

Before the Disarmament Commission met in London on 13 May 1954 a preliminary meeting of American, British, French and Canadian representatives on 10 May considered the question of public information about nuclear weapons and their effects, for which Nehru had called. The British did not wish to initiate the discussion as they were behind in nuclear weapons development. They saw little difficulty in giving information on known effects; information on unknown but probable effects, and possible worldwide radioactive contamination, was more difficult. There would probably be confusing differences of opinion among scientists; public opinion,

especially in Britain, might become so inflamed as to hamper the government's nuclear weapons policy; and damaging differences might
arise between American and British public opinion. On the other hand, a
lack of official information would leave the field wide open to alarmist
exaggerations.

On 24 September 1954, seven months after *Bravo*, one of the crew members
of the *Lucky Dragon*, Aikichi Kuboyama, died in hospital in Tokyo. He had
been suffering from radiation sickness ever since returning to Japan. The cause
of death was hepatitis, not radiation sickness, but since the infection was due
to a blood transfusion necessitated by his condition he was perhaps a radiation fatality, even if indirectly, and was mourned in Japan as the world's first
H-bomb victim. Angry demonstrators in Tokyo carried signs demanding an
end to tests in the Pacific. The Japanese were angry too about the severe
effects of the testing on their important fishing industry. President
Eisenhower expressed the nation's regret and the American government paid
compensation for the loss of Japanese life and property.[8]

In October 1954 Plowden, Cockcroft and the British ambassador, Roger
Makins, met American officials in Washington to discuss a bilateral agreement
following the minor but significant amendment of the McMahon Act in
August.[9] The three representatives emphasized that Britain faced being locked
into permanent nuclear inferiority as a result of international pressures for a
moratorium, or even a total ban on testing and production of nuclear
weapons. Nevertheless, they said, British public opinion strongly favoured a
moratorium. It was therefore necessary to accelerate the whole British nuclear
weapons programme; testing in Australia was being stepped up, plutonium
supplies were to be increased by constructing six new production reactors; and
the Cabinet had recently decided to develop H-bombs.

Meanwhile at Aldermaston the scientists were working to early 1958 as a
target date for the first British H-bomb test. But it was painfully obvious that
the programme might be abruptly cut off at any time before 1958 by an international agreement on a moratorium. If and when the strategic advantages to
the West – even if not to Britain – proved irresistible, if political pressures
were too powerful, and if the Soviet Union agreed, the British could hardly
refuse. It was of course unlikely that the Russians would agree before catching
up, qualitatively, with American H-bomb development. But meanwhile the
British, as the third power, must make haste or risk being at a permanent disadvantage, vulnerable to a Soviet threat and excessively dependent on the
United States.

The Chiefs of Staff considered the latest information on H-bomb fall-out in
November 1954 and decided that there was no time to be lost in bringing the
problems formally to the attention of ministers. They would have to decide
how the secret decision to develop a British H-bomb could best be presented

to the public in the Defence White Paper due to be published in February 1955. The Foreign Secretary, Lord President of the Council, Home Secretary and Minister of Defence met with senior officials on 9 December 1954. The United States administration, they noted, had already started to introduce the American public to some of the civil defence implications, and the civil defence administrator, Val Petersen, had broadcast on television a description of the effects of the H-bomb and the protective measures possible. (The BBC was arranging a feature programme on the H-bomb for January 1955.) Dulles would be asked informally not to make any dramatic government announcement without giving the British advance warning.

Fall-out fears

A small group of officials led by William Strath (of the Treasury and the Cabinet Office) was set up to study the problems. Cockcroft gave the Strath working party a USAEC report dated January 1954 on 'Project Gabriel' (an expurgated copy with the passages relating to megaton bombs blacked out). The objective of Project Gabriel had been 'to evaluate the radioactive hazards from the fall-out of debris from nuclear weapons detonated in warfare . . . either in local fall-out or in the superimposed long-range fall-out from many weapons', but its findings were relevant to weapon tests as well as warfare. The report described a worldwide but secret survey, begun in 1953, of the distribution of strontium-90 from all nuclear detonations to date. Monitoring of soil, air and water had been carried out, at about 150 domestic and overseas stations, and extensive radiobiological experiments had been conducted.[10]

The Strath report was circulated in March 1955, but a month earlier another important USAEC report on fall-out had appeared.[11] Its publication had been held up by disagreements in Washington about releasing the information: the USAEC and the Federal Civil Defence Council had favoured disclosure; the State Department (and the military, for a time) had been reluctant, in case relations within NATO might be adversely affected, and because the report might increase public demand for a ban on nuclear weapons. Finally the President approved publication. However, the report was scooped by a long article on 11 February by the nuclear scientist Ralph Lapp in the *Bulletin of the Atomic Scientists* and on 13th in the *New Republic*, describing the fall-out from *Bravo*. Lapp's article estimated that if a bomb similar to the *Bravo* shot were dropped on Washington it would cover the entire state of Maryland with lethal radioactivity.

The USAEC report, appearing five days later, generally confirmed the accuracy of Lapp's analysis. It estimated that the debris from a shot like *Bravo* would cover an area 220 miles long and up to 40 miles wide, and that half the people living up to 160 miles downwind from the explosion would be killed.

The American press seized on these 'local' effects and on radiation hazards in war. It paid little attention to the major part of the USAEC report, dealing with global fall-out caused by megaton bombs (which send radioactive debris high up into the stratosphere, from where it is very gradually distributed world-wide). This new threat to the health of populations was not a potential hazard from a hypothetical nuclear war, but a real hazard from actual weapon testing.

The USAEC report identified the main radioactive hazard as strontium-90, a fission product with a half-life of 28 years, which can enter the food chain and so become incorporated in human bone, with possible long-term damaging effects, though not posing a genetic threat. The report concluded that the amount of strontium-90 resulting from all nuclear explosions to date would have to be increased many thousands of times before it had any noticeable effect on human beings, and the radiation hazard from other fall-out substances was too small to cause concern. Such risks as existed were, it judged, minute compared to the advantages for 'the security of the nation and the free world'.

Public response was mixed. Few people showed any interest in global fall-out, but one who did was the biochemist and Nobel Laureate, Linus Pauling, who warned publicly that it might cause cancer and who stressed that leukaemia was one of the dangers.[12]

The British government's Defence White Paper[13] published in February 1955 informed the public for the first time that Britain too was developing H-bombs and would be carrying out tests (Chapter 5). It described the destructive effects of such weapons if used in war, including the indirect effects of fall-out, and argued the need to build up 'the most powerful deterrent we can achieve' and to work for peace through strength. At the same time, it said, the government would continue to strive for a practical scheme of disarmament, with the 'ultimate aim' of 'abolition of the use, possession and manufacture not only of all nuclear weapons, but also of other weapons of mass destruction, together with simultaneous major reductions of conventional armaments and armed forces to agreed levels which would redress the present Communist superiority'.

In a famous speech in the House of Commons debate that followed,[14] Churchill saw mankind 'placed in a situation both measureless and laden with doom', but believed that with hydrogen weapons in their arsenals no major power would dare to resort to war (see Chapter 5). After a strong opposition challenge, Parliament voted to support the government's H-bomb programme. But public anxiety about nuclear weapons and pressure for disarmament continued throughout 1955.

The public would have been even more anxious had they been able to read the Strath report on the implications of fall-out, which ministers considered on 29 March 1955. The Strath report examined every aspect of the problems of fall-out in the event of nuclear war. A Harwell scientist who was co-opted as a member because of his Los Alamos experience and his radiation expertise, Dr W. G. (Greg) Marley, recalled many years later the stunned expressions around him when he presented a detailed scientific appraisal of the damage and loss of life after a hypothetical H-bomb attack on Britain's major cities with, say, 10 bombs each of a megaton yield. The Strath estimates were mostly based on extrapolation from British A-bomb trials, but they were largely confirmed by the USAEC report of February 1955.

Political pressures, in Britain and world-wide, were building up for an end to nuclear tests. On 28 June the Prime Minister (Anthony Eden, who had succeeded Churchill in April 1955)[15] was asked if, in view of prospects for general nuclear disarmament, he would be willing to halt British research and development on H-bombs. No, he said; it was only since the Western Powers had increased their efforts to build up their military strength that the outlook had improved. A month later Labour MPs began a new line of questioning: whether the government viewed a suspension of all nuclear weapon testing as desirable. The government did not; it would be a matter of the utmost gravity for the position of the country. The Opposition then urged the government to approach the governments of the USA and USSR 'with a view to concluding an agreement for cessation of further experimental explosions of the H-bomb'.

Questions in Parliament hitherto were merely irritating for the government but if public pressure grew too strong it might cause real difficulties for the test programme. Meanwhile more information about the effects of H-bombs would certainly have to be made public in order to put in hand the various civil defence measures recommended by the Strath report; however it should be released only to the extent necessary.

But a good deal of information was making its way from the United States to Britain, and was being read with attention, not only by the Aldermaston scientists. A British physicist, Joseph Rotblat,[16] who had been at Los Alamos and after the war worked in physics as applied to medicine, was quick to make deductions from information from Japan on *Bravo* fall-out. The amount and character of the fission products in the fall-out indicated, he wrote, that the bomb owed much of its yield to the fission of uranium-238 by fast neutrons from a thermonuclear reaction. It must therefore be a fission-fusion-fission device. This was confirmed when the USAEC commissioner, Dr Willard Libby – distinguished chemist, inventor of carbon dating and later Nobel laureate – gave an address at the University of Chicago on radioactive fall-out.[17] He explained how radioactive materials were produced by the explosion of a nuclear bomb; how they were diffused and precipitated in the case of aerial shots and ground shots; the effects of wind and weather; the fundamentals of the effects of fall-out on living systems; and the question of safe levels. He described a nuclear explosion with a fission yield of 10 megatons, producing 1,100 pounds of fission products which would be disseminated over the whole earth's surface but 'locally' over some 100,000 square miles. He then outlined the protective measures that would be necessary. While noting the particular hazards of strontium-90, he was dismissive of genetic effects of nuclear weapon tests (as distinct from nuclear war). In London, on 14 June, *The Times* published a full and detailed report of the address.

The United States administration was making great efforts to reassure the public but the fall-out debate continued vigorously, and so did the world-wide protest against nuclear tests. In July 1955 there was wide press coverage for a conference in London at which the Russell-Einstein manifesto against nuclear weapons[18] was read. It was to have important sequels in the next two or three years, in the development of strong anti-nuclear groups and the creation of the international Pugwash movement – still active over 40 years on – to promote co-operation among scientists in the pursuit of peace.

Thinking about a test ban

On 29 November 1955, a week after *Joe 19*, a commentator on Moscow radio announced that the Soviet Union would be willing 'here and now' to discontinue testing nuclear weapons if America and Britain were prepared to do the same. Reports on a talk in Moscow between Khrushchev and the Labour politician Harold Wilson suggested that the broadcast offer was just a propaganda ploy, but it sharpened British interest in the idea of limiting H-bomb explosions, to minimize harmful effects of increases in environmental radioactivity. A special committee of the Medical Research Council, the Himsworth committee on 'hazards to man of nuclear and allied radiations', had been announced in March 1955[19] by Sir Winston Churchill. In the United States, a much bigger committee set to work (under the aegis of the National Academy of Sciences and chaired by Dr Detlev Bronk) on biological effects of atomic radiation. An important United Nations scientific committee on the effects of atomic radiations (UNSCEAR) followed in December 1955.[20]

Immediately after the November 1955 Moscow broadcast, Clement Attlee, the Leader of the Opposition, asked the Prime Minister whether he would follow the test ban idea up with the American and Soviet governments. But Eden replied[21] that there had been no official Soviet communication. The offer, he added, might have appeared in a better light if made before rather than after the recent Soviet test; the British government was always ready to discuss these matters but with due regard to the number and nature of the tests already made (as well as proposed) by each country. He emphasized that a test ban proposal must not apply to *atomic* tests; such a prohibition would seriously damage the whole British programme. (The British had so far carried out only three detonations, none thermonuclear.)

The *Manchester Guardian*, reflecting popular fears of genetic damage from fall-out, commented on 3 December 1955 that the Prime Minister had been strangely reserved about H-bomb explosions:

> He will not take the initiative in proposing a meeting between the nuclear powers – why ever not? How long will the competition go on, and what might be its price in terms of more people with mental disabilities, more infants with malformed limbs, and adults who are sterile? The need is simply to limit large explosions, not to prohibit all nuclear weapon tests of whatever size. Why not propose a limit of one explosion each annually? Regrettable as it may be, one British explosion may be the price of impressing Congress and the Pentagon.

The *Manchester Guardian* writer misunderstood the nature and purpose of testing but the Prime Minister took the article seriously and asked the Minister of Defence to reconsider the ideas in it. The Ministry objected strongly to any limit of one explosion a year. It pointed out, reasonably, that the first British H-bomb test *must* have a successful result; other objectives – such as developing an operational weapon – must take second place. H-bomb trials were extremely expensive to mount, and so must be planned to maximum advantage; the Americans had always had a series of explosions in their trials. Limiting trials to a single detonation a year would make them prohibitively costly in money and resources.[22]

As more Parliamentary Questions followed during December 1955, the Prime Minister maintained that the government would welcome discussions but was not prepared to accept agreements that would put Britain in a position of decisive inferiority to other great powers. However the government was prepared to discuss methods of regulating and limiting test explosions, which took account of the British position as well as that of other powers.

Early in 1956 the Prime Minister prepared to visit Washington to meet President Eisenhower. Regulation and limitation of tests had been under consideration by the American government, but it had not yet come to any positive conclusion on the highly technical questions involved. Secretary of State Dulles reiterated on 11 January that the United States had not yet found any basis for suspension of tests, as it was imperative to keep in the forefront of nuclear developments pending general acceptance of a trustworthy disarmament system. This view was repeated next day in the announcement of further United States tests in the Pacific, in May–July 1956 (*Operation Redwing*).

The British too were planning weapons tests in 1956 in Australia – *Mosaic* in the spring and *Buffalo* in the autumn – and their first megaton tests in 1957 in the Pacific. It was all-important to the government's defence and foreign policy to carry out the planned tests as soon as possible, and to demonstrate Britain's ability to exercise the major deterrent. But if megaton tests were banned, it would be quite impossible for the British to make a megaton weapon. The Americans were sympathetic, but the British wanted a reassurance that their attitude would not change after completion of *Redwing*.

Nevertheless, despite the vital necessity of the megaton tests for Britain, there were attractions in the idea of making proposals for test limitation. Political pressures at home and abroad were increasing. The Afro-Asian countries, at their first conference at Bandung (West Java) in 1955 had appealed for a moratorium on testing, and in the United Nations India had introduced a resolution proposing negotiations for a test ban; though the General Assembly had not passed it, it had been remitted to the Disarmament Sub-Committee, which was resuming its meetings in London in February 1956.

So much uncertainty about prospects for testing made life difficult for the scientists responsible for the British programme and, from 1955 on, the pressure was intense to bring it to completion before an international test ban cut it short.

The aspect of H-bomb tests that caused ever-increasing public anxiety was global fall-out – the worldwide dissemination of radioactive fission products from the high altitude clouds caused by megaton explosions. (Radioactivity from the relatively lower clouds from atomic explosions on a kiloton scale was limited to fairly well-defined areas.) What people most feared was the cumulative genetic effect on world populations. According to the best scientific opinion in Britain at the time, radioactive contamination from all nuclear tests to date was well below any danger level, but there was still not much scientific information on which to base an accurate assessment of the levels at which it might begin to have serious genetic effects.

The Prime Minister responded to public concern in a broadcast message to the nation on 21 January 1956, just before leaving for Washington:

And now I want to speak to you about a very grave problem ... the H-bomb. You know that we are making the H-bomb in this country just as one of the previous governments made the A-bomb. I don't think there is any party difference about that, but we are making it because we believe that the H-bomb is the most powerful deterrent to war that exists in the world at the present time. It is strange, isn't it, to think that the only way to restrain man from some act of supreme folly is to threaten him with a weapon more destructive than we've ever known. But so it is, and so we have to build up the deterrent power. And I must tell you something else. You cannot prove a bomb until it has exploded. Nobody can know whether it is effective or not until it has been tested. That is why I have said that there should be tests; that is why I have said that I couldn't put us in a position of inferiority to other countries; but that doesn't mean that I wouldn't like an agreement to limit, or restrict, or regulate tests, if we could reach one.[23]

British ideas on test limitation

The American press reported widely that the Prime Minister wanted an international agreement on restricting tests and the State Department immediately asked to have the text before the forthcoming discussion in Washington. The tentative British scheme was that the three nuclear states should agree to limit their tests to a specific amount of fission energy per year (with the possibility of averaging the release over more than one a year). The proposals seriously disturbed Sir Roger Makins, British Ambassador in Washington. Britain alone of the three nuclear states, he said, had not yet tested a megaton weapon and could not do so before 1957. Therefore Britain had most to lose from curtailment of tests. Certainly, it would be very satisfactory to obtain both American support for the 1957 test plans *and* the propaganda advantage of seizing the moral initiative from the Soviet Union and India. But, alas, he said, these aims were fundamentally incompatible.[24]

Pressures on the government were still increasing at home. As he left for Washington, the Prime Minister received a strongly worded letter from the Archbishop of Canterbury about the 'anxious and growing opinion among the churches' that the British and American governments must take a fresh initiative at once in the field of disarmament and atomic warfare if the situation was to be kept under any kind of moral control:

> The use of the H-bomb in a war would destroy and devastate both sides beyond endurance. Since its only use would be a final act of suicide, the H-bomb is losing its power as a real deterrent. A local war could be conducted with impunity since neither side would dare to use the H-bomb, thereby making the local war into a global war of mutual extermination. Thus any moral justification of the H-bomb daily decreases and the revolt of the Christian conscience against the very existence of such an inhuman and nihilistic weapon multiplies.

The Archbishop believed the disarmament discussions had reached a critical point where ground might be lost, not gained, unless the British government could give a vigorous lead when the Disarmament Sub-Committee reconvened. The immediate problem was three-fold: some reduction in all armaments; the prohibition of manufacture or use of certain means of destruction; and a control which would ensure that any agreement was observed. No progress was possible unless the most powerful nations could move together. The British and Americans must recapture the moral initiative.

The Archbishop considered the prohibition of all nuclear weapons unrealistic. He called for a clear distinction between atomic bombs for limited and tactical use, and strategic use of H-bombs, so that the situation could 'come under moral control once again'. Could an investigation be authorised, he asked? If at the same time there could be an agreement to prohibit any more experimental explosions of H-bombs this would greatly help both the moral issue and the public morale. He questioned whether these experimental explosions served any practical purpose?

Penney, immersed in *Grapple* problems, was asked to comment on the Archbishop's letter and did so in some detail. He suggested that the Archbishop would be better able to wrestle with his terrible problem if he came to Aldermaston.[25] 'He ought not to argue spiritual matters with an incorrect or incomplete technical background. If we put him straight on technical matters he can then understand what we are up against.'

Eden goes to Washington

In Washington, on 1 February 1956, the Prime Minister talked to the President and then, with the Foreign Secretary and British officials, met Secretary of State Dulles, Governor Stassen (the President's special adviser on disarmament), Admiral Strauss (chairman of the USAEC) and Admiral Radford (chairman of the Joint Chiefs of Staff) in the White House. They discussed weapon tests among various nuclear matters. The Americans were not planning major trials in the Pacific during 1957 but would conduct smaller tests in Nevada; they had no intention of testing weapons of 40–50 megatons as was rumoured. Future trials would be directed to more economical – not larger – bombs, and to testing the defensive use of nuclear weapons against aircraft.

The Prime Minister outlined British plans for a megaton test in spring 1957. Christmas Island seemed a suitable site; aircraft for the test would be based there and Malden Island would be used as an observation area. He felt he should inform Mr Dulles, as the sovereignty of the islands was a dormant issue between the two governments.

The British public, Eden said, was inclined to think that there might be a real risk from tests. Unfortunately, Strauss commented, some writers and journalists were unscrupulous in encouraging such fears, especially fears of genetic effects. The impact on health, he asserted, was insignificant, and scientists like Libby were in a position to present a reassuring picture based on present scientific knowledge. The American government was opposed to a joint study of the possibility of controlling tests; it would appear to justify public apprehensions, and it would raise security problems. But, said Dulles, if it were shown that nuclear tests harmed the human race, the two governments would certainly do something to control them.[26]

Waiting for Himsworth

On his return, the Prime Minister told the House of Commons:

> We also discussed the question of the possible limitation of nuclear weapon tests. ... The House will perhaps recall that a special committee appointed by the Medical Research Council is still examining whether [they] give rise to any appreciable hazard. A similar examination is taking place in the United States. But I am bound to report that HMG and USG at present share the conviction that the radiation dose to human beings arising from the testing of megaton weapons at the present rate is insignificant compared with the radiation dose received from natural causes.

He stopped short of claiming that, properly conducted, the tests were not harmful, in deference to Sir Harold Himsworth, who sent Downing Street a warning note.[27] His committee, he said, was at a critical stage of its work and had not yet reached firm conclusions on the tests; a premature statement that the explosions were harmless might well lead to the committee's resignation and, even if it did not, might conflict with the eventual report. Besides, influential American scientists would be unlikely to allow such a statement to go unchallenged.

While ministers waited anxiously for the Himsworth report pressures against H-bomb tests continued. Following a resolution of the Japanese Diet, the Japanese government formally requested Britain not to carry out tests in the Pacific, and expressed profound anxiety. 'The Japanese people', it said, 'have taken note that Her Majesty's Government will make every possible effort to avoid any harm to life or property but ... can hardly believe that any precautionary measures, however scrupulous they may be, can guarantee complete safety.' It recalled *Castle Bravo* two years earlier, and emphasised that, even if no contamination occurred, the extensive exclusion zones would be very detrimental to Japan's vitally important fishing industry, the main source of protein for the population. The Japanese government continued to press its case strenuously, both at the Foreign Office in London and at the British Embassy in Tokyo, protesting repeatedly against the proposed Pacific tests.[28] The Foreign Office gave the ambassador no hope that the British would change their intentions and, further, questioned the legal basis for any claims to compensation for inconvenience or delays to shipping.

Meanwhile, scientists were anxious about the continued build-up of strontium-90 in young children's bones, if the test explosions went on indefinitely.

Cockcroft told the Foreign Office that if megaton explosions continued at the present rate for some years, the strontium-90 level would certainly go beyond what the scientists would consider desirable.

By May 1956 the lack of any official British statement about the 1957 Pacific tests was causing considerable embarrassment in Washington, adding to the difficulties of the American authorities on whose help the *Grapple* operation depended. The Foreign Secretary, the Minister of Defence and the Lord President all urged the Prime Minister to make an announcement. But Eden was unwilling to, until the Himsworth report had been received and considered, and he wanted his public statement to include an undertaking to try to secure international limitation of tests.

The Himsworth report was not essentially about weapon tests or fall-out. As its title implied, it was about the hazards to human beings of ionizing radiation from *all* sources – natural, medical, industrial and military. Nor was it simply about genetic effects (though Churchill always called it 'the genetic committee'). But what ministers wanted urgently was its views on weapon tests. Would the committee have good news for them, they asked Himsworth.

The report was submitted to ministers on 24 May 1956 and brought them good news, but with a warning, especially about strontium-90.[29] The report was especially concerned about strontium-90 because it is a fairly abundant product of nuclear fission and, because it follows calcium through the human food chain, is easily absorbed into bone; and has a half-life of 28 years so that, once absorbed, it is stored for long periods and continues to irradiate the body. Children are especially sensitive to its harmful effects. The Himsworth report estimated the level of irradiation, in Britain, from strontium-90 from all test explosions to date; it concluded that it would cause no detectable increase in harmful effects. But if the current rate of firing continued for several decades the level might increase ten-fold; any signs of rising much beyond that would require immediate consideration.

To the relief of the government and the weaponeers, 'several decades' allowed a good deal of latitude. The Lord President, Lord Salisbury, wrote to the Prime Minister on 26 May:

From this report one rather disturbing fact will emerge – evidence of a marked increase in the amount of radioactive strontium in the soil throughout the world ... As a result of thermonuclear explosions which have already taken place not only has this strontium increased in amount, but it is increasing at a rate which, if tests were intensified, might approach a level at which ill effects could be produced in a small number of the population within the lifetime of some already living. I thought you ought to know this before finally deciding on an announcement [about *Grapple*] in Parliament ... *on balance I am personally still in favour of the test to make certain that we have a bomb that will explode.* [Emphasis added.] But I should be much more doubtful of anyone continuing tests beyond that point, to get an improved weapon. That would be a matter for further consideration between us, the USA and the Soviet Government.

Getting all our ducks in a row

Prospects for *Grapple* had been in the balance and, with the Prime Minister undecided, were still precarious. Ministers and officials met the Prime Minister on 28 May to consider whether the announcement of *Grapple* should be postponed until publication of the Himsworth report on 12 June. It was accepted that the strontium-90 risk could not be ignored if firing continued, but Sir Frederick Brundrett thought it unlikely that test firing would continue at the rate of recent years; the Americans had, he said, carried out most of the tests they wanted to make. But there would be no cause for anxiety even if tests continued for 10 more years at the level of the past three. It was agreed not to delay the *Grapple* announcement; but to say that the government had taken full account of the Himsworth report before deciding to proceed. It would sharpen the demand for some international agreement on H-bomb tests, and the government might be well-advised to take the initiative in proposing discussions between the three nuclear powers.

The Washington Embassy reminded the Foreign Office that it was 'important that the Americans and ourselves get all our ducks in a row' on the question of the Himsworth and Bronk reports. Himsworth believed that the consensus of American scientific opinion would probably agree with this report, but Dr Libby's reaction was uncertain; he had said publicly that he would not worry if strontium-90 levels in bone in the general population rose to the maximum permissible for radiation workers. World scientific opinion would not accept this, Himsworth thought, but apparently now believed that levels were most unlikely to reach one-tenth of the occupational maximum.

The Embassy informed the United States authorities of the forthcoming announcement and showed them extracts from the Himsworth report (which could not be given to them in full before it was presented to Parliament). Strauss left Makins in no doubt of his displeasure at the passages relating to strontium-90.[30] It would be easy enough, Strauss said, to 'tear the MRC document to shreds'. He hoped publication could be deferred, in view of the current American tests in the Pacific; and the coming Presidential election campaign when the Democrats would make a major issue out of nuclear tests limitation. The head of the FBI, Edgar J. Hoover, was almost more scathing. Tests at the present level, he insisted, were not dangerous and were absolutely necessary for the West to keep ahead of the Soviet Union in nuclear weapons. The United States authorities 'would have no difficulty in demolishing the

MRC statement', but would not want to make a public issue of it. A British initiative on limitation would embarrass the United States, and the British were reminded that they had recently asked for considerable assistance. Makins himself, as we saw, disliked the idea of a unilateral initiative on test limitation and thought if the roles were reversed the British would very much resent it.

It was decided on 5 June to announce the *Grapple* plans in the House of Commons two days later, and to declare the government's willingness to discuss limitation and control of tests; subject to this, every effort would be made to meet United States views. But the Americans took a very serious view of the proposed British initiative, nor did they believe that the Himsworth report justified such action. Strauss gave a statement to Makins affirming that testing could be continued indefinitely at the present rate, without increasing the exposure of human beings throughout the world to radiation from strontium-90, above the level cited in the Himsworth report.

Announcing *Grapple*

The Prime Minister duly made his announcement in the House on 7 June. He stressed that a limited number of tests were essential in providing ourselves with thermonuclear weapons; they would be so arranged as to avoid danger to persons or property and would not involve heavy fall-out. The government had given full weight to anxiety about the indefinite continuance of tests; he again emphasized its readiness to discuss methods of limitation and control, and promised to seek every opportunity of doing so.

Pressed by Hugh Gaitskell (Leader of the Opposition) and other MPs for information on fall-out, on strontium-90, on the local dangers of testing, and on the possibilities of international agreement to limit testing, he advised MPs to read the MRC report when published, and the joint Anglo-French proposals for limiting and ultimately banning nuclear tests, which had been submitted to the Disarmament Commission in March and would shortly be discussed in New York.

Press reactions to the Prime Minister's announcement were mixed. Some were critical, asking why, if the government was really seeking every opportunity for limiting bomb tests, it had never proposed direct discussion with Russia and the United States. Some were wildly inaccurate suggesting, for example, that Britain was about to test a simpler, more effective weapon than the Americans, and that this H-bomb would put Britain in front of the other nuclear powers.

The Bronk and Himsworth reports were published simultaneously on 12 June 1956. There had been some concern about possible discrepancies, especially on strontium-90. But when Himsworth had met Detlev Bronk during the previous week – Bronk was visiting Cambridge to receive an honorary degree – they concluded no serious disagreement between the reports was likely. American, like British, scientists would not want to see the average concentration of strontium-90 in bone in the population – currently about one unit – go above 100 units, but up to 50 units need not cause concern. Neither report indicated any immediate cause for alarm; they differed only on the future point at which anxiety might become reasonable. It was not surprising that these two independent reports were not unanimous, but they were essentially very close in their findings, despite what Strauss and Hoover had said.

The Himsworth report got a very good press reception. Comments focused on nuclear weapon testing, and some noted that radiation exposure to the population from medical X-rays was a greater health hazard than fall-out. (This finding delighted Lord Cherwell – a vociferous supporter of nuclear weapons who had no sympathy with fall-out fears.) The Bronk report too was thoroughly covered by the *Manchester Guardian*; a long article by Alistair Cooke on 13 July 1956 described it as the work of six committees of the National Academy of Sciences which had carried out the most thorough survey yet made of the effects of radiation.

A few days later, on 19 June, the second *Mosaic* shot – a boosted weapon yielding 60 kilotons – was fired at Monte Bello off the north- west coast of Australia.

Reducing fall-out

Just before the two reports appeared, the Prime Minister had news from Makins that the Americans were working towards reduction or even elimination of fall-out hazards; it might be possible to remove the greatest impediment to further testing. Fear of fall-out was the basis of all that opposition to nuclear weapons tests that was not purely political and anything that could offset the fall-out scare would be helpful. Public fears, though not creating anything approaching panic, inevitably conditioned discussion of both nuclear strategy and nuclear testing. But what was this secret of reduced fall-out? Penney and Cockcroft were puzzled. Was it a matter of test techniques – very high altitude bursts, perhaps – or something new, intrinsic to the design of the weapons themselves?

The House of Commons debated the Himsworth report[31] on 16 July. Some medically qualified MPs expressed concern about strontium-90; one noted that the Bronk report said that 'the concept of a safe rate of radiation does not exist if one is concerned with genetic damage to future generations'. Barbara Castle thought the government complacent, using the report as 'proof that we can go on making the tests without any check'. Opposition speakers drew attention to some alarming evidence on fall-out given by a United States General to a Senate sub-committee, extensively reported in the American press.[32]

Disarmament discussions ended inconclusively in New York, and the Soviet authorities again announced their readiness to negotiate the cessation of

H-bomb explosions. To counter the idea of a ban, the Cabinet decided to pursue the limitation or regulation of tests. British officials suggested an annual, combined total of 15 megatons of fission yield – safe, they thought, for five to ten years at least. An arrangement might be sought whereby each of the three nuclear powers restricted its tests to produce, on average, no more than 5 megatons of fission a year. American agreement to putting forward such a proposal would be essential. But, at any moment, the Americans might have learnt so much about nuclear weapons that they decided they needed no more tests. Then, without warning, and whatever the current state of the British programme, they might declare their willingness to abolish tests and leave the British high and dry.

Eden reviewed foreign and defence policy at length on 23 July 1956, and made a statement in the House of Commons about nuclear weapon tests. The Himsworth and Bronk reports, he said, were reassuring for the present. But there was still a problem. All the powers concerned should try to work out the best method of limiting and controlling test explosions to avoid the risk that, over a long period, they could affect human health. The British government would have preferred to handle the matter in the context of a disarmament convention, but was quite ready to discuss it separately, and had no rigid ideas. Loud cheers greeted Eden's statement in the House and it had a good press next day, though some critics thought the offer should have been even more positive and unconditional.

But across the Atlantic, Lewis Strauss was much disturbed; were the Prime Minister's remarks *extempore* or the result of a change of policy? Makins explained to him that the government had been under very heavy pressure; the Prime Minister had wished to take an initiative earlier when he announced the British H-bomb test plans, but had refrained then in deference to the United States government's views. Since then pressures had been renewed and the Prime Minister had felt obliged to announce his willingness to discuss test limitation outside the disarmament forum.

The United States Administration had been under pressure too, Strauss replied, and now the Prime Minister's statement was being used to increase the pressure on it. Limitation by megatonnage was impracticable; tests could not possibly be detected and controlled, and any such scheme was bound to work to the Soviet advantage.

'Clean bombs'

Shortly before this, Strauss had issued a statement about the test series (*Redwing*) nearing completion at Eniwetok and had mentioned 'real progress ... towards the objective of making weapons with reduced fall-out, and achieving maximum effect in the immediate area of a target with minimum widespread fall-out hazards'.[33] An article by the well-informed William Laurence in the *New York Times* – which Makins sent to the Foreign Office on 1 August – revealed the secret which had puzzled Cockcroft and Penney. The reduction, Laurence wrote, was achieved partly by high altitude detonation – so preventing the huge fire-ball from drawing thousands of tons of radioactive earth into a gigantic mushroom cloud – but also by radical changes in weapon design. Hydrogen bombs could be made as fission–fusion bombs – deriving their yield mainly from the fusion of light elements which does not create radioactive fission products – instead of as fission – fusion – fission bombs, which depend largely on fission of natural uranium and so create vast quantities of fall-out. The former, clean, type removed the strongest objection to nuclear weapon testing, and even to the operational use of H-bombs as a defence against an aggressor.

Cook, after reading the *New York Times* article, said that the Americans appeared to be able to obtain a large proportion of the yield from light element reactions rather than from fission of uranium, but the British did not yet know how to do this. Brundrett doubted if the Americans had carried out a pure fission–fusion explosion, but thought that without more definite knowledge it would be unwise to tell ministers of any startling new development. It did, however, appear that the Americans had somehow largely reduced the proportion of secondary fission in fission–fusion–fission explosions, and this would be of major importance. Strauss' reference to undetectable tests perhaps meant tests in which the fission element was so small that there was virtually no long-distance debris to be collected. Plowden and Makins were more convinced than Brundrett and Cook that there *had* been a major design development, as the Laurence article suggested. Cockcroft, visiting North America in October, got some enigmatic hints from Libby.

The Soviet Union resumed testing in August 1956, with a megaton explosion on 24 August, and a few days later President Eisenhower released a statement about the Soviet test programme. Of 13 Soviet tests listed by the United States authorities, only three had been announced by the Soviet Union – two after a previous American announcement. The President again emphasised the necessity of international control of atomic energy and such measures of adequately safeguarded disarmament as were feasible.

Quotas for test fall-out?

All through the summer and autumn of 1956 British officials, as instructed by the Cabinet in July, continued to study ideas for limiting tests by international agreement. The idea of sharing 15 megatons of fission yield annually was examined and Himsworth was asked to advise on the health implications. His panel on atomic bomb explosions again highlighted strontium-90 and also caesium-137. If the world total of nuclear explosions was reduced from the current estimated 17.5 megatons to 15 megatons, it would take only a little longer to reach the warning level. But with an annual total of only 9 megatons valuable time would be gained and the danger level might not be reached at all. A draft scheme was considered by the Cabinet on 25 October and was remitted for further study.

The Cabinet thought that the United Kingdom need not seek parity with the superpowers; and a total of 11 megatons might be divided in the ratio 4:4:3. But officials could not agree to less than parity. The United Kingdom, being in arrears, really needed a higher figure than the United States, not a lower; especially as the Americans, with their new clean bombs, could get many more tests for the same fission yield. The starting figure, they argued, should be 15 megatons shared equally.

Penney's comment on the proposed scheme for limitation was a lugubrious one. In the past year he believed tests had been at a higher rate than expected. On admittedly scanty evidence he estimated the superpower total for the year at about 60–65 megatons (50 American), and thought the fission yield component must be at least twice the suggested 15 megatons. Since the tide of opinion was running so strongly against testing, the Americans might press on with tests as fast as possible and then declare that more would be dangerous. A month later he made a more promising analysis believing his earlier estimate of 60–65 megatons too high. But, even with substantially lower figures, an individual 5-megaton limit would, for the Americans at least, mean a large scale reduction.

By Christmas 1956 ministers finally approved a proposal on which discussion with the United States government should begin.

Penney and the Aldermaston men were all too conscious of the urgency of their programme. Mass protests and the ban-the-bomb campaigns were still to come, but the political pressures to end nuclear tests were increasing. Sooner rather than later, test limitation or a moratorium appeared inevitable. But meanwhile at the end of 1956 the way seemed clear for Britain's megaton test in the spring.

Part IV
The Pacific Trials

10
The First Trial – *Grapple*

Purposes and early planning

The purpose of the new Pacific range was to test four prototype weapons, each of the order of a megaton, in the spring of 1957. As detailed preparation for *Grapple* began, the design of the weapons had yet to be settled, but in the autumn of 1955, 18 months away from the trial, this fact did not affect planning. Christmas Island would be a theatre for which any kind of nuclear act could be booked. In the event, it would be decided only in the week or two before each test which device would be fired, and in what precise configuration.

Between the 1954 decision and the first *Grapple* trial, weapon development went on in parallel with finding and developing the new range, and planning the test methods. Of the four weapon designs initially favoured in November 1955, three were boosted weapons:

1. *Green Bamboo*, a single spherical device with a thermonuclear component.
2. A version of G2, the second round to be fired in June 1956 in the *Mosaic* trial[1] at Monte Bello (the *Mosaic* G2, was intended to have a lead tamper, but a uranium tamper was planned for the *Grapple* version).
3. *Orange Herald*, a megaton boosted fission round.
4. *Green Granite*, a cylindrical bomb, a hydrogen bomb employing a radiation implosion technique – a design discussed at Aldermaston at least as far back as January 1955.

All four weapons, it was hoped, would be ready for firing by 1 July 1957.

From the outset, *Grapple* trial planning included detailed analysis of all aspects of trial safety. The Aldermaston staff had considerable experience of safety planning for atomic weapon trials on the Australian mainland and the

131

offshore Monte Bello Islands.[2] But the megaton trials in the Pacific would be on a very different scale, and the problems of airdrops and airbursts would be new; so far all the British atomic trials had been on towers (or in a ship in the case of *Hurricane* in 1952). The Atomic Weapons Trials Executive was especially concerned about safety during the bombing aircraft's take-off, and asked for proposals for ensuring the safety of the islanders and of those servicemen who would have to remain on Christmas Island. Charles Adams, the Aldermaston Chief of Research, responded with a paper on radiation hazards that personnel might face if a weapon test did not go according to plan. What would happen if, instead of a successful airburst, there was either a surface burst (with a full or partial yield) on the target near Malden Island, or else a surface burst (with partial yield) at Christmas Island resulting from a crash on take-off?

If the trial went as planned, Adams wrote, the risk of serious contamination was believed to be very small. However, a full yield surface burst would cause serious contamination over very large distances, and it would hardly be possible to clear or to patrol the area affected by such an accident. An explosion of kiloton order must be assumed if the Valiant bomber crashed on take-off. Then the prevailing easterly wind would ensure that – in terms of the radiation dose limits medically approved for trials generally[3] – a large area of Christmas Island would be safe, and personnel remaining on the island could be evacuated to the south-east corner, but the Port London area might be uninhabitable for up to six months. So the native villages in the area were 'operationally an embarrassment'; nevertheless there were political misgivings over evacuating them before the trial. These accident possibilities, however remote, required the most careful study.

To assess the performance of each device as it was fired, arrays of instruments and cameras would have to be aimed at the burst. The kinds of measurement to be attempted included:

1. Radiochemical analysis of samples from the mushroom cloud taken by high-flying Canberra jet bombers.
2. Measurement of the performance of the weapon electronics.
3. Ciné photography of the expansion of the fire-ball.
4. Measurement of blast pressure.
5. Measurement of thermal, gamma ray and blast effects on the Valiant bomber dropping the weapon.

To meet the 1957 date for the trial, the scope of these measurements would have to be kept down to the minimum consistent with obtaining essential data – a recurrent theme.

By January 1956, the programme had been revised, but everyone was confident that by 31 December the experimental weapons selected for testing would be ready for loading for the long sea voyage to Christmas Island. Besides the live warheads, six inert weapons would be needed to test the weapon telemetry system, and, for operational rehearsals, six replica weapons containing high explosive charges only. The RAE and Aldermaston accordingly planned to have 22 complete 'skins' (or bomb casings).

The Treasury too was counting numbers, and costs. On 12 January, Chancellor Harold Macmillan wrote to Eden expressing concern over the cost of *Grapple* – why, he asked, test three megaton weapons? He accepted the case for testing the one-megaton warhead for the ballistic missile, but thought the case for the free-falling or powered guided bomb was weaker. Rather lamely, he ended by hoping that Eden would stipulate that the experiment must be carried out as economically as possible.

Penney answered Macmillan's criticisms in a letter on 17 January to Edwin Plowden, quoting the Chiefs of Staff to justify testing warheads for both free-falling and powered guided bombs. To fit a megaton warhead to the latter – required to extend the effective life of the V bomber force – meant restricting the weight and size of the device. *Orange Herald*, the boosted fission device, was necessary because *Green Granite* as originally envisaged would not fit into the nose cone of the intermediate range ballistic missile (IRBM) then under development.

Penney also told Plowden about the 'special assembly' that might be fired at *Grapple* if necessary. The object would be to demonstrate to the world that the United Kingdom was capable of dropping a megaton bomb from a military aircraft. Because of Britain's extremely limited experience of nuclear weapons there was a good chance, Penney thought, that the experimental weapons might produce yields of 200–300 kilotons or even lower, and the world would then know the United Kingdom had failed and was not in a position to produce and use megaton bombs. If *Green Bamboo* failed to achieve a yield approaching a megaton then the 'special assembly' would be fired, to make sure of a big bang. However, should *Green Bamboo* be successful, the experimental ballistic missile warhead *Orange Herald* would be fired, not the 'special assembly'. *Green Bamboo* – described as a single spherical thermonuclear weapon – and *Orange Herald* – the boosted fission warhead – were very extravagant in terms of costly fissile material. The more speculative double bomb design, *Green Granite*, offered the possibility of a megaton yield from a much smaller quantity.

That made three devices to test (not counting the modified G2 round which, it was thought, was likely to exceed the limits on what could be fired in Australia and so would have to be fired at Christmas Island).

In January 1956 Graham Hopkin, the chief of the materials department at Aldermaston and a key figure in the manufacture of the hand-crafted test devices, noted that he had yet to be given details of the radioactive components needed for the *Grapple* shots. He doubted if these components could be made in time for the shipping date of 31 December 1956.

Questions of safety

Scientific requirements for *Operation Grapple* were discussed at a meeting in Penney's office at Aldermaston on 25 January. Besides the five measurements already decided on (see above), radioflash measurements would also be taken and United States co-operation in analysing samples from the radioactive cloud would be sought.[4]

The weapons would have fixed time, clockwork fuses, not barometric ones, and for an airburst at 8,000 feet each weapon had to be dropped from an altitude of 45,000 feet. The same fuse timing was set into all the live rounds. If a clockwork fuse did not function, the weapon would be safe but, as an added precaution, each was fitted with an 'impact sterilising switch' or 'ISS', which would disable the firing circuit on impact with the sea.

After each shot, high-flying 'sniffer' aircraft would collect samples from the highly radioactive cloud. The health and safety aspects were demanding. The crew would be subjected to a flux of radiation, and radioactive particles would lodge in the myriad of crevices on the surface and in the engines and systems of the Canberra jet bombers to be used. To reduce this contamination, and the risk to both aircrew and ground crew, detailed procedures for flying, handling and cleaning the aircraft had been devised, based on experience of 'sniffing' gained at earlier American and British tests. A special unit would be built at the Christmas Island airbase for the purpose. Guarded to control access to the aircraft, it would contain changing rooms and showers for the crews. It would also have facilities for preparing radioactive samples, either for analysis at Christmas Island or for immediate non-stop flight to Blackbushe airport (near Aldermaston) in the bomb-bay of a Canberra – *Operation Falcon*. All sniffer aircraft would be coated in a specially developed barrier paint, to be cleaned off at the end of the whole operation or if an individual aircraft became unserviceable. A special method would have to be developed for cleaning the Canberra's Rolls Royce Avon engines *in situ*, instead of returning them to the United Kingdom or – the other alternative – burying them on land or at sea. Effluent from the aircraft decontamination process or from washing and laundering would be treated to remove radioactivity and then stored. A team of RAF tradesmen to form the active handling flight would be specially trained at Aldermaston.

The area that might be affected by radioactive fall-out would depend on meteorological conditions at the time of the explosion, and accurate weather information was essential. At least as important for safety at *Grapple* was how this information would be used in deciding if it was safe to drop the live weapon at a particular time; an expert on fall-out prediction, Ernest Hicks from the Aldermaston theoretical physics division, would be at Christmas Island to work with the meteorological staff.

Demarcation of the danger area was a safety issue requiring much consideration. In April 1956 Pilgrim (an experienced trials man since 1946 who was to be the trials director for *Grapple*) was concerned that he still lacked the necessary information to define the areas of the Pacific which could become dangerous to shipping because of *Grapple*'s fall-out, or from any possible accidents. He could not interpret the data he had received from theoretical physics division. 'I am a simple man', he told Corner, 'and would like a simple yield figure for each weapon under crash conditions.' On 18 April he presented his conclusions on the size of the danger area to a meeting at Aldermaston. It would be a rectangle 150 miles by 20 miles, downwind of the burst, together with a circle of 40-mile diameter centred on ground zero. This allowed for a surface burst of 250 kilotons and took account both of the Christmas Island airfield and the target area some 400 miles away. A Coastal Command officer present thought this would require 18 aircraft to search and patrol both the Malden and Christmas Island areas.

For Royal Naval personnel, ships and helicopters, precautions included positioning the ships and aircraft 30 miles upwind of the airburst, and ensuring that exposed personnel wore the prescribed protective clothing and had their backs turned to the explosion. Detailed plans were worked out in the following months, covering the types of clothing and eye protection, and the monitoring instruments to be used. There would be no guinea-pig ships.

By 19 June 1956, a meeting chaired by Cook decided the area to be announced as dangerous to shipping and aircraft during *Operation Grapple* would be some 540 by 660 nautical miles.[5] The Task Force Commander would be recommended to search the area 300 nautical miles downwind in the direction of the mean wind, before a live drop; in the event of a surface burst, the search would have to be extended to cover the whole area defined. But two months later new information about the wind structure in the mid-Pacific showed that the danger area would have to be even larger; additional Shackleton aircraft would be needed for patrol and search duties. Meanwhile detailed contingency plans were made for evacuating the airfield and camp areas if an accident occurred, and embarking personnel from Port Camp.

The target date and the test devices

The target date for *Grapple's* first live drop was still 1 April 1957. HMS *Narvik* was to be the technical control ship, but *Narvik* – a veteran of *Hurricane* – was to take part in *Mosaic* in the spring of 1956; if she was delayed in leaving the Monte Bello Islands it might be impossible to complete her refit at Chatham docks in time to meet the *Grapple* schedule. The *Narvik* saga was to become one of the *Grapple* cliff-hangers.

Meanwhile the debate on weapon design continued at Aldermaston, focused in Cook's newly established and highly effective Weapons Development Policy Committee (WDPC – see Chapter 6). At the end of February 1956 Challens, the superintendent of weapons electronics, was worried about including the double bomb, *Green Granite*, in the trial; if it was to be ready in time, work on the necessary electronics equipment would have to start without delay, but he needed to know what warhead was intended for the first stage (the Tom) and also whether the whole assembly was to be housed in a *Blue Danube* case. Cook said that the first stage would be a *Red Beard* (a smaller and more efficient fission bomb developed from the Mark I weapon) and a *Blue Danube* case would be used. By the end of April there appeared to be no outstanding problems on *Green Granite*; approval was given to freeze the design and issue drawings.

Modifications to the spherical device, *Green Bamboo*, were still being mooted: inclusion of a lithium tritide powder, if the industrial group could produce it in time; and the use of steel balls – over 700 pounds of them – into the fissile core cavity (to be withdrawn before arming) as a safety measure. Uncertainties of tritium supply prompted Graham Hopkin to stress that changes could not be introduced into *Grapple* weapons easily. The *Green Bamboo* design was therefore declared frozen. Hopkin's plea was often repeated throughout the tortuous weapon development process, as designs were repeatedly unfrozen for further tinkering – or so it seemed to the materials scientists and engineers. By mid-June 1956 it was decided that *Green Bamboo* would be shipped to Christmas Island during the third week of January 1957, but this allowed no margin for delays. The sailing could not be postponed and if *Green Bamboo* was not ready the components would have to be flown to Christmas Island and assembled on site; that would mean an additional assembly team of three men and another building with de-humidifying equipment.

On 15 May the Task Force Commander, Air Vice-Marshal Oulton, asked Noah Pearce, Superintendent of Trials Planning at Aldermaston, to prepare a complete check-list for the conduct of the operation for the 36 hours before each drop. Long hours of discussion and exploration of alternatives followed, which would pay off eventually, in the amount and quality of vital data collected on this complex and costly operation.

Meanwhile *Operation Mosaic*[6] was taking place in the Monte Bello Islands. Its purpose was to test two small boosted fission weapons (G1 and G2). They had been intended to be fired with lead rather than uranium tampers, in case the yields exceeded Australian limits but, as the G1 shot on 16 May had only produced 15 kilotons, a uranium tamper was used for G2 on 19 June. It yielded approximately 60 kilotons. It may be remembered that one of the *Grapple* shots originally proposed was a version of G2 with a uranium tamper. 'By using a uranium tamper', Penney wrote to Brundrett at the Ministry of Defence, 'we have saved one round at *Grapple'*.

Two versions of the boosted fission bomb were by now developing, *Orange Herald (Large)* and *Orange Herald (Small)*. The difference was in the size of the high explosive supercharge, not the boosted fissile cores, which were similar. Both designs were frozen in July. *Orange Herald (Large)* would be kept in the *Grapple* programme in case of a poor yield from *Green Bamboo*, but if the full production programme could not be met it would have to be deleted. *Orange Herald (Small)* would continue but the feeling was that 'we should be lucky to get half a megaton'. (In the event it gave three-quarters of a megaton.)

The double bomb design, *Green Granite*, was still far from settled. The *Red Beard* primary might be modified, and this modified version might be tested in the *Antler* trials[7] in Australia in September 1957, but these would be well after *Grapple*. The design of the secondary (Dick) was still undecided.

Uncertainties about *Green Granite* continued. Corner put forward a new idea at a WDPC meeting on 3 September 1956, for a close proximity version of the double bomb. Hulme had questioned whether the *Green Granite* casing need be so massive; perhaps it could be shorter and lighter, with Tom and Dick closer together. The Dick, or secondary, would have to be spherical, for easier calculation; any idea of a cylindrical Dick would have to await delivery of a new computer, on order from the United States, in mid-1957. This close proximity version of *Green Granite* was *Short Granite*.[8]

Right up to the end of 1956 there were calculations and discussions about the various *Granite* possibilities, especially about different designs of the spherical Dick – the fissile and thermonuclear materials to be used, in exactly what quantities, and the number of concentric spheres. In early January 1957 the Director-General of Atomic Weapons in the Ministry of Supply, Eric Jackson, summed up the current options for *Grapple* (then only four months away), listing them in firing order:

1. *Short Granite* – the two-stage thermonuclear bomb.
2. *Green Bamboo* – the single, spherical, thermonuclear bomb.

3. *Orange Herald.*
4. *Green Granite I* – the heavy version of 1.

If *Short Granite* succeeded there would be no need to fire *Green Bamboo*. But it would still be necessary to fire *Orange Herald* (since the *Granites* were too big to use in a ballistic missile or guided bomb). If *Short Granite* failed then *Green Bamboo* would have to be fired, as the second round. For the third round Jackson would have preferred *Green Granite I* to *Orange Herald* but Aldermaston would not be able to produce the round until the end of the trial as it was planned.

Grapple planning continues – safety and other matters

The final hectic weeks of weapon development and manufacture were approaching, while the operational planning of *Grapple* continued against the wider political background described in Chapter 9.

Major preoccupations of the *Grapple* planners were radiation safety standards; finalising the danger area; the possible contamination of fish in the ocean; action to be taken in the event of an accident, or if for any reason a Valiant bomber could not drop its bomb;[9] over-flying permissions to transport the weapons by air to Christmas Island; and measurements at the trial, in which the Americans would participate.

Radiation safety standards for trials personnel, based on the current recommendations of the International Commission on Radiological Protection (ICRP), had been approved by the British Medical Research Council before the first nuclear weapon test in 1952. They were not, as is sometimes thought, more permissive than ICRP standards at the time – or indeed 25 years later. From these basic standards for radiation exposure, secondary standards were derived, defining fall-out deposition so that if this derived limit was not exceeded then the prime requirement – the limit on radiation exposure – would not be exceeded either. These limits were revised in 1957, but the corresponding primary values remained the same. So though fall-out calculations and distances changed, the basic standards did not (see Appendix 4).

A new problem, which had not arisen in the case of atomic trials in Australia, was the possibility of radioactive fall-out contaminating fish in the Pacific Ocean. The Japanese government was greatly concerned; it could cause a loss of earnings for their fishing fleets. The risks were thought to be grossly exaggerated, but precautions were necessary, if only to refute any possible claims. (The Americans were sensitive on this point also, after the *Castle Bravo* experience.) The danger area might have to be larger, and arrangements would be necessary for catching fish for analysis over a wide area of the ocean. *Grapple* task force ships were given orders to catch fish every day – tuna whenever possible – and to dissect and check them for radioactivity, and local 'fish catchers' might be hired as well.

Work on accident procedures continued and the emergency evacuation plan for Christmas Island was finally issued on 1 April 1957, prefaced by the statement that measures for the safety of forces on the island in the unlikely event of an accident to the aircraft carrying the weapon were not to be allowed to prejudice the operation or the essential support of it. This was a reminder, if one were needed, that *Operation Grapple* – though carried out for the Ministry of Supply – was a quasi-military operation.

For purposes of evacuation, there were three categories of personnel. Category C – those not directly concerned with the operation or its support – would muster for a roll-call and then board transport at the Main Camp, or stand by craft at the Port Camp, ready to move to a safe area immediately if an accident did occur. Category B personnel would get under cover of a building and stay there until the danger had passed. Category A must remain at their posts. If an accident occurred, fall-out might begin to reach the Main Camp after 15 minutes and Port London after 30 minutes.

Another urgent question was, what must be done if a Valiant was unable to drop its weapon? If the aircraft could not bring the weapon back to base, would the crew have to bale out into dangerous shark-infested waters? What would happen if an aircraft landed back on Christmas Island with a weapon on board that had failed to detach itself from the bomb shackle? The Task Force Commander was given the authority to decide whether a bomb should be brought back or jettisoned, or – if the bomb could not be released – whether the aircraft should then be abandoned.

On 11 October 1956, in Australia, Britain's first nuclear airdrop, of a fission bomb, was carried out with an accuracy of 350 feet (*Operation Buffalo*). Its success had been encouraging news for the *Grapple* task force. They would, however, have far more powerful bombs to drop – in the megaton range instead of 3 kilotons.

Some new concerns were expressed by the Admiralty and Aldermaston as late as February 1957. If a Valiant with a bomb on board crashed a mile off the north shore of Christmas Island and the maximum possible surface burst resulted, they thought that there might be a tidal wave and serious flooding, especially in the airfield. But the Atomic Weapons Trials Executive decided that this risk added little to the other risks; Air Vice-Marshal Oulton must 'take such precautions as he can'.

A practical problem, which involved the Foreign Office, was that of transporting the test weapons to Christmas Island. There would not be time to send them by sea, as originally intended; they would have to go by air, possibly carried by Valiants, by a westabout route to avoid flying secret stores over the Middle East so soon after the Suez war. (The same considerations would apply to flying radioactive samples back to Britain for analysis.) In January 1957 the State Department was not entirely discouraging when the British Ambassador asked them about flying the weapon components through United States airspace, but there were fall-back plans to approach the Canadian government about routing courier flights over Canada if necessary. However, the American authorities agreed in February to flights over the United States.

Plans for American co-operation were developed at two meetings with United States representatives in mid-January 1957. The British told them about the plans to airdrop four weapons in the megaton range, and the test dates, and it was agreed that American scientists should measure radioflash, make acoustic recordings, and take radioactive cloud samples, using two especially equipped B-36 bombers. A 20,000 pound trailer containing all the necessary ground equipment was to be airlifted to Penrhyn Island in a C-124 Globemaster.

Test devices

At Aldermaston work continued on the design of the test devices – *Green Bamboo* (the spherical thermonuclear bomb); *Orange Herald (Large and Small –* the boosted fission weapon); *Short Granite* (the lighter, close-proximity double bomb); and *Green Granite* (the original heavier version). In December Cook suggested a third *Granite* to the Ministry of Supply – *Green Granite II*, light enough for use with *Yellow Sun* (a new bomb casing under development) and as a warhead for the powered guided bomb later known as *Blue Steel*. However, it could not be ready in time to reach Christmas Island before 26 June 1957, and to fire it, *Operation Grapple* would have to be extended, at a cost of some £1.5 million. Furthermore, it seemed less likely than *Green Granite I* to be successful.

The Director-General of Atomic Weapons, E. S. Jackson, preferred *Short Granite*. But the secondary (or Dick) for *Short Granite* was still unsettled. At the end of December Keith Roberts produced a design with an increased number of concentric shells, but Shackleton, the engineer design authority, was far from happy; in a service weapon, he thought, routine assembly might present great difficulties.

By mid-January 1957 manufacture of the *Granites* was in hand. Any further design changes in the outer layers of the Dick would, in Hopkin's mild words, cause embarrassment; certainly no alteration of the outside diameter could be contemplated.

Early in February Roberts reported that the latest implosion calculations had shown serious weakness in the inner shell designs for the *Granite* secondaries, and he now wanted to alter the number of shells, but his ideas were not yet firm. Cook insisted that the design must be frozen almost immediately as the device was due to be shipped on 29 April, but even at this late stage he was still prepared to listen to any new idea that might improve the chances of success. Was Roberts' proposal practical, he asked? Fabricating the secondary – with 14 concentric shells of various esoteric materials – in thicknesses ranging from 0.034 to 0.971 inch – would be exacting, and the worst problem would be the lithium deuteride shell. Cook said the design must be final by 12 February. This date left very limited time to manufacture and assemble the devices for transport to Christmas Island, but by early April *Short Granite* was being assembled.

Even as late as the end of April, Penney put forward a new idea for *Grapple*. Before long, he said, there might be restrictions on nuclear testing which would prevent any major trials after *Grapple*; so, if *Short Granite* was successful, they should try to fire a 1-ton, 1-megaton double bomb at the end of the trial. However, this came to nothing.

How many double bombs should be fired? Cook thought that if *Short Granite* succeeded, firing a second double bomb might not be justified. Corner disagreed; even if *Short Granite* was successful, *Green Granite* would provide valuable additional data. Cook's view was both pragmatic and economical but, given the huge cost and effort of mounting the operation, there was much to be said for Corner's view that the maximum value should be extracted from it. (He believed, rightly, that a well-conducted, well-recorded trial could yield valuable information for many years.) The question was left open, to be decided during the trial.

Meanwhile provisional plans were being made for two experimental, *Grapple*- related shots (R1 and R2) to be fired during the *Antler* trials in Australia in late 1957. They would be double bombs, with standard Toms, but the Dicks would not contain thermonuclear materials. They would only be fired if *Short Granite* and *Green Granite* failed at *Grapple*, and they would give invaluable help in diagnosing what was wrong with the *Granite* devices – whether a failure to implode the secondary, or a failure due to Taylor instability[10] in the layered secondary.

Difficulties with the double bombs were expected since the concept was advanced and highly speculative. But it was not all plain sailing for the other less advanced devices. *Green Bamboo*, the spherical thermonuclear bomb, suffered from persistent assembly difficulties, and it was decided that, though *Green Bamboo* would be sent to Christmas Island, it would not be fired if *Short Granite* gave a satisfactory result.

The *Orange Herald* design was revised because of concern about criticality 'in a resting state', due to the large fissile material content. The earliest date that *Orange Herald (Small)* could be despatched to Christmas Island was 25 May, and the parts would have to be flown there by Hastings aircraft, in three separate loads. It would take 10 days; Valiants would have taken only three days but could not accommodate the big packing cases. On arrival two and a half weeks would have to be allowed for assembly and so the earliest possible firing date would be about 23 June.

The yield of *Orange Herald (Small)* was calculated by Corner as 0.6, 0.7 or 0.9 megaton, depending on certain variables. His 0.7 megaton estimate turned out to be very accurate. *Orange Herald (Large)* was a 'political bomb', included not because it was a good design but because it could be relied on to give a big bang if all else failed. It was only to be fired as the last hope of a megaton or near-megaton burst. But because of the time-scales it could not be fired last, and a decision to fire it or not would have to be taken before the *Green Granite* shot. However, the firing order was not yet final.

Activity continued round the clock at Aldermaston, especially in the hard-pressed workshops – where stress and overwork took their toll in morale – but now the preparatory period was coming to an end and the operational phase was beginning.

The operational phase begins – the first shot

Grapple was the biggest Combined Operation since World War II, with the added complications of a large civilian element as well as the three services, and a complex scientific task undertaken for a civil department, the Ministry of Supply. Though not exactly a military action, the work and living conditions would be hard and – however careful the safety planning – there would be some undeniable hazards. For some servicemen the absence from home would turn out to be much longer than expected. Such disadvantages as poor and inadequate food and lack of simple amenities were not inevitable but, to get better rations, Oulton and his staff had to argue forcefully with an often unimaginative and parsimonious officialdom in London. Compensations included interesting travel, the novelty of the experience, the sunny (but sometimes rain-swept) beaches of a coral island, swimming, fishing, occasional trips to Hawaii by courtesy of the RAF, and the feeling of camaraderie which developed, skilfully fostered by the task force commander.

By December 1956 there were nearly 4000 men on Christmas Island, and more than 2,000 members of the Task Force spent Christmas away from home.[11] By early January 1957 almost all the domestic, technical and operational facilities of the base were complete. The next four months were a time of intense activity on the islands, filled with scientific and operational tasks – testing equipment, getting instrumentation set up, continuing the special training of the Valiant crews, and establishing the meteorological station on Christmas Island, with its network of outstations and reporting centres (the most important on Penrhyn, 600 miles south, and Fanning Islands).

During January HMS *Narvik* – the veteran of *Hurricane* and *Mosaic* – sailed from Portsmouth after a refit at Chatham, where she was given a helicopter platform and a great deal of complex instrumentation and recording equipment. She was to be stationed off Malden Island, to act as command post and scientific control for the live drops. Crossing the Atlantic in bad weather, she developed an ominous crack in her deck plating but was able to reach Kingston, Jamaica, for repairs, and was only a few days late at Christmas Island.[12] The aircraft carrier, HMS *Warrior*, sailing a month later, also ran into heavy Atlantic storms and had to put in at Kingston for repairs. She then passed through the Panama Channel, since there was not time to go round the Horn and the Suez Canal was impossible in 1956–57. The Panama Canal was a tight squeeze for a big ship, with only a few inches of clearance in places. She arrived at Christmas Island at the beginning of March,[13] just as the operational phase began.

There were inert drops of dummy bombs during April, for the scientists to test their telemetry equipment and the Valiant crews to perfect their bombing runs and bomb aiming. Accuracy was especially important if the instruments were to be able to make the necessary measurements, since they had to be focused on the point in space at which the detonation was planned to occur. It was a different matter from taking measurements from the detonation of a device on top of a tower.

The first shot – *Short Granite*

On 10 May a Valiant courier delivered the final components of the *Short Granite* double bomb. It was three days late because of severe head winds between San Francisco and Honolulu. The first possible firing date now appeared to be Thursday 16 May, and by this time the firing programme had been altered by a decision at Aldermaston – *Orange Herald (Small)* would be fired before *Green Bamboo*, and *Orange Herald (Large)* – the 'political' bomb – would not be fired at all. (It may have been because Aldermaston was now confident of getting a big yield without having to fall back on *Orange Herald (Large)*; or it may have been too difficult to extend the operation and produce the device in time.)

Penney wrote to Plowden on 13 May on the current situation. Generous time had, wisely, been allowed for assembling of *Short Granite* and there should be no difficulty in being ready for firing about noon on Thursday 16 May. Results should reach Aldermaston early on Friday morning. Reports from Cook (who had arrived at Christmas Island at the end of April) were of very good weather, with favourable winds and no cloud over Malden Island. Practices were going well and everyone was in good heart. Cook had added that, if Australian objections precluded continued use of the Maralinga Range, Christmas Island would be very suitable for kiloton as well as megaton trials.

Australian and New Zealand observers arrived in time for the operational rehearsal on 11 May of the *Short Granite* drop, using a high explosive round. The rehearsal included the evacuation of all personnel from Malden Island, the withdrawal of the naval ships to their operational stations, and the subsequent return of ships and scientists.

At 11.30 am on 14 May the meteorological conference decided that the weather outlook continued to be favourable, and at 12.30 the Task Force Commander ordered the firing phase to begin. Foreign observers were directed to embark on the spectator ship, HMS *Alert* (on loan from the Naval Commander-in-Chief, Far East). The rest of the day was taken up with the planned movements of ships and personnel, more meteorological flights and weather assessments, and the bombing up of the Valiant. At H-11 – that is, 11 hours before the planned time of the drop – the countdown started. At H-10, the Shackletons got ready to search the danger area, and at H-8 they took off, followed by other Shackletons on low level weather reconnaissance and a Canberra on a high level weather reconnaissance mission. The Valiant crews were given their final briefings; so were the crews of the Canberra 'sniffer' and photography aircraft. By dawn on 15 May the scientists finished their last-minute check of the weapon telemetry. At first light, a helicopter from HMS *Warrior* evacuated the remaining men – Aldermaston personnel and Royal Engineers – from Malden Island by 7.45 am. At 8.25 am a Dakota aircraft landed Oulton and Cook on Malden Island, where they were picked up by helicopter and immediately taken to the control ship, HMS *Narvik*. By 8.30 am – H-3 – all the scientists were on board *Narvik* and *Warrior*. By 9.30 am all ships were on station and in a state of readiness, with all personnel in protective clothing and equipped with film badges, and those on deck wearing anti-flash gear, goggles and respirators.

The sea search Shackletons reported that the danger area was clear; the meteorologists updated their weather information and remained confident; the scientists made their last checks on the bomb before the firing circuit batteries were inserted and connected and the bomb doors closed. At H-2 the bombing Valiant, and the 'grandstand' aircraft that was to accompany it, took off for Malden Island. When they reached Malden Island there was still an hour before the drop and they began circuits of the 'race track' to make signal and other checks. Search and rescue helicopters stood ready, final weather flights were made, and the Canberras took off. The instruments on Malden focused on a precise point in space a mile and a half offshore and at 8,000 feet altitude. The Valiant pilot needed to know his position accurately for the drop, and his track from bomb release to the instant of burst, so that he could carry out the essential escape manoeuvre. He was guided by radar on HMSs

Narvik and *Warrior*, which also determined the bomb trajectory. Flying at approximately 200 yards per second he dropped the bomb on his third run, at 10.38 am on 15 May. It was later estimated to be 418 yards short of the target ground zero.

The release of the weapon automatically started (via the *Narvik* control desk) recording instruments on board *Narvik* and on Malden Island. The fire-ball was to be photographed from two sites on Malden and, from this record, a radius time curve could be plotted to give an estimate of the yield. By H+10 minutes, the cloud was fully formed, rising slowly, and gradually degenerating into a vast ring of frozen particles centred on Malden, where it remained for most of the day before drifting slowly away to the east. On HMS *Warrior*, the noise of the burst was surprisingly small, sounding like a double report of distant gun-fire, but the blast wave was noticeable both on deck and below, felt as a sudden increase and release of pressure on the ears.

As the first re-entry helicopter from HMS *Warrior* got to about 17 miles from Malden Island, the dust cloud began to clear and at 15 miles a large fire in the camp area, and several smaller fires, were apparent. Hovering at five miles out, the Aldermaston scientists on board considered it safe to continue. Over the main camp area and stretching out to sea for two to three miles there was a low dark cloud, underneath which the atmosphere was tinted bronze. Odd pieces of debris floated in the sea. Fall-out readings were at a safe level and the re-entry continued. Some old boats were found to be burning. The runway seemed to be undamaged and the road in good condition. A pig, apparently unharmed, lurked behind a disused vehicle.

Lights were still on in some of the buildings but a large marquee had completely disappeared leaving behind three oily brown stains on the grass. The re-entry party landed and soon afterwards Ken Bomford, the scientist in charge of Malden Island, gave permission for both *Warrior* and *Narvik* to approach the moorings off the island to facilitate the re-entry operation. Radioactive contamination was light but many fires were still burning the next day.

The first sniffer aircraft over Malden Island entered the cloud about an hour after the explosion, and the Valiants meanwhile landed back at Christmas Island. After the drop, continuous radiation measurements of air and sea samples were taken on HMS *Warrior* until midnight, with negative results, and no radioactive contamination above tolerance levels were found on any re-entry helicopter returning from Malden Island.

Penney promptly wrote to Brundrett about the yield of *Short Granite* – 300 kilotons (plus or minus 5). The diagnostic instruments had worked well. More important than the actual yield, he said, it was 'quite clear that our principles [were] right'. The test had achieved a 'radiative implosion'. This, Penney said, was something the Russians did not attempt until their third or fourth big shot. Since receiving the news late on Friday night, he and many of his senior staff had been in continuous session. They now saw that, although they did things correctly, they had made one stupid mistake (he did not specify) which must have reduced the yield by perhaps 100 kilotons. They had learnt much from the post-mortem, and now the main question was how to get the most out of the remaining *Grapple* shots. Since *Short Granite* had proved that they could implode at short distance there was no point in 'going to the longer distance of *Green Granite*', which was unlikely to give any improvement. 'I have therefore cancelled *Green Granite*', he wrote. 'We are now proposing *Purple Granite*, which in most respects is identical with *Short Granite*.' This was a new idea, putting right (Penney thought) the mistake made in *Short Granite*. The Dick component would be modified, with extra uranium-235 and with the outer layer replaced by aluminium. Without expecting any sensational improvement on *Short Granite*, he thought it should be worthwhile. However, it would not be easy to achieve a megaton without a further test, though they should get well over half a megaton.

The second shot – *Orange Herald (Small)*

The proposed new *Granite* round was now being made at Aldermaston. Hopkin was confident that the modified Dick could be made and assembled in a *Short Granite* case ready to fly out to Christmas Island by 20 June or earlier. Meanwhile *Orange Herald (Small)* was to be fired as soon as possible, using some thermonuclear boosting material if possible but as a pure fission device if there were safety problems. Press representatives, including the formidable Chapman Pincher, were to be present for this shot and would be accommodated on HMS *Alert*.

The components, in three separate loads, were delivered to Christmas Island on 13 May, and taken to the assembly building. Unpacking, dismantling, inspecting and partially re-assembling the device continued for nearly two weeks, and on 27 May Oulton and Cook went with Challens to watch the final assembly.[14] RAF and Aldermaston personnel fitted the high explosive sections round the fissile core and then placed the outside hemispheres with great precision round the whole. These hemispheres each had a small flange with a fine screw thread, to enable them to be screwed together. The RAF warrant officer responsible for this task gently rotated the upper hemisphere. It stuck. He was unable to reverse it to try again, and after two hours of unavailing effort, there was still no movement. At last the warrant officer told Cook and Challens that there was 'only one thing left to do – clout it!' It seemed a desperate measure. With the task force commander's approval he took a small sledge hammer to *Orange Herald*. It worked. The device was care-

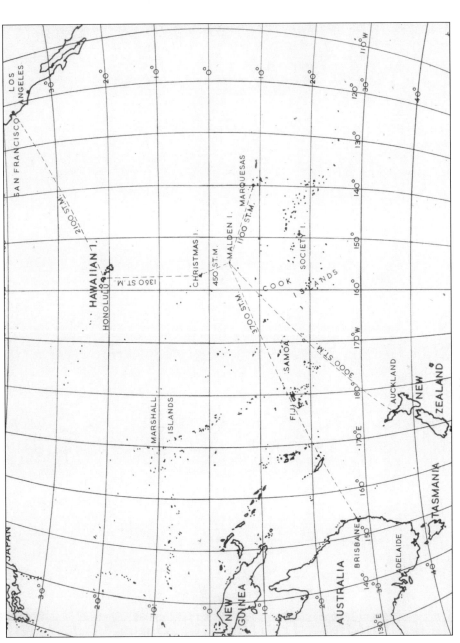

1 *Map of the Pacific Ocean, showing positions of Christmas and Malden Islands.*

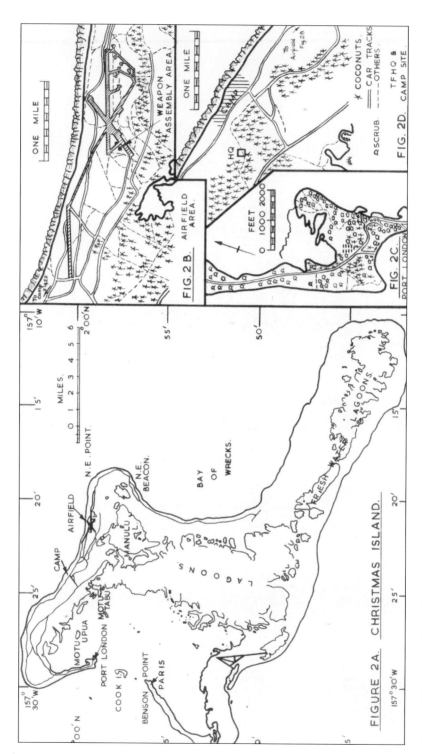

2 Map of Christmas Island, during the *Grapple* trials of 1957–8.

3 Port London, Christmas Island.

4 Coconut palms in Christmas Island – a striking picture illustrating the terrain by
Aldermaston photographer Ted Baker.

5 Sir William Penney, director of Aldermaston from 1950 to 1959.

6 William Cook (*centre*), deputy director of Aldermaston, at *Grapple* talking to John Challens (*left*) and Noah Pearce (*right*).

7 Sam Curran, Chief of Nuclear Research at Aldermaston.

8 Henry Hulme, special adviser to the director of Aldermaston.

9 Graham Hopkin, chief of materials at Aldermaston.

10 John Corner, head of theoretical physics at Aldermaston.

11 Charles Adams, chief scientist, with John Challens (*right*), scientific supervisor at *Grapple* (and a future director of Aldermaston).

12 Roy Pilgrim, scientific director for *Grapple Y* and *Grapple Z*.

13 Prime Minister Harold Macmillan (*left*) visits Aldermaston, August 1957. He is seen here with Ken Allen (*centre*) and R. Batchelor, one of Allen's scientific staff (*right*).

14 Keith Roberts, one of the two theoretical physicists at Aldermaston who 'practically invented *Green Grapple*'.

15 Bryan Taylor, theoretical physicist, who worked closely with Keith Roberts.

16 A Valiant V-bomber of 49 Squadron at Christmas Island. The flat end of the tail-cone contained two cine cameras which were used to film the detonations.

17 Air Vice Marshal Wilfrid Oulton, task force commander, arrives at Christmas Island.

18 Air Vice Marshal John Grandy, William Cook and Air Vice Marshal Wilfrid Oulton (seated left to right) at *Grapple X*. Standing is Ken Bomford, scientific superintendant at *Grapple X*.

19 Air Vice Marshal John Grandy, task force commander, at Christmas Island for *Grapple Z*.

20 *Blue Danube* bomb-casing used for the *Grapple* airdrops – it measured over 24ft long and over 5ft in diameter.

21 *Short Granite*, the first *Grapple* test device, dropped off the coast of Malden Island in May 1957.

22 *Orange Herald*, the second *Grapple* test device, May 1957.

23 The explosion of the *Halliard* device – the second *Grapple Z* test in September 1958.

24 *Red Snow*, produced after the 1958 bilateral agreement, was a British-built version of the American MK 28 warhead.

25 Meeting at the Sandia National Laboratory in September 1958. *Left to right*: Dr N. F. Bradbury (Los Alamos), Sir William Cook (UKAEA), Dr Edward Teller (Livermore Laboratory) and Major-General Herbert B. Loper (Department of Defense).

26 *Grapple* badge.

fully screwed together, and by the end of the day the bomb – with its core, electronics, firing circuit and telemetry instruments – was fully assembled.

During the two weeks since the *Short Granite* shot, there had been much work for the scientists and the RAF air and ground crews to prepare for the *Orange Herald* shot. The USAF monitoring team was settling in on Penrhyn Island, where there was excellent Anglo-American co-operation. Heavy rains and flooding on Christmas Island, an outbreak of flu, and a worsening of the fly plague, hindered preparations, but the programme of high explosive and inert airdrops went ahead. The dress rehearsal was on 28 May. By this time the rain had stopped and the weather was hot and dry. The live drop was scheduled for 31 May and procedures for the preparatory and firing phases were the same as for the first shot.

On D-Day all went smoothly, and the Valiant bomber made a good and accurate drop, but in the escape manoeuvre after the drop a malfunction on the pilot's instrument panel resulted in a high speed stall. Disaster was avoided by superb airmanship.

The yield of *Orange Herald (Small)* was estimated at 700–800 kilotons, a record for a pure fission weapon. But it was uncertain whether there had been any boosting effect at all, or whether the yield was all due to fission of uranium-235. It was very close to Corner's estimate for an unboosted yield. Back at Aldermaston the WDPC thought the boosting had failed because of Taylor instability and any further work on core boosting by this method would be pointless. Hulme thought it would be a mistake to assume that there had been any contribution at all from the boosting.

The third shot – *Purple Granite*

At Aldermaston they hoped that *Purple Granite*, the second double bomb – with a modified Dick containing an additional quantity of uranium-235 – would give a better yield than *Short Granite's* disappointing 300 kilotons. *Purple Granite* was fired on 19 June and operationally was a complete success, but the scientists at Christmas Island made a preliminary estimate of the yield at only 200 kilotons – even less than *Short Granite*. *Grapple* had been valuable; but undeniably disappointing, as the American observers too were well aware.

Looking ahead

That evening, Oulton recalls, Cook had a private talk with him.[15] 'We haven't got it quite right', he said, 'and we shall have to do it all again, providing we can do so before the ban comes into force; so that means as soon as possible.' He emphasized that this immediate need was not all; a programme of further tests might be necessary. Oulton, who knew it had been an operational success, was at a loss for words as he contemplated the exhausted service elements, the ships that would not be available, the men who had been on duty at Christmas Island for over a year, the patched up and worn out equipment and depleted reserves, the demands of the *Antler* series in the autumn.

The next morning Cook flew back to the United Kingdom to talk to Penney and his colleagues, to explain to the government, and to try to get political and financial authority for another test.

It had been hoped that no more megaton trials would be needed after *Grapple*, but it had never been a very realistic hope. Penney, and the government, had always been aware that further tests might be needed. After the two *Granite* results there was now no doubt of this. But it would be wrong to think of *Grapple* as a failure. The *Granite* shots had been useful proofs of the principles of staging and radiation implosion, operationally the airdrops had been highly successful, and the trial had been conducted with admirable safety.

Present policy was to move everything worth removing from Christmas Island after *Operation Grapple*. However, if facilities had to be rebuilt, a megaton trial could not be planned in less than about 18 months, and if there was to be yet another trial at Christmas Island in 1959, a decision must be taken in 1957.

On 21 June, two days after *Purple Granite*, the Ministry of Defence sent Prime Minister Macmillan an assessment of the position. From nuclear tests carried out so far, Britain had acquired the knowledge to make a megaton warhead for a ballistic missile – this was the *Orange Herald* device or a variation on it – but it would be extremely expensive. Britain could also produce a large yield, free-falling bomb, or warhead for a propelled bomb, but it was appreciably heavier than desirable and could only be carried in V-bombers. Britain lacked the knowledge to produce lighter and cheaper megaton weapons. If it was not prevented from carrying out the planned kiloton tests (*Antler*) in the autumn of 1957, minor improvements in the current megaton weapons might be achieved, but it would still not be in a position to make efficient use of fissile material. Both America and the Soviet Union would be able to produce larger stockpiles from the same quantity of fissile material. There was therefore a real need to continue both megaton and kiloton tests for at least two years, but kiloton tests were very much the more important. A few days later Penney wrote to Brundrett: 'Certainly we have learned a lot, but as always happens we now see a further long programme which could be done, policy considerations permitting.'

After much discussion of the two *Granite* results, it was agreed that this type of warhead should not be abandoned. A step by step development programme was the only way forward, with individual rounds fired at intervals. Cook considered it technically feasible to fire them off the southern tip of Christmas

Island, rather than off Malden Island; this would greatly simplify the logistics. The theoretical physics division was investigating the safety aspects; up to 3 megatons were probably acceptable bursts.

Theoretical physics division staff believed that *Granite*-type weapons could be made to work well provided the secondaries were designed for higher compression and reduced Taylor instability. More detailed implosion calculations were essential for a proper understanding. Cook suggested another test round with a simpler Dick than either of the *Granite* rounds, but in an otherwise similar device. If it achieved half a megaton or more, it could be used for the interim weapon the RAF wanted. Then they could try building up extra layers on the Dick, and could consider three-stage designs. If it failed, then perhaps the *Granite* concept should be abandoned.

Cook wanted a simple design, to be largely settled by mid-September, and he wanted to fire this first round in November, with others at two-monthly intervals. He stressed the importance of extracting all possible information from the *Short* and *Purple Granite* results, and asked all the members of his hard-working WDPC to prepare separate analyses of them. Corner thought the new design could not be optimized so quickly, but that there might be sufficient time to do calculations on, say, three designs from which the best could be selected. Cook's plan was agreed in principle but there might of course be political or financial objections to it.

He met service representatives and E S Jackson of the Ministry of Supply on 2 July to discuss a new series of trials in October or November. December 1957 was suggested as a possibility, but only if *Antler* (in September/October) was cancelled; if *Antler* had to go ahead, the Christmas Island trial could be delayed to February/April 1958. But Cook had already told Jackson and Brundrett that such dates were not realistic. The First Sea Lord and the Chief of Air Staff had assured Brundrett that an earlier date could be met, with Air Vice-Marshal Oulton again as Task Force Commander.

By mid-July 1957 Whitehall had agreed that Christmas Island should be prepared for a progressive series of megaton tests beginning with one or two firings in November. The Minister of Defence, Duncan Sandys, had decided that the services must meet Aldermaston's date and the Chiefs of Staff had no doubt that it could be done. Sandys warned that further *Granite* rounds might give away the fact that the earlier ones had been disappointing, and asked if Aldermaston could fire an extra round testing a different megaton technique. Cook agreed to look into this possibility.

Sandys had, of course, questioned Cook closely on the reasons why Aldermaston wanted to continue double bomb tests after having tested a fission bomb, *Orange Herald (Small)*, which yielded nearly a megaton and would fit into *Blue Streak*. Cook explained that double bombs offer a bigger yield for a given quantity of fissile material, and that fission bombs cannot yield much above 1 megaton whereas double bombs have a much greater potential. Though not greatly impressed by these arguments for persisting with the double bomb, Sandys agreed nevertheless to further tests. So did the Prime Minister. Sandys stressed that two matters were to be regarded as 'more than Top Secret' – that Britain was considering further tests after *Antler*, and the disappointing results of the *Grapple* firings. An operational success was fine but the deterrent needed 'a bigger bang for less bucks'.

Cook confidently awaited instructions to prepare for tests in November. But the Foreign Office warned that a cut-off for nuclear weapon trials might come in the latter half of October. Even so, Cook was certain that November was the earliest that useful trials could be held. He explained the basis for the new trial to his Aldermaston colleagues on 15 July. Another *Granite* device must be fired, he told them, to provide a better understanding of the system. The target yield would be 1 megaton, but 'we should not attempt to get 1 megaton by guesswork' and the yield would be less important than fact-finding. That the scientists wanted to continue with *Granite* showed their confidence in the basic design, even though they did not yet know in detail why the *Short* and *Purple Granite* shots gave low yields. To meet Sandys' request, Cook said, Aldermaston should try to prepare another round embodying a different megaton technique. (What technique Cook might have had in mind is not clear.) It would be fired if the next *Granite* shot demonstrated that a double bomb with a spherically imploded, layered Dick could not be exploited after all. A fission bomb should *not* be considered as an alternative; no significant increase in yield was likely from an *Orange Herald* type of device, even with boosting or with improved high explosive.

Once the Prime Minister had given his approval for *Grapple X*,[16] the Ministry of Defence asked the Ministry of Supply to set up a planning staff and make the necessary arrangements. Although specific approval had been given only for one trial, in October or November 1957, planning should allow for the possibility of further trials early in 1958 and at intervals thereafter. The Prime Minister had stressed that no publicity should be given to these decisions, and knowledge of *Grapple* results, and the reasons for mounting another megaton trial so soon, must be limited to the very small circle of officials who had already been informed.

There was now little time, and a daunting amount of work to be done both by the services and by Aldermaston, to prepare to mount *Grapple X* in November and to have new designs and hardware ready.

11
'We shall have to do it all again' – *Grapple X*

Purposes

The *Grapple* results, and the reasons for a further trial, were restricted on the Prime Minister's instructions to the small circle already in the know. The Minister of Defence even hoped there was no need for the moment to inform the Americans, and he also asked the Atomic Weapons Trials Executive to see if it was possible to avoid declaring a danger zone in advance.

Whatever operational and propaganda success had been claimed for *Operation Grapple*, the scientific reality could not be concealed, for weapon debris, radioflash data and microbarograph readings were available for anyone with the necessary expertise and equipment and they showed that the trial had been only partially successful. A 'thermonuclear bluff'[1] had never been seriously contemplated; the Americans had regularly been assisted to take measurements and collect data at several British trials, including *Grapple*. For *Grapple X*, arrangements were again made with the United States about collecting data, Aldermaston was committed to producing a full megaton a yield from the *Granite* type of double bomb, and the British desperately wanted to be able to demonstrate their thermonuclear maturity. The launching of *Sputnik I* by the Soviet Union in early October 1957 encouraged hopes of renewed nuclear co-operation with the Americans, even the exchange of nuclear weapon design information. Prime Minister Macmillan began to reach out for the 'great prize'. Success at *Grapple X* might help him to grasp it.

Sputnik I, the first artificial earth satellite, caused immense alarm and a widespread feeling of national humiliation in the United States. The launch vehicle, a large and relatively crude ICBM, was already in limited service – unlike *Atlas*, the American equivalent, which had failed on its first flight. The Soviet Union had shown itself capable of hitting targets anywhere on the surface of the earth. This afforded Britain a brilliant opportunity to seek improved nuclear defence co-operation, and Eisenhower responded sympathetically to Macmillan's approach. The presence of United States observers at *Grapple X* was essential to winning Congressional approval for modifications to the 1954 Atomic Energy Act, and the trial was no longer merely a matter of making a double bomb work – that had already been done at *Grapple* – but of making it work very well indeed.

Grapple X would be different from *Grapple* in several ways. Though *Grapple* had been urgent, now the increasing fears of an imminent moratorium had produced an overwhelming sense of time running out. The new trial would be conducted off the coast of Christmas Island instead of Malden Island, as HMSs *Warrior* and *Narvik* would not be available. The change dictated an extremely tight schedule for the *Grapple X* planners, Aldermaston and the three services. The Royal Engineers had a major construction task before them, since the Christmas Island facilities had to be improved, and the Malden instrumentation sites had to be duplicated there.

Another difference was how the weapons were developed. Nuclear weapons design was increasingly being supported by computer calculation, although there were (and still are) differences of opinion about the extent to which it was necessary then. According to one retired Aldermaston scientist, the new IBM 704, delivered in the summer of 1957, played a vital part in designing the test device for *Grapple X*, the success of which (he believed) effectively secured the 1958 Anglo-American agreement.

A further significant change was in weapon development management. On returning after *Purple Granite*, Cook had had the embarrassing task of explaining to the Government the disappointing outcome of *Operation Grapple*, and without doubt he was determined not to repeat the experience. From this time on Cook took a more personal grip on the H-bomb work as Penney took less part in it.

One requirement for *Grapple X* was an improved design for the primary (Tom), but this could be done with little or no further research. Tom was to be a modified *Red Beard* fission bomb, with a higher yield, say 45 kilotons. It would use improved high explosive, and a beryllium[2] tamper, and it was to have a cartridge loading tube (a safety device allowing last-minute loading – LML).

As for the Dick, Cook told the WDPC, if the *Granite* type of weapon was to have a future, several improvements appeared essential. The yield must be enhanced. Taylor instability must be reduced. The production of fast fission neutrons must be improved. Compression must be increased, and criticality possibly delayed. To achieve these aims, it would be necessary to augment the amount of uranium-235, and to increase the thickness of the lithium deuteride layer or layers.

K.V. Roberts thought that two layers of lithium deuteride in the secondary would be enough, but the idea of a single lithium deuteride layer was favoured for fact-finding purposes, since it would lend itself more easily to calculation. Modifications to both Tom and Dick were discussed but some, especially the beryllium tampers, might present manufacturing difficulties and the improved high explosive supercharge would require new dies and presses.

The objectives of *Grapple X*, Cook insisted, must be quite clear. Firstly, fissile material must be saved; megaton yields must be achieved without the extravagant amounts of fissile material needed for *Orange Herald* and its (untested) derivative, *Knobkerry*. This would be essential if – as seemed possible – fissile material production for weapons were to be stopped by an international agreement. Meanwhile Aldermaston must learn to make a 1-megaton double bomb without worrying about its weight or fissile content; both would then have to be scaled down without reducing the yield. Secondly, Aldermaston had to find out how to make weapons of 5 to 10 megatons. Thirdly – and this was most important – a warhead immune to attack by radiation-intensive enemy nuclear weapons had to be produced.

Cook was convinced that these objectives could only be attained through step by step experiments checked with theory. He wanted to start with three investigative rounds, in logical sequence, based on a double bomb with a five-layer Dick – or a three-layer Dick if, even with the fast new IBM computer, the five-layer calculations could not be done in time. In each of the first two rounds, different thermonuclear layers would be replaced by inert material, so that effects could be clearly identified. It was decided to do the five-layer calculations on the IBM 704, taking four weeks; the three-layer calculations (estimated at five weeks' work) would be done on the older and slower Ferranti Mark I.

Then K. W. Allen, the head of nuclear physics and an innovative and original scientist, produced a brilliant new idea for a 1-megaton device, and was strongly backed by his senior, S. C. Curran (who later became Aldermaston's chief scientist). We shall see later what this idea was. However, Allen's bomb would require implosion studies on the IBM, and Cook said it must be deferred, perhaps to the spring of 1958. At the time, Cook had no other option; he had to go for the conservative idea most likely to succeed; after *Grapple*, he could not afford to take any chances or try anything novel. If a ban had cut short the testing programme at the end of 1957 Allen's idea would never have been vindicated, but the moratorium held off for another 12 months, and Allen's bomb was exploded with spectacular success in April 1958 (Chapter 12).

Planning and preparations

Meanwhile, in late July, the planning staffs went into action, with an inflexible target date of 5 November for the first drop. All construction and installation work had to be finished by 23 October, and there was much to be done by then. Twenty-six blast-proof steel shelters were to be erected on Christmas Island; 18 were already on Malden Island, some were in Australia, and some were being manufactured in the United Kingdom. Some of the Malden shelters would be used to construct a control room, fitted out with equipment from HMS *Narvik*, used earlier at *Grapple*. A tented camp for 100 men, including 28 Aldermaston staff, would be established on the east coast of Christmas Island, 15 miles from the intended ground zero. Ken Bomford, remembering the primitive conditions on Malden Island during *Grapple*, and the complaints about the Christmas Island facilities, urged that the standard of food should be as high as possible, and Air Commodore 'Ginger' Weir ordered the number of cooks and butchers to be doubled.

By the end of July 1957 it was clear that construction work on Christmas Island would take three or four weeks longer than previously estimated. The most important item was the shelter programme and here Aldermaston's requirement had risen. There were also many staffing problems, including shortages of trained RAF personnel for the active handling flight (responsible for dealing with cloud samples) and for the 20-strong aircraft decontamination team. Then there were difficulties over the meteorological service since the staff were reluctant to stay on at Malden and Fanning Islands for 10 days after the explosion – not surprisingly, considering the isolation and bleakness of the islands. The absence of a weather ship was a matter for concern, but in early October New Zealand offered the frigates *Pukaki* and *Rotoiti*, whose work at *Grapple* had been officially commended by the Task Force Commander.

The deadline of 23 October for completing the construction work was just met (in spite of delays in the shipping programme) thanks to dedicated hard work by the Army and the Aldermaston trials staff. More than half the control equipment taken from HMS *Narvik* was found to be faulty, much of it damaged in unloading, but most of it was repaired in time by staff who had literally lived with their equipment, sleeping on camp beds in the shelters.

Programme and test devices

While the task force personnel were working against the clock and the calendar to meet the target date and to have everything ready for the trial, so were the Aldermaston staff who had to design and manufacture the devices which were the operation's raison d'être. One matter of debate was whether to fire the investigative five-layer or three-layer Dicks with the inert shells first, or the complete weapon. Hulme argued for the complete weapon in case there might not be a later opportunity. Cook firmly maintained his logical step by step method and refused to be panicked into a more pragmatic approach by the threat of a moratorium; as it turned out, the moratorium was not until November 1958, giving time for six more shots at Christmas Island.

By early August, the sequence of rounds was beginning to take shape. The first round (A) would have a three-layer secondary. Its results would determine the rest of the firing programme by a process of elimination in a systematic diagnostic sequence.[3]

If the yield of fast neutrons in Round A was satisfactory the next shot would be Round B, with a five-layer Dick (providing the calculations could be done in time).

If the Round A fast neutron production was below expectations, the defect might be due to the Dick's uranium-235 component. This could be checked by firing Round C – with a three-layer secondary but with an inert layer instead of lithium deuteride. If Round C showed a low uranium-235 yield, then a fourth round – a primary alone – might be fired to check its separate yield.

At the worst, if the Round A fast neutron yield was disappointing, yet the uranium-235 yield was satisfactory, the reason would almost certainly be the mixing of the layers. In that case the *Granite* type of device, with the layered secondary, might have to be abandoned.

Round A would be in a case of the same size as the *Short Granite* case, but thicker, and the primary would be 50 per cent more powerful than that used in *Short Granite*. Various ideas were discussed for reducing the overall weight – using a smaller, boosted Tom, and/or reducing the amount of filling in the casing between the Tom and the Dick. It might even be possible to eliminate the filling altogether. Might not an air gap transport enough energy from the Tom to implode the Dick? This idea was later to be tried successfully at *Grapple Z* (see Chapter 13).

The engineers and the materials scientists waited anxiously for details of the physicists' requirements. By mid-August Graham Hopkin (chief of the materials division) was worried. Lithium-6 stocks were insufficient for current tentative designs of the *Grapple X* rounds, and enough could not be manufactured in time to meet the existing deadlines. He was short of the special personnel he needed. Delays in providing firm information on the *Grapple X* devices added to the difficulties, and were going to be embarrassing. It might be just possible to get three rounds made by November, but only two might be ready. Bill Lord, his deputy, was also worried by the problems of working on the *Grapple X* devices while manufacturing fission bombs for the stockpile, and said the only solution seemed to be day and night shifts throughout September and October. Even so, he could not promise uranium-238 castings before 20 September, and even that was doubtful if there were difficulties in commissioning a new smelting furnace. Hopkin told Cook that time for fabricating the tampers was getting very short, and it seemed increasingly likely that only two rounds would be ready for the trial.

Cook's range of options was dwindling from the original four rounds. Calculations for Round A were not going well, Pike said, and as it had top priority he would have to switch the calculations from the Ferranti to the IBM 704 (which was then working on Round B). There was no hope of completing the Round B calculations in time on the Ferranti, and the five- layered Round B now looked impossible for *Grapple X*.

The programme was down to three rounds, and Hopkin questioned whether Round C, with an inert layer, was really worthwhile. Cook thought it would be if Round A's yield was as low as 200 kilotons (the *Purple Granite* result). But Hopkin could not wait for an answer until after Round A had been fired; he needed 'an early firm decision' about the lithium-6 requirement. Cook promised him an answer by 9 September.

At a special meeting on 9 September, the WDPC was presented with the configuration chosen for the Round A Dick. It had been partially dictated by the size of the press tools available. Alternative suggestions were made for the design of the fissile layer – should it be in one part or two 'nesting' parts? – and its composition. John Corner thought there was just enough time for calculations to decide these points and Cook agreed. Hopkin's feelings can be imagined but he is recorded merely as saying that he would require the final details by the end of the week. Round B was ruled out for *Grapple X*; by 16 September Round C was settled and dates of delivery of the bombs were estimated. The Round A components would meet the 5 November firing date.

Two policy decisions

By the end of September, the Prime Minister had approved the area of the danger zone (based on the assumption that no yield at *Grapple X* could exceed 2 megatons). It was to take effect on 1 November; the Notice to Mariners was to be issued at the last possible date, and in no circumstances before 15 October. The next question for ministers was how the trial should be announced. They agreed that a forthcoming speech by the British representative at the United Nations Disarmament Commission would provide an opportunity to explain Britain's attitude to nuclear testing and then to say that more trials during the winter were planned.

Another policy question was whether foreign observers should be present. The United States did not want to send an observer, and E. S. Jackson at the Ministry of Supply thought no other country should be invited. With so little time and with already harassed staff working to their utmost capacity, the presence of observers would be an added difficulty. Besides, the dates of shots were always subject to unavoidable change at short notice, and observers might be kept hanging about for some time. There was also some security risk involved.

However, there was to be a last minute change of mind by the United States, in the new circumstances created by the Washington talks in late October 1957 and the publication of the Declaration of Common Purpose (Chapter 14). A week before the target date for the first shot, the Ministry of Defence was informed that General Herbert Loper was very anxious to receive invitations for United States observers. Loper, the Assistant Secretary of Defense for Special Weapons, was highly influential and a strong supporter of Anglo-American nuclear co- operation, and his position in the Washington battle for the amendment of the United States Atomic Energy Act might be weakened if the invitations failed to materialise. The British Joint Services Mission in Washington advised that everything should be done to meet this request by inviting two observers of General rank.

The trial

The Personnel Safety Plan for the trial was issued towards the end of October. It was similar to the *Grapple* safety plan, but with some modifications since the point of burst would be off the south-east of Christmas Island and not off Malden Island, 400 miles away. The native population of Christmas Island would be embarked on HMS *Messina* during the shots – a precaution not necessary for *Grapple*. Task force personnel remaining on the island would have to cover as much of their bodies as possible, during rehearsals as well as live drops, by wearing hats, long sleeves, trousers or overalls, and socks and shoes. Access to the forward area would be strictly controlled and everyone entering or leaving would have to pass through a radiation monitoring process. The chief health physicist, Ed Fuller, would lead the re-entry into the forward area after the blast.

On 18 October, consignments of weapon components began to arrive by Hastings transport aircraft. These included not only the components for the nuclear weapons but also the 'rehearsal rounds' containing only high explosives. (Some of the HE rounds were refurbished surplus items from *Grapple* which had been stored on Christmas Island for possible future use.)

The firing programme at this point, it may be remembered, consisted of Round A, with the three-layer secondary; then (depending on Round A results) Round C, with one inert layer in the secondary; and then, perhaps, a separate Tom. There would be no Round B. Nearly all the (dismantled) components for Rounds A and C were delivered to Christmas Island on 24, 27 and 29 October and were taken to the weapon assembly area for inspection and radiography. Only the primary for Round C was still to come.

Radiography showed a small fault – which might have developed in transit – in the Round A primary, and there was little time to spare before the round was due to be fired. The Christmas Island staff reported back urgently to Aldermaston, where Cook was on a flying visit home. If the fault was confirmed, the Round C primary would be taken for Round A. A replacement primary for Round C would have to be sent out later, if Round C was to be fired. But a decision whether or not to fire it could not be made until some radiochemical results were available, four or five days after the Round A firing. (Mass spectroscopy results would take longer.) It was decided to rule out the possibility of a third shot (the separate Tom). The programme was down to two shots, or even one.

Before leaving to return to Christmas Island, Cook wrote a handwritten letter expressing his appreciation of the tremendous efforts that Hopkin and his staff had made to meet the *Grapple X* schedule, and asked 'Hoppy' to pass on his thanks to all concerned.

One consignment, delivered on 29 October, posed a serious problem for the Christmas Island scientists. The fissile core for the Round C Tom – now wanted urgently for Round A – was stuck fast and would not come out of its special container. The container was reassembled and placed in a few inches of hot water, and 15 minutes later the ball came out without any trouble. 'Difficult to persuade Tom to leave his bed', said a signal from the island to Aldermaston. 'Success by means of hot bath'. After radiography, precise measurements of the core began at 1.00 am on 30 October.

Eight hours later, the core was taken to the explosives assembly building and fitted into the Tom. Work went on round the clock, and on Thursday 31 October the complete Tom was brought into the weapon assembly area, and – after the addition of fillets of plasticine to parts of the exterior – it was installed in the Tom part of the casing. The extensive cable array was fitted by evening. Next day, 1 November, the cabling checks were complete and more plasticine was used to fill the remaining hollows. A mobile crane then brought the Dick from its humidity-controlled building, and the Tom and Dick ends of the casing were bolted together. On the following day, Saturday, the complete warhead was installed in the *Blue Danube* bomb casing, the firing unit and wiring harness were fitted, and more plasticine was generously applied before fitting the remaining panels of the ballistic casing. (Nuclear bombs have some surprising ingredients.) Round A was ready for firing on 5 November, as scheduled, but torrential rain affected the instruments and delayed the operation by three days. Cook asked Penney to let the Prime Minister's office know how sorry they were to have missed 'his date' when they were so close.

Penney's preoccupations during these weeks must have been overwhelming: the *Antler* trials,[4] which ended on 9 October; *Grapple X* in early November; the urgent investigation of the Windscale reactor fire[5] which took up all his time from 17 to 26 October; the crucial Anglo-American talks of late October, and their immediate consequences (Chapter 14).

The final operational rehearsal was on 5 November. Then came D-1, on Thursday 7 November. Round A was loaded into the Valiant ready for D-Day. To prevent unauthorised re-entry a barrier guarded by military police was set up on the road between C Camp and the Health Control Point at C-site. All movement in the area beyond this point was to be reported to the Joint Operation Control.

The day of 8 November, D-Day, was a bad day for the task force commander. He had to cope with the sort of crisis that is liable to occur when political considerations override operational ones. Because, as we saw, ministers had been so anxious to avoid publicity for this trial, they had refused, despite all argument, to allow the Note to Mariners to be sent out in good time to keep shipping clear of the designated danger zone, and it had gone out very late. Now, at 1.00 am on the 8th,[6] Oulton was woken up with the news that a Shackleton on routine sea search had found a Liberian ship in the danger area and heading towards Christmas Island. *Effie*, an old World War II Victory ship, had probably sailed from her last port before the notice was issued. The Shackleton, unable to get any response from the crew, was keeping *Effie* under observation; the task force frigate, HMS *Cossack*, was sailing to intercept her and hoped to reach her in about four hours. If *Effie* could not be turned away in time there would be no question of a live drop that day. Oulton had few kind words for politicians just then.

The D-Day preparations went on, with the meteorologists and Aldermaston's fall-out prediction expert, Ernest Hicks, updating their assessments every 15 minutes. There was heavy rain, and wind gusting up to 30 knots, but they forecast that the weather would clear sufficiently, and so it did. Everything was ready by 6.00 am, but there was no news of *Effie*. Then, at 6.15 am, came a signal from the Shackleton tracking her. The Shackleton captain had at last managed to rouse the crew and drop leaflets, and *Effie* was turning south and steaming away at 12 knots. She would be clear of danger in time. Round A was dropped shortly after 8.46 am local time.

A megaton airdrop

It was a dramatic event. As the *Blue Danube* with its warhead was released from the bomb shackle and began its fall, filmed by cameras in the Valiant's bomb-bay, there was an immediate change in the frequency of a tone being transmitted from the weapon. This turned on the telemetry recording instruments that were focused on the point in space where the bomb was planned to explode, some 8,000 feet above the ocean. Its release from the shackle also switched on the clockwork timing mechanism which, 53 seconds later, would set off the firing sequence. Extensions to the fins on the tail of the bomb snapped into place and began to damp down its oscillations to a graceful arc through the morning sunlight. The radar beam found the weapon as the Valiant bomber and companion grandstand aircraft each turned into its escape manoeuvre.

The firing sequence began a series of events – what the older weapon scientists from Fort Halstead would have called 'phenomena of very short duration' – lasting only a few millionths of a second but capable of being analysed, calculated and, to a large extent, directed. First, at 42 seconds past 8.47 am, the high explosive lens system of the Tom – the modified *Red Beard* fission weapon – exploded, and then the high explosive supercharge, squeezing the beryllium tamper. This in turn crushed the composite fissile core with enormous force, reducing it to a ball of ferociously hot, super-dense liquid metal. The core was now in the ideal state for an uncontrolled chain reaction. This was triggered off by the 'urchin', a small polonium and beryllium device; crushed by the implosion process, the polonium and beryllium began to mix, emitting neutrons which initiated fission in the highly compressed core. This implosion phase had taken some 70 millionths of a second after the firing sequence began. Round A's casing remained intact but had expanded by a few centimetres. Now followed the explosion phase, taking just three hundred millionths of a second. A great flux of X-rays poured out, compressing the Dick to a twentieth of its previous volume in less than two millionths of a second and, as it imploded, the uranium-238 outer case crushed the thermonuclear fuel.

The fast neutrons produced by the fusion reaction then began to initiate fast fission in the uranium-238 layer, which was now acting as a tamper, holding the Dick intact long enough for each of the reactions to make its contribution to the total yield. When this process – described by one weapon scientist as 'vicious physics' – had gone as far as the design would allow, an intense, searing white flash dispersed the ionized remains of the weapon casing. Within a second they erupted into the morning sky as an incandescent fire-ball, more than a mile across. Being much less dense than the surrounding air, it soared upwards, first taking a doughnut shape as the cooler upper air rolled the outer surface of the fire-ball in on itself, and then it became a classic mushroom cloud as it burst into the stratosphere and rose rapidly to a great height. The cloud was so high that the sniffer pilots found sampling extremely difficult, especially since they were unable to use rocket- assisted Scorpion Canberras as the task force commander had hoped.

Results

After the hard work and disappointments of *Grapple*, and the enormous effort needed to mount *Grapple X* at all, this must have been a very special moment for Cook and for his staff. The yield surprised everyone – 1.8 megatons, much bigger than the predicted 1 megaton, but still well within the 2-megaton limit on which the safety calculations had been based. The bomb had exploded at the correct height, but some 320 yards to the left and 32 yards beyond the target. All the planned measurements had been obtained and there was no contamination of the island, as Cook's jubilant signal assured Penney. For personnel closest to the explosion, the exploding weapon had produced an integrated radiation dose calculated as well below the minimum level of detection of the most sensitive dosimeter. A health physics survey team led by Ed Fuller made the initial re-entry into the forward area and subsequent re-entries were made by teams in full protective clothing, each member provided with a film badge and a quartz fibre dosimeter. The team leaders were equipped with gamma survey meters and instructed before re-entry on how to use them. No dosimeter carried by any member of any re-entry party recorded a detectable gamma dose. Measurements of air and ground contamination were also taken at the Main Camp Officers' Mess and at Port London, and none indicated radioactive contamination. A survey of the forward area by helicopter the next day failed to reveal any ground contamination.

Some damage had been done and repairs would be needed. Helicopter windows had been blown out, the aircraft fuel storage tanks at the airfield, some 26 miles from ground zero, had been damaged, and a considerable area of land close to ground zero had been scorched and devastated. Damage – unspecified – to the personal property of Gilbertese natives living on Christmas Island was subsequently assessed at four pounds Sterling.

It had been the opinion of Aldermaston scientists that if the yield of Round A was about a megaton, Round C should not be fired. Now, in view of the much higher than expected yield, Cook saw no point in firing Round C, and after consulting Penney he cancelled the shot. *Grapple X* was over, with one shot. On 9 November, Penney sent him a signal on Christmas Island: 'Glad you got it off Friday. This took out some of the sting of Windscale. [That is, the Windscale reactor accident of October 1957.] On Monday there is a small meeting with Powell to work out the next move with the Americans. Plowden and I expect to get to Washington about Sunday 17 November . . . and [I] am hoping you can join us there provided you are not still busy at Christmas'. Clearly Penney thought that the success of *Grapple X* had restored, in the eyes of the Americans, some of the prestige lost after the Windscale accident. Cook replied on Sunday morning, 10 November, that he expected to be back on Tuesday morning.

Then, with Air Commodore Wilson (a pioneer of radioactive cloud sampling since *Totem*,[7] who had directed the *Grapple X* sniffing operation), he climbed into the cramped cabin of a Canberra for a rapid trip to Honolulu, the first stage of the journey. A bag containing most of the records of the trial was placed on board. But the pilot lost his way. After flying on one engine to conserve what little fuel remained, he managed to land on a small airstrip some 100 miles south-west of Honolulu, and Cook and Wilson were then taken to Honolulu by a United States aircraft. In a deeply critical report Wilson said they had faced the fearful prospect of losing both the scientific director and the early results of the trial, if they had not had the exceptional good fortune to find land when they did. Back at Aldermaston, Cook signalled Air Vice-Marshal Oulton saying that he was 'now making slow recovery'.

A week after his return, Cook told the WDPC that *Grapple X* had been very successful and he read out a letter of congratulations from the Prime Minister to Penney. Reporting on the early experimental results, Aldermaston's chief scientist, Charles Adams, said that the yield measurements ranged from 1.4 to 1.6 megatons, but the Americans had estimated 3 megatons by comparing it with their estimates of 3 to 5 megatons for certain Soviet test explosions. Photographic measurements of the *Grapple X* fire-ball suggested a yield closer to 1.8 megatons than 1.6. Radiochemical and mass spectrographic analyses were not yet completed and, unfortunately, the samples obtained by the sniffer aircraft were poor and not really representative. The current best estimate is 1.8 megatons. But whatever the precise figure, it had undoubtedly been a big bang – 75 times as powerful as the 1952 *Hurricane* device.

Aldermaston held a post-mortem on the trial on 10 January 1958. Although the yield had been higher than expected, there was a measure of agreement between theoretical predictions and observed results which showed that they were beginning to understand the processes involved. Two papers by Keith Roberts and Bryan Taylor, 'on the efficiency of thermonuclear bombs', made notable advances in the understanding of the physics of the H-bomb. The second paper, in early 1958, made invaluable use of *Grapple X* data.

The trial proposed for early 1958 would advance that understanding. But what was the outlook for a further trial or trials?

Future trials?

The Ministry of Defence, in its directive on *Grapple X*, had intended that preparations for that trial should make it possible to hold further tests early in 1958 if the government decided that they were necessary. 'It should therefore be our policy', E. S. Jackson wrote to Sir Richard Powell of the Ministry of Defence, 'to make appointments and provide equipment on the basis that people sent there for the series may have to stay at Christmas

Island for some considerable time, and all necessary material resources should be provided on the Island'. It was not suggested that a permanent establishment should be set up comparable to Maralinga, in South Australia, but it was the clear intention of the Prime Minister that if the government did want further tests they should not be made impossible by lack of preparations at Christmas Island.

However, the Atomic Weapons Trials Executive, as well as the Task Force Commander and the service departments, wanted more clarification. Preparations for megaton tests in the first half of 1958, and the necessary expenditure, were indeed authorised, but there were several questions outstanding. Many installations at Christmas Island would not be usable after the November 1957 test. Considerable building and runway resurfacing would be necessary. Spending 30% above the bare cost of these basic preparations for tests in the first half of 1958 could provide semi-permanent facilities that might last for several years, but if this money was not spent now, it would cost much more in the long run to make the facilities last.

The service departments could see no difference between making preparations at Christmas Island on the assumption that tests might continue more or less indefinitely, and setting up a permanent establishment there. They wanted to be told precisely what provision they had to make. Unless instructions were immediately forthcoming, tests at Christmas Island could not be carried out in the second half of 1958, and much time and money would be needed before tests could be mounted again. Plans must be made on a long-term basis. The Navy wanted to know which ships it would have to keep in commission for the tests. The Army had to know about construction and maintenance loads; would it, for example, be necessary to withdraw units from the British Army of the Rhine? The RAF needed to know what aircraft would be required. If tests at Christmas Island extended into the second half of 1958, the services would not be able to support any tests at Maralinga the same year.

Jackson sent Air Vice-Marshal Oulton a memorandum on planning megaton trials after *Grapple X*. The Prime Minister, it said, had given 'verbal approval' for planning future megaton trials, and it should be assumed there would be trials in February and May 1958. But in the 18 months from May 1958 to October 1959 there would be no trials and therefore no need for operational forces on Christmas Island. A small care and maintenance party would maintain the facilities. The services should assume that, if there were to be any nuclear tests *after* October 1959, they would know well in advance. Meanwhile, the roads and the airstrip on Christmas Island should be patched; huts with a life of at least two years should be provided for the care and maintenance party, but other personnel would be accommodated in tents. There was no intention of holding future kiloton trials at Christmas Island rather than Maralinga, but possibly one of the explosions at Christmas Island in 1958 would be in the kiloton range. Plans could – and did – change drastically as the possibility of a special nuclear relationship with America unfolded, and as a test moratorium loomed ever closer. But, despite long-term uncertainty, the trials seemed set to continue in the immediate future.

12

Britain's Biggest Explosion – *Grapple Y*

Objectives and options

Grapple X had exceeded expectations. It had been a big bang, at 1.8 megatons. But was it a real hydrogen bomb or, as K. W. Allen suggested, more like a double boosted bomb? Did that matter? Did it fulfil the remit given to Aldermaston in July 1954 and was it the superbomb the Chiefs of Staff wanted? Cook simply concluded that it showed a measure of agreement between theoretical predictions and observed results which indicated that Aldermaston was beginning to understand the processes involved. This, after all, was a prime purpose of nuclear weapon tests (see Preface).

The idea of further tests after *Grapple* had, as we saw, been super-secret. Plans for *Grapple Y*, and even Z, to follow *Grapple X* – approved informally by the Prime Minister – were still more secret. Even the Chiefs of Staff were excluded from the very small circle of informed officials. This was extraordinary given their prime interest in the H-bomb programme and also the service commitments involved in mounting more tests or even maintaining a minimum facility at Christmas Island.

Peter Chadwick of the theoretical physics division later said that already the design of the *Grapple Y* device was essentially complete before *Grapple X*. Much work had indeed been done by then but a great deal was still to do, and his comment perhaps exemplifies how 'design' meant rather different things to theoretical and nuclear physicists and to the chemists, metallurgists and engineers who actually had to make the devices. At the early WDPC discussions of *Grapple Y* in September 1957 Cook had outlined three possible lines of development.

The first was another double bomb, with a spherical, layered Dick calculated to find a satisfactory compromise between too thick shells (which would slow down the fast neutrons from the thermonuclear reaction), and too thin shells (which would risk interfacial instability – the notorious Rayleigh- Taylor

165

effect). The next option was like the *Grapple X* device (Round A) but with improved compression. The third option – technologically very difficult and requiring far more complicated calculations – was to abandon separate shells of fissile and fusile materials in favour of shells made of intimate mixtures of the materials, consisting of micron-sized particles of uranium-235, uranium-238 and lithium deuteride. Little or nothing was known about such mixtures; if this third option was chosen Hopkin doubted the possibility of meeting the February 1958 deadline. If one of the other options was followed, he thought three or four months would be required to manufacture the new Dick assembly.

A decision on a February 1958 trial would have to be taken by 1 November, so Cook concluded that the *Grapple Y* gadget would have to be a layered type. If mixtures were to be investigated they would have to feature in a later trial in, say, May 1958. Calculations should meanwhile be carried out on various different layouts of a layered Dick – including a five-shell device; a cylindrical secondary using lithium-7 deuteride; and another (non- cylindrical) using 'a lot of lithium-7 deuteride' and less uranium-235. The latter two were suggestions by Ken Allen which Cook had had to rule out for *Grapple X* but was now ready to consider. The last was the one eventually adopted, and it was sometimes called 'the Dickens',[1] because it used Ken's Dick concept.

The computing power available to Aldermaston, though improved, was still seriously limited, and by mid-October 1957 it was clear that the five-layer calculations could not be completed by February, but a simpler three-layer calculation could be finished in time. It was therefore decided that a device similar to Round A (*Grapple X*) should be used, but incorporating a greater quantity of lithium deuteride. The five-layer system, as well as systems using intimate mixtures of metals, could be considered for later test series.

Cook called a special meeting at the end of October with one question on the agenda – had theoretical design studies advanced far enough for a weapon trial to be carried out in February 1958? It was agreed, first, that the design of the primary was not a problem; an adequate yield might be about 50 kilotons and if higher yields were required in future, boosting would provide them. Next, it was agreed that the main objective of *Grapple Y* was not just to produce a high yield, though this was an important consideration; the main objective was to develop a system in which the light element reactions were used more successfully. Therefore, diagnostic measurement would be crucial in determining exactly what processes had taken place and in distinguishing the fission and fusion contributions. Allen was concerned that the interpretation of radiochemistry results would be complicated by the presence of uranium-238 in both primary and secondary, making discrimination between them difficult, so he suggested that thorium be substituted for a natural uranium tamper.

It was agreed that the configuration of the *Grapple Y* device should be similar to that of Round A (with a three-layer Dick) but with a larger radiation case and perhaps with Tom and Dick closer together. Hopkin was assured that the design of the shells would be decided in time to allow for manufacture but, as he pointed out, it would take 10 to 12 weeks to obtain new dies and other equipment needed to fabricate the components. Lack of the necessary experience, too, would cause some delays. It was agreed, however, that plans should go ahead for a test in February 1958.

Cook again emphasised to the WDPC that the main objective of *Grapple Y* was to determine whether, with the compression that could be achieved, a worthwhile yield could be obtained from the lithium deuteride, so that more of the total yield was obtained from the thermonuclear reactions, without relying so largely on the uranium-235 in the Dick and on fission of natural uranium by fast neutrons from the thermonuclear reactions. Reducing the uranium-235 would make greater compression possible, and a trade-off would be necessary. The degree of enrichment of the lithium deuteride was also an important question.

There was again a safety limit of 2 megatons, and Cook asked for an estimate of the maximum likely yield. K. V. Roberts thought the yield could reach 3 megatons, but it could be restricted if necessary by modifying the tamper. Cook opposed the suggestion that the design should be modified to ensure that the yield was less than 3 megatons. He wanted to fire the best round that could be designed and, if necessary, to revise the firing conditions to permit a larger yield. But this would be difficult, as Adams pointed out; ground zero would have to be moved by about ten miles, so reducing the measurement possibilities and, as Curran and Allen both emphasized, accurate and detailed diagnostic measurements were of the essence of this trial.

Workshop problems

Producing these one-off experimental rounds, always urgently required and always subject to frequent alterations, was not easy. Besides design changes, and problems of materials and special equipment, there were novel technical difficulties in dealing with unfamiliar materials whose properties were not well known. The technique of hot-pressing thick layers of lithium deuteride, for example, had not been worked out. Then there was the human problem of the workshops. Each test was treated as a special occasion and the establishment relied on heroic efforts by an under-strength work-force to complete the components on time. There were limits, Hopkin pointed out, to what could be expected and what the men could put up with, as one urgent demand succeeded another. Some resistance to long working hours was now developing. Because of staff shortages some men were having to do work that should have been done by lower grades, if they had been available. The situation was aggravated by a 'flu epidemic in October.[2] There was a risk of mistakes; some slips had been made. Hopkin was convinced that more staff must be found.

Dates and devices

The planned firing date for *Grapple Y* was still 28 February 1958, but it might have to be delayed to March or even April because the Christmas Island runway needed resurfacing. Corner urged minimum delay since the very recent discussions in Washington between President Eisenhower and Prime Minister Macmillan opened up such great new possibilities for the renewal of Anglo-American nuclear co-operation (see Chapter 14). This made it especially important for Britain to be able to demonstrate significant advances, which would be evident to the United States scientists (and hence to the policy-makers) from the analysis of debris from the British tests.

The delay of *Grapple Y* was soon confirmed. First it was postponed to 19 March, and then to just before or just after Easter Sunday (16 April). Whatever the eventual date, what was to be fired? Design of the *Grapple Y* Dick continued in December. Cook feared that cutting down the uranium-235 content, with the object of obtaining a large yield from the thermonuclear material, might cause the round to fail. Corner thought there was no real risk; later, it might be worthwhile testing a device with much less uranium-235 to determine how far the quantity could be reduced. Corner, Hulme and Roberts gave their preliminary rough estimates of the yield. A reasonable figure, they agreed, was 2.5 megatons; the upper limit was 5 megatons, though 7 megatons could not be entirely ruled out. There would be no need to change the weapon design or to move ground zero, Cook thought, but the safety of the delivery aircraft needed study; Pilgrim and Hicks would consult the Royal Aircraft Establishment (RAE) at Farnborough.

By mid-December aircraft safety criteria had been worked out, on the basis of an expected yield between 2 and 2.5 megatons, with an upper limit of 4 to 5 megatons. It was decided to raise the dropping height and height of burst by 1000 feet.[3] Challens pointed out that this would be at the maximum altitude for a Valiant bomber – that for a Vulcan was little more – and that performance decreased as the aircraft ceiling was approached. The idea of retarding the fall of the bomb by using a parachute was suggested but Cook feared it would make accuracy in aiming impossible. Another suggestion, discussed with RAE but rejected, was to slow the fall, by replacing the *Blue Danube*'s pointed nose with a flat nose. No other gravity bomb case was available with a slower rate of descent. However, as long as higher yields than *Grapple Y* were not contemplated for the time being, the situation might just prove to be satisfactory. The plan was given a cautious endorsement.

Island hardships

Living conditions at Christmas Island had always been unsatisfactory. During the *Grapple* series it had been regarded as a temporary base for one trial series only, and facilities had been fairly primitive. By the spring of 1958 they still were, despite some recent amelioration in accommodation and messing facilities. If the island were to become a permanent base, there would be more money to upgrade it, but the government had only sanctioned expenditure on the minimum repairs and improvements to make it usable for a limited period.

However, the civilian scientists, unlike the servicemen, were in the position of being able to refuse to take part and there were signs that their *Grapple X* experience had stretched their enthusiasm and goodwill. It was bad enough being repeatedly away from their homes and families for long periods, without having to put up with such poor living conditions. They were beginning to make their complaints heard about inadequate rations – the ration allowance was still being discussed in Whitehall – and about the difficulty of getting meals outside normal working hours. Pilgrim, the trials director for *Grapple Y*, pressed for improvements and on 28 January Cook wrote in trenchant terms to the new task force commander, Air Vice Marshal John Grandy, who had been appointed to succeed Air Vice Marshal Oulton:

Immediately after *Grapple X*, I made strong representations to the DGAW and yourself on the need for a considerable improvement in the quantity, quality and variety of food at Christmas Island for civilians from AWRE.[4] I urged the messing allowance (I believe 4s 6d per diem for food) to be at least doubled. At *Grapple X* and since I've had protestations from staff here in the strongest possible terms against going again to Christmas Island unless the situation is rectified. Staff contrast the conditions regarding food with those at Maralinga. [There is] no reason why they should have … conditions so far inferior … I must urge you to get approval for an increase if I am to persuade AWRE staff to man *Grapple Y*.

The Aldermaston men wanted, among other things, better tented accommodation, ablutions, showers and latrines; adequate laundry facilities; a NAAFI shop; and opportunities for recreation. A modest request for an ice-making machine was ruled out by Whitehall as too expensive at $800. However, a second-hand ice cream machine from a British post at Benghazi was returned to Britain for overhaul and then sent out to Christmas Island –

not in time for *Grapple Y*, but no doubt it came in useful later. The supply of newspapers was to be increased.

Early March brought an increased ration scale, an additional allowance for local purchase of food, mainly from Honolulu, and a round the clock meal service. Aldermaston would send out '12 teapots and 50 knives' to remedy the shortage of crockery and cutlery. The library was to have 250 extra books; a radio and a record player (only one?); and records would be provided. There would be a new projector and films, and a new manager for the cinema. More basically, pipes were to be installed for water-borne disposal of sewage and the latrines were to be maintained in a 'serviceable and sanitary' state.

Two policy questions

Two policy questions arose during February. First, were any observers to be invited to *Grapple Y*? American observers had been present at all the British trials – though not for all the shots – since *Buffalo* at Maralinga in 1956. Representatives from Canada, Australia and New Zealand, which had given much help, had attended the first *Grapple* shot. Those countries had been excluded from *Grapple X* in favour of the Americans, and the reasons had been explained to them, but they had been invited to one round of *Antler* at Maralinga in 1957. Press representatives had been invited to *Grapple*, for the *Orange Herald* shot. If invitations to *Grapple Y* were issued, it would have to be stressed that the accommodation was going to be 'rugged' and there would be no VIP treatment. It was agreed that nine observers could be invited.

The second question was a familiar one – the announcement of the trial and the issue of the danger area warning notice. Again, it was feared that a long interval between announcement and test would create opportunities for hostile political activity, but nobody wanted another *Effie* situation. In any case the movement of white-painted Valiant bombers through Honolulu to Christmas Island, beginning about six weeks before the operation, would reveal that a test was due. The task force commander, Air Vice Marshal Grandy, thought the notification should be made on 17 March, to take effect from 21 April, a week before the intended firing date, but ministers preferred to follow the *Grapple X* pattern. The Minister of Defence, Duncan Sandys, wrote to the Prime Minister:

At your meeting on 4 March it was agreed that the arrangements for announcing the intention to hold a further test and for notifying the danger area, should be the same as for the last test in November.

On that occasion, the MoD issued a press statement on 26 October announcing the intention to hold a test in the near future. The notification of the danger area was issued on 1 November and the danger area was brought into effect on 3 November, 48 hours before the planned date of the test, which had, however, to be postponed for a few days owing to bad weather.

The minister recommended that the intention to test on 28 April 1958 should be disclosed on 22 April in a Parliamentary statement, and the danger area should be announced on 24 April and brought into effect on 26 April. Once again, very little margin was to be allowed for ships at sea.

'Intruders' were detected on the periphery of the danger area at the time of the shot who did not respond to signals. But it is not clear whether they were inquisitive submarines or inquisitive whales.

Measurements and monitoring

Scientific activity at *Grapple Y* was to be broadly the same as at *Grapple X* but with an increase in the number of scientific measurements. Greater effort would be directed to determining the early output of gamma radiation from the weapon, and the effects of the explosion on the dropping aircraft would be fully investigated. The latter task involved the use by RAE Farnborough of considerably more instrumentation than was used at *Grapple X*.

Extensive programmes of measurements and monitoring were arranged, both for weapon diagnostics and for safety purposes. On Fanning Island, facilities for measuring radioflash from the exploding weapon had been provided for the electronics measurements group – a mobile caravan and cooler unit, an air-cooled hut, three generators and a Land Rover. Radiation measurements and microbarograph readings were to be taken at several sites.[5] Arrangements for sampling air, water and fish were made in Honolulu, Fiji, Samoa and Raratonga, and on Kwajalein Atoll and Christmas, Canton, Penrhyn, Malden and Fanning Islands. Equipment needed for fall-out monitoring included motor-driven air filters, 'sticky papers' and rain-water bottles. The RAF – with a little help from the United States Air Force – was to have a busy time maintaining communications and supplies and collecting samples and records.

The primary aim of the sampling was 'to confirm that the fall-out consequent upon a Christmas Island test firing [was] negligible'. This was to be expected, since a high airburst of a megaton weapon would create little fall-out: the explosion would be too high to draw up large quantities of soil and water into the radioactive cloud; the cloud itself would rise to such an altitude that the radioactive material it contained would remain for some consider-able time in the upper atmosphere, losing much of its radioactivity, before returning diffusely to earth. Post-firing radiation measurements and fall-out sampling confirmed these expectations.

A very important operation at nuclear tests was cloud sampling, by highly trained Canberra crews who flew through the cloud shortly after the explo-sion. But megaton tests posed a problem. With such large explosions the clouds rose to proportionately high altitudes and it was doubtful whether the aircraft would be able to fly high enough to enter the most turbulent part of the cloud at some 63,000 feet. A rocket-assisted aircraft could fly higher, and in August 1957 a Canberra fitted with Napier Double Scorpion rocket engines had set the world altitude record for aircraft, at 70,310 feet. Conversion work on two Canberras was put in hand, one of them the record-breaking aircraft itself. The plan was that, one hour after the burst, the conventional Canberras would obtain samples from the cloud at about 50,000 feet and, two hours later, a Scorpion-assisted Canberra (with another in reserve) would attempt to get samples from about 60,000 feet. After much preparatory work and special training, two Scorpion Canberras arrived at Christmas Island in the first week of April 1958. However, an accident to another Scorpion Canberra elsewhere made Air Vice Marshal Grandy unwilling to use one at Christmas Island until the cause of the accident was known. The air sampling task had to be left to the conventional Canberras flying at a lower altitude.

Operations

There was a busy shipping schedule during January and February 1958. Meteorological flights began in February. By mid-March the Joint Operations Centre at Christmas Island was up and running. At the end of March practice bombing began at the range. The *Grapple Y* Tom was on its way to Christmas Island by sea, and a second stand-by Tom (in case of a possible small fault in the first) would be flown out to Christmas Island on 20 April, followed two days later by the Dick.

Because *Grapple Y* was expected to be a very large detonation, even larger than *Grapple X*, safety of personnel had been reviewed. Thousands of anti-flash hoods, gloves and white boiler suits were provided. After the experience at *Grapple X*, when more material damage was caused by the explosion than had been foreseen (see Chapter 11), special attention was given to protection against blast, and where possible additional venting to existing buildings had been provided. But some damage to buildings was inevitable and would have to be repaired later.

The programme of flyovers, HE drops, and operational rehearsal continued through April, and the live drop was scheduled for 28 April. On 21 April, Task

Force Headquarters issued safety instructions. 'After the weapon has exploded and the thermal flash has passed, it will be followed approximately one to two minutes later by a loud bang and a blast wave. This blast wave will cause loose material, rubbish, etc. to be blown before it and it may cause some damage to buildings.' To avoid unnecessary damage from the blast, loose items were to be secured, glass windows, doors and partitions were to be removed and stowed, and all electrical equipment not essential to the test was to be switched off. Tall cupboards had to be laid on one side and secured. Telephone handsets had to be tied to the receiver cradle. Vehicles were to be parked with the rear end facing ground zero, and all windows left open. Pets were to be placed in 'suitable humane containers' and taken to the owner's place of duty. Every endeavour was to be made to round up stray domestic animals, and they were to be secured in similar containers and kept in the evacuation convoy vehicles until the test was over.

Another directive was issued on action in the event of fire, damage to building and installations, and casualties which might occur during or as a result of the test. It covered the period from 60 minutes before the Valiant bomber's take-off time to 'stand down', and it set out in great detail the emergency procedures for each part of the Task Force on Christmas Island including, of course, the scientists. All were divided into Categories A, B and C according to their responsibilities at the time of the test (as at *Grapple X* – see Chapter 11), and nominal lists included everyone on the island, each with his individual station at the time of the test.

The *Grapple Y* device was fired on 28 April 1958 at five minutes past ten local time, after a delay of one and a half hours because of cloud conditions. Dropped from the Valiant bomber flying at 46,000 feet, it fell for 53 seconds and exploded at an altitude of 8,000 feet. The commander of the Valiant squadron, Group Captain Kenneth Hubbard, described the blast wave:

Had we been standing without protection, there is no doubt we should all have been blown off our feet … the majestic build-up of the mushroom shaped cloud … towering to a great height.

The fire-ball [he wrote] appeared as a huge red and orange cauldron of fantastic energy, which gave the impression of revolving. As it did so it emerged at its apex into a stream of orange-coloured cloud mass moving upwards all the time, and as it ascended the colour changed to white. Then somewhere in the region of 50,000 feet it curved and fanned outwards from its centre making a cap similar to the top of a mushroom. All the time this fantastic formation moved upwards, progressively increasing the spread at the top until it stabilised, then the edges of the actual mushroom shape partially drifted from the main structure as upper winds began to carry these white whiffs downwind.[6]

He had witnessed all five *Grapple* shots to date, but this was much the most impressive; not surprisingly as it was much the biggest detonation – at 3 megatons, it gave the highest yield of all the British test devices.

The task force commander reports

The task force commander reported to the Atomic Trials Executive on 15 May that the operation had been a success. The RAF had 'delivered [the weapon] to the right place', it had exploded at the correct height, and the measurements obtained were, he said, gratifying to Aldermaston. Immediately after the shot the weather had deteriorated and had there been any further delay the operation could not have taken place during the rest of that week. As it was, cloud conditions reduced the number and quality of the photographs obtained.

There had been no damage to personnel or to buildings, and the special venting of the latter had proved extremely effective. Telling all the personnel exactly what to expect, and issuing white suits, had been well worthwhile. The health record had been generally very good. Morale on the island was very high among servicemen and scientists. Service personnel now knew the length of their posting there; there was an appearance of permanence at the island, with the appointment of a Base Commander, and there were obvious signs of improvements. Food was very much better, and was cooked and eaten under cover. Though improved living accommodation and proper sewage could not be constructed as soon as had been hoped, living in tents was not uncomfortable in good weather; however, in bad weather the situation could deteriorate rapidly.

Results

The scientists had already shown, at earlier *Grapple* trials, that they could design and test a two-stage device using radiation implosion and thermonuclear reactions. But with *Grapple Y* they had demonstrated their ability to design and test an effective multi-megaton warhead with an enhanced thermonuclear yield and much less dependent on the fission components. This was without question a successful hydrogen bomb.

Corner's second-in-command in the Aldermaston theoretical physics division, Herbert Pike, was at Christmas Island for *Grapple Y*. (Apparently Cook wanted to show his appreciation of some especially valuable advice given by this wise and experienced physicist, and was told 'Pike likes trips'. He had a good time riding round the island on a motor cycle.) When asked whether he was pleased by the 3-megaton yield, close to that predicted, Pike said that if it had been a lot higher 'we should really have had to think and that would have been great fun'. But first someone would have had to think very hard about the Valiant bomber and its crew!

It had been a success, but there was more still to do. Aldermaston's next task was '1 megaton in 1 ton', in a warhead immune to intense radiation from defensive nuclear missiles. *Grapple Z* was to follow.

13
Mission Accomplished – *Grapple Z*

Aims and objectives

Weeks before *Grapple X* in November 1957, and months before *Grapple Y* in April 1958, the next trial – *Grapple Z* – was already being considered. All three trials were part of a programme of development which had to be flexible because plans for later shots, and the order in which they were fired, depended largely on the results of the earlier ones. They also depended on larger contingencies – the encouraging prospects of renewed Anglo-American nuclear co-operation, and the pressures of public opinion and worldwide concern about fall-out which would make a test ban or moratorium inevitable sooner rather than later.

Grapple Z, if it could beat the ban, would be critically important. To complete their programme, and to build on the results of *Grapple X* and *Y*, the British urgently needed further tests – as many as Aldermaston and the services, overloaded as they were, could manage. Moreover, as the possibilities of Anglo-American nuclear collaboration began to take shape in October 1957 (see Chapter 14), the British scientists were well aware that the amount and value of the weapons information they would receive from the Americans depended crucially on the quality of what they themselves had to offer. This was the background to Britain's last, biggest and most complex test series.

The RI effect, immunity and boosting

Cook had defined the essential purpose of *Grapple Z* as early as October 1957, in a paper on megaton warhead development. It was to produce the promised 1-ton, 1-megaton warhead, which also had to be 'immune' – invulnerable to radiation damage, or the so-called RI effect.

Early in 1956, two of the young physicists in Corner's division, K. V. Roberts and J. B. Taylor, had been revisiting some early work done by HER in the

1940s. They came to a startling conclusion – that there was a high risk that British nuclear weapons could be disabled by an intense flash of radiation from a nearby nuclear detonation, that is, from a defensive enemy warhead launched for this purpose. Fission weapons with plutonium cores – like all the early British bombs – were particularly vulnerable because of plutonium's susceptibility to pre-detonation. Moreover, neutron and X-ray penetration of a warhead could damage or distort the fissile components and might reduce the yield or even prevent a nuclear detonation. (The weapon's electronic systems might also be affected – a separate problem.)

This clearly had extremely serious offensive and defensive implications. If the Russians knew about it, and had themselves developed an immune ballistic missile warhead while the British had not, Britain's nuclear bombs had virtually lost their deterrent value. Nor was there much hope of Britain developing an anti-ballistic missile defence. Cook's paper pointed out the gravity of the defence situation.

The Aldermaston scientists' immediate concern was for the effectiveness of the future British nuclear deterrent that was planned to succeed the V-bomber force – a high-yield warhead to be carried by a large ballistic missile called *Blue Streak*. Fission warheads – whether as single bombs or as primaries for double bombs – now seemed to be dangerously vulnerable.

This discovery was at once assigned a special degree of secrecy; the two scientists were strictly enjoined not to disclose the information even to their closest colleagues, and one was sent to London 'hugger-mugger' to explain it to Lord Mountbatten, the Chief of the Defence Staff. A very secret project, known simply as 'R', was set up to analyse the processes involved and to provide the data needed to design nuclear weapons immune to intense bursts of radiation. Over the next three years, an increasing proportion of Aldermaston's computing capacity was committed to this project.

To make an immune warhead required knowledge of certain techniques imperfectly understood at Aldermaston at this time. One was boosting, the addition of thermonuclear materials to a fission bomb in order to enhance the efficiency of the fission process and so increase the yield. Aldermaston made several attempts in the mid-1950s to increase the yield of fission weapons by boosting. (The Russians had apparently not yet solved the boosting problem and Aldermaston had no evidence of American methods.) But there was another way to look at boosting. Instead of using it to *increase* the yield of a warhead of given size and fissile content, it could be used to *reduce* the size and fissile content of a warhead while maintaining or even improving the yield. This would have obvious advantages – economising in scarce and costly fissile material, making smaller, lighter bombs, and making more of them for the same expenditure. There would be a further very important advantage, of reduced vulnerability.

So a small, light, boosted bomb, if it could be made, would be the ideal primary for a double bomb. Corner believed that such a bomb could be made and might be tested by mid-1958 but Cook was less optimistic. He considered it unlikely that a primary of this kind could be made as yet, and thought that to get sufficient yield to ignite the secondary, the primary itself would have to be in two (fission) stages – making three stages in all. (In the event, Corner was right.)

It was agreed that a design for a three-stage weapon, with an immune two-stage primary, should be included in the *Grapple Z* plans. The search continued for methods of improving the design of primaries, with the exploration of new systems of high explosive detonation (perhaps eliminating high-explosive lenses) and of external initiators – a device first used for *Orange Herald* – to start the chain reaction in the fissile core with greater precision and better effect than the internal initiator (the 'urchin') could do.

When boosting was discussed at Aldermaston in September 1957, neither of the methods suggested – either gaseous tritium, or layers of solid thermonuclear material placed inside or outside the core – had appealed to Cook, and there were many difficulties, both of supply and handling, in using tritium gas. But only a year later both methods were to be successfully tested at *Grapple Z*, in the *Pendant* and *Burgee* shots.

The programme for *Grapple Z*

By December 1957 Cook felt that work on the *Grapple Z* rounds would soon have to start, and in the next six weeks he wanted four lines of development to be discussed by the WDPC – employment of thermonuclear reactions, reduction of warhead weights, immune primaries, and multi-point or lensless initiation. But a firing programme designed to meet scientific requirements was bound to be affected by resource limitations. There were shortages of some materials, and there were limits to what the workshops could manage. Besides making experimental rounds for trials, they had to continue the production of service weapons – *Blue Danube*, *Red Beard* and an 'interim weapon' in the megaton range – and the tests absorbed a seemingly disproportionate amount of time and resources.

Planning and logistics

Meanwhile the task force commander, Air Vice Marshal John Grandy, and his staff had to begin the operational planning and preparation, whatever the eventual decisions on the rounds to be fired. Though unavoidable, this sometimes led to difficulties because some practical matters – such as equipping balloon sites or installing telemetry and communications equipment – would depend on the nature and number of the shots. Before turning to the choice of warhead designs and the firing programme, we look at some of the practical arrangements for the operation.

Grapple Z turned out to be the biggest of the four *Grapple* trials, the most complex, and also the one most beset with problems. There was an even greater sense of urgency than previously, to complete the task before an international moratorium rang down the curtain on testing. This time the threat was sharper and more imminent; it even appeared at one time that the ban might come as early as September 1958. The trial must be mounted as quickly as possible, yet there were difficult scientific questions to be answered first, before a programme could be decided and the design and manufacture of the test devices could begin. It was all the more important to get the answers right, and to gain the maximum value from this trial, because it would almost certainly be the last opportunity. (Nevertheless, contingency planning continued for further trials in 1959.)

The materials department and the engineers waited impatiently to hear what they would be asked to provide, and how many devices, and Hopkin and Lord worried about whether they would have enough of some vital materials.[1] Once the scientific programme had been decided, sufficient time would have to be allowed for fabrication of the test devices, the long sea voyage, and assembly on site for firing. So options for *Grapple Z* were uncomfortably squeezed between the scientific decisions that were pending and an inevitable test moratorium at an early though unpredictable date.

Against this background of uncertainty, various other difficult operational and logistical problems arose. A major one was the planned replacement of several hundred servicemen at Christmas Island during the second half of July. After a long tour of duty they had been promised a return home, and the task force commander insisted that nothing must prevent it; that, he said, would be a breach of faith. Some of the scientists, too, had been away from home for up to five months and some had applied for transfers to the Atomic Energy Research Establishment at Harwell where overseas trials would not interfere with their careers and family lives. For the most part, Roy Pilgrim commented, the Aldermaston men put up with difficult conditions 'stoically in silence', but there were limits beyond which goodwill ought not to be taken for granted.

Transport to Christmas Island was another cause for anxiety for months, and *Grapple Z* eventually required more freight movements than any other trial. Crucial shipments were held up for weeks by a dock strike, and large quantities of stores had to go by air, stretching the RAF's Transport Command to the limit even though much 'unclassified' material was carried by civil aircraft.

One demanding feature of trial planning was the balloon programme. Of the five test methods the British had used – detonating the weapon underwater in a ship, or on the ground, or mounted on a tower, or dropped from an aircraft, or suspended from a high altitude balloon array – each had its advantages and disadvantages and was appropriate for different shots. The British had fired one balloon shot at the Maralinga Range in South Australia, in the *Antler* series in October 1957, and it was decided that one of the *Grapple Z* shots, a boosted fission bomb, could best be fired in this way.

W. M. (Bill) Saxby – an Aldermaston scientist and former Army officer – was in charge of the balloon programme. Preliminary training of balloon crews began at Cardington in Bedfordshire in January 1958. Besides these crews, the balloon shot would require additional facilities at Christmas Island for health and safety control of personnel, and 50 extra specially trained servicemen would be needed to decontaminate equipment. A new camp for the crews would have to be provided, near ground zero.

One question to be considered was, what was the best method of shooting down any balloons that broke loose – a problem familiar from the *Antler* trial.[2] Even more questions were to arise as the design of boosted devices progressed. Charles Adams, the chief scientist at Aldermaston, questioned the use of balloons at all; he thought they would offer few advantages over an airdrop and would cost significantly more. But on present designs, Penney said, it would be difficult to fit the complete boosted device into a suitable bomb case for an airdrop, and Adams agreed that, without significant progress in design of the weapon electronics, the balloon method would have to be accepted.

The programme, including practice night flying, went forward at Cardington, and in May 1958 the manufacturers handed over the balloons to the task force. New winches and other equipment were delayed, but by the end of June they were delivered and tested at Cardington, where practice flying continued when weather permitted. Shipping the supplies of hydrogen for the balloons would leave no reserve of cylinders in England; the empties would have to be returned quickly if more balloon shots were wanted for trials in 1959.

The test devices and the firing programme

The story of the *Grapple Z* scientific programme and firing plans is a tortuous one. This account of their vicissitudes is drastically simplified but, even so, is not altogether simple. In late 1957 it was envisaged that the series would consist of two shots. The first would be a double (two-stage) bomb, which would be a scaled-down version of *Grapple Y*; the second, a boosted fission bomb of the type cryptically called DP,[3] intended as an immune Tom for the 1-ton/1-megaton weapon. By March 1958, three shots seemed more likely – the double bomb, now named *Flagpole*, and two boosted bombs (one gas-boosted and the other boosted with solid thermonuclear material). A month later there were even tentative suggestions that two variants of *Flagpole* should be tested.[4] But an international summit meeting proposed for September increased fears of a test moratorium in the autumn. *Grapple Z* would have to be accelerated and simplified – on 8 August a single balloon round (a solid-boosted fission bomb called *Pendant*);[5] and *Flagpole* on 1 September. Could these dates be met? The last ship for Christmas Island would sail on 19 June and arrive about 17 July, too late for a firing date of 8 August. The replacement of a substantial part of the task force during July would be an added difficulty. The earliest date seemed to be 15 August 1958. Plowden told the Prime Minister on 16 April that the autumn test would consist of two shots, one to be fired on or about 15 August and one in the first week of September.

However, if the summit meeting was postponed, or if agreement on a moratorium was delayed, there might be later firing opportunities in October 1958, or even December, extending the *Grapple Z* programme from two shots to four. One of the additional rounds which the scientists had in mind, to follow *Pendant* and *Flagpole*, was a gas-boosted fission bomb of the kind originally contemplated but then ousted by *Pendant*. This other round, to be tried if *Pendant* failed, was a novel concept – a triple, or three-stage, bomb which would, in effect, have two small, immune primaries with a combined yield sufficient to ignite thermonuclear fuel in the third component.

The idea of doubling the number of rounds, and perhaps extending the trial period to four months between August and December, was a very tentative one. It did not have political sanction and it would be a logistical nightmare for the task force, as Grandy pointed out forcefully. It would mean keeping people too long on Christmas Island; some of them would already have been there for months before the first firing date. Tented accommodation would be unsuitable in the winter. The Valiant squadron would have great difficulty with maintenance schedules and some aircraft, especially the indispensable helicopters, would run out of flying hours.

If a second balloon shot was to be fired, urgent action would have to be taken. At present there was only provision for one. More men would be needed at Christmas Island, another balloon assembly would have to be procured and shipped and an additional vessel would be required just to transport the extra 1,200 cylinders of hydrogen. However, it was uncertain for many weeks whether one balloon shot was to be fired, or two. By mid-May the Prime Minister had only approved two shots in all, for 15 August and 1 September, and submissions about the purpose would have to be made before financial approval would be given. Provisional planning meanwhile went forward assuming a maximum of four shots, at intervals of two weeks from 15 August, and *not* extending beyond October. The new working timetable was:

Round 1	15 August	First balloon shot	*Pendant*
Round 2	1 September	First airdrop	*Flagpole*
Round 3	15 September	Second balloon shot	*Ensign*
Round 4	1 October	Second airdrop	*Halliard*

Pendant, with two possible versions, was a fission bomb, boosted with solid thermonuclear fuel, intended as a primary for a megaton double bomb. *Flagpole* – again in two versions – was a double bomb based on a scaled-down *Grapple Y*, with a small unboosted primary, *Indigo Herald*; (though *Pendant*, if successful, would be adopted later). *Ensign* was a variant of *Pendant*, also with solid boosting. For *Halliard*, there was a double bomb version as well as a triple bomb version (and eventually, two triple versions) but, even if it was included in the provisional programme, *Halliard* might not be fired. Provided that *Pendant* results showed that it could be used as a model for a small boosted primary, an efficient, immune, double bomb would be practicable, and *Halliard* would then be unnecessary. But if *Pendant* gave poor results, a triple bomb might be preferable to a double bomb. A *Halliard* triple bomb, an insurance against the failure of boosting, would be fabricated and sent to Christmas Island for Cook to make a decision there when he knew *Pendant*'s results.

However, at Aldermaston doubts about the triple bomb were increasing, and a strong case was made for improving the chances of boosting by introducing *Burgee* – using gas-boosting (instead of the solid boosting in *Pendant* and *Ensign*). If *Pendant* and *Flagpole* both succeeded, then *Ensign* and *Halliard* would be withdrawn. *Burgee* would be fired next, making a series of three shots. If *Pendant* failed, *Halliard* would be fired. Four shots would be the maximum.

Whatever was to be fired, Grandy was most anxious to keep to the present timetable of fortnightly shots from 15 August to 1 October. By mid-June, however, it was clear that, because of a protracted dock strike, the dates could not be met. Loading had begun at last, but the firing dates would almost certainly have to be deferred a week – to 22 August, 8 and 22 September, and 8 October. July brought a serious warning from the Foreign Office that tests might have to be stopped before the United Nations General Assembly meeting in September. There was a grave risk that *Grapple Z* might be cut short. Could the programme possibly be accelerated?

Various modifications to the programme were still being suggested. Hulme thought *Pendant* might be dropped and replaced by *Burgee*, but this seemed risky. Cook and Roberts thought *Ensign* could be dropped. By July, the programme the scientists favoured consisted of *Pendant*, *Flagpole*, *Burgee* and

Halliard. But which *Burgee*, large or small?[6] It did not seem possible to do both. And which *Halliard*? The three versions were: (1) a triple bomb with a heavy case; (2) a double bomb; and (3) a new design – a triple bomb with a light case. These were difficult decisions, and some could only be made, whether at Aldermaston or on the spot, during the trial. So variants of the test devices would have to be fabricated and flown out to Christmas Island so that choices could be made and components could be mixed and matched as required.

RAF Transport Command was having trouble in meeting all the increased demands, with frequent changes of dates and the extra burden of air freight due to the dock strike. Furthermore there were overflying problems with the United States authorities, who were concerned about the movement of high explosives and radioactive (though non-fissile) materials in the same aircraft, and who now also asked for 96 hours' notice of flights. Transport continued to be a constant source of anxiety. But somehow dates were met, and fortunately for *Grapple Z* the September test ban did not materialise. Still, timetables were desperately tight: *Burgee*, for example, was due to leave the United Kingdom on 5 September, to be delivered on 10 September and assembled and tested by 15 September; it could not possibly then be fired before 20 September. (It was actually fired on 23 September.)

Burgee was a very exploratory device and exceptionally difficult to handle. Designing and making it had been a formidable chemical engineering task because of severe incompatibility problems with tritium and plutonium. It was difficult to contain and control highly reactive tritium gas at high pressure, and to design and manufacture a mechanism for inserting the gas into the core just before firing. The talented Welsh chemist D. T. Lewis ('Dai Trit') thought three to six months' scientific work would be needed to test components with inert gases before tritium could be safely used for boosting; he saw no likelihood whatever of producing a successful assembly in 1958. In June, the cautious Hopkin had reported on experiments on the corrosive reaction of tritium with plutonium, but he remained confident that gas boosting was practicable, and greatly preferable to solid boosting. A promising new gas generator device (*Daffodil*) was being developed. However, *Ensign* was still kept in the production programme in case of insoluble problems with *Burgee*.

For the trials director, Roy Pilgrim, safety in firing *Burgee* was an urgent question. What was to be done if, at the end of the countdown, *Burgee* failed to fire for some reason? He wanted a hazard assessment from Lewis. If the injected gas remained in the core, its condition would very quickly become dangerous; there would be little time for action, but lowering the assembly from its balloon cage would take about two hours. What was needed was a fail-safe method of destroying it in the air without causing further hazard in the process. He, Challens and Lewis worked on this problem, which was then referred to the Aldermaston weapons safety panel. It made recommendations and arranged for two of its expert members to be present at *Grapple Z*. Lewis was also invited to be present – to act, he said, as a kind of chemical safety officer.

At the end of July a decision was finally taken on *Halliard* – not on which version to fire as the fourth round but on what criteria should determine the choice (based on results of earlier rounds). Cook would himself be at Christmas Island to make the decision on the spot. (As we shall see in Chapter 14, he would be in constant movement between the Pacific islands, the United Kingdom and the United States). The criteria agreed were complicated but logical. (Readers who may wish to work through the logical steps will find them detailed in the end-notes.)[7]

However, if the three powers agreed on a moratorium starting on 1 October, it would be impossible to fire *Halliard*, and even the earlier shots might be in jeopardy. *Pendant* too might be delayed because replacements were needed for equipment lost or damaged in transit; the firing harness had been lost after clearing San Francisco customs on 1 August. For *Burgee* the limiting factors were the tritium gas generator and the weapon control system, but it was hoped to have them both ready for despatch on 5 September and delivery at Christmas Island on 10 September. The *Burgee* fissile core would be ready by 4 or 5 September and would be sent out on a Valiant courier flight, but there were still some uncertainties about the emergency destruction unit for use in case of a misfire. Ten days would have to be allowed for installation and testing and, at the earliest, the assembly would be ready for firing on 20 September. It was all desperately close. The firing dates were now very near, with many questions of weapon design still unanswered. However, at Christmas Island preparations for the trial itself were well advanced, though here too there were plenty of problems of a different kind.

One problem was the familiar one, of the announcement of the trial and the timing of the warning to mariners. The task force commander would have liked ample warning, for the convenience of merchant shipping and in the interests of safety. But, as usual, political considerations prevailed and ministers decided that the notification should be only four days before the first planned firing date.

Pendant

The repeated changes of plan, and the dock strike which had held up shipments, meant that supplies arrived at Christmas Island in anything but a precisely planned order. The freighter *Tidecrest* had reached Christmas Island on 20 July but her cargo of balloon equipment was not cleared until 2 August and work was also delayed by important air consignments being held up for two weeks in customs at San Francisco airport.

The fissile core for *Pendant* arrived on 12 August, was radiographed, taken to the balloon site and radiographed again. The weapon stillage was erected and fitted with the firing unit, telemetry and external neutron initiator (ENI) equipment.[8] The stillage had to be lifted into the balloon cage by a large fork-lift truck for each rehearsal and for the drop; it took a first-class driver to load it without a hitch. Because of the loss, late arrival or unserviceability of some minor but crucial items, skilful make-do-and-mend was required. A complete cable harness had to be manufactured on site, and replacements for missing nuts and bolts had to be found or made.

The preliminaries for *Pendant* began with a high-explosive ground shot to test the ENI equipment, followed by a scientific rehearsal on 16 August and an operational rehearsal on 19th. Then came D-Day. On 20 August the *Pendant* device was lifted 1,500 feet into the air. A countdown, beginning at minus 40 minutes, was relayed over loudspeakers to the many spectators assembled to witness the test. At minus 30 minutes, the master safety link was inserted into the control desk. At minus 10 minutes all personnel were instructed to turn their backs to the weapons site. At minus 40 seconds they were told to close their eyes and cover them with their hands. At minus 10 seconds, the countdown continued at one-second intervals. At 0900 hours local time, sus-pended from its four balloons, *Pendant* exploded. In a moment, the fire-ball had expanded to a diameter of 1,300 feet. The early stages of this expansion were captured on Kerr-cell camera pictures which clearly show the lower balloon above the explosion and 'precursors' flashing like lightning down the cables coming from the weapon cage. Two Canberras collected samples from the cloud at 18 and 30 minutes after the burst. The sampling aircraft were quite heavily contaminated but their barrier paint afforded good protection.

Access to the forward areas contaminated by the balloon shots was, as usual, controlled by a mobile health control and decontamination centre. After the firing, suitably protected personnel, under the direction of the health physics group, carried out a survey to establish the boundary between 'clean' and 'contaminated' areas. A health control point was then set up near the bound-ary; entry and exit to and from the contaminated area could only be made through this facility. For movement within this area, the so-called 'yellow' vehicles, based at Health Control, were used. They never travelled outside the contaminated area, and clean vehicles were not allowed inside it. If any *did* enter for any reason, they would automatically become 'yellow' and could not be driven into clean areas until decontaminated. During the operation period, 'yellow' transport had to be serviced and maintained within the contaminated area.

The physicist responsible for theoretical predictions of fall-out distribu-tion, E. P. Hicks, had mapped out an area of sea in which, on the basis of the wind structure, the greatest contamination from fall-out could be expected within 80 miles of ground zero. He later expressed some reservations about the exact choice of site; the south-west point of Christmas Island would have been ideal. Eight hours after the shot, a Shackleton mapped the fall-out plume; and readings on the map clearly showed that if ground zero had been at the south-western tip of the island, the plume would all have blown away out to sea.

The yield of *Pendant* was estimated at 24 kilotons. On Saturday 23 August the results arrived at Aldermaston, and Cook called special WDPC meetings for Sunday and Monday to review the firing programme in the light of the *Pendant* result and the latest political situation. The United Kingdom had recently made a carefully worded offer of an agreement to halt nuclear tests, conditional upon a reciprocal offer from the Soviet Union, and 31 October was the date proposed for a meeting. So maximum information must be extracted from the rest of *Grapple Z* in the shortest possible time.

On the assumption that *Flagpole* would be a success, preparations were to be made to fire the thin-case triple bomb, *Halliard 3*. If *Flagpole* failed, *Halliard 1* (the thicker-case version) would be fired. Hopkin thought that this conversion could be carried out at Christmas Island in about three days, with the appropriate staff and equipment. The double bomb, *Halliard 2*, would be abandoned. The small version of *Burgee* would be fired. On Sunday, Cook sent a signal to Grandy on Christmas Island explaining all the changes. A flurry of signals between Grandy and Aldermaston next day established that *Flagpole* would be fired on 2 September and *Halliard* on 11 September. Pilgrim had been sent details of how component and equipment deliveries would be arranged to meet these new dates.

Then, at short notice, Cook called another special meeting on Sunday 31 August. He reported that, during the very successful talks in Washington (see Chapter 14), the United States representatives had said they could provide information on lightweight megaton weapons that would make the firing of *Halliard 3* (the thin-case triple bomb) 'unprofitable'. But they had expressed considerable interest in *Halliard 1* (the heavier version) and Cook had offered to change the firing programme in return for a firm promise by 1 September of information on lightweight megaton weapons; the prospects, he thought, were favourable. He would then instruct Pilgrim, at Christmas Island, to take appropriate action. Components for both weapons would be on Christmas Island in time for the first possible firing date of 11 September. The Prime Minister had approved the firing of *Flagpole*, but not yet of *Halliard* or *Burgee*, and American interest in *Halliard* made a strong case for it. It was suggested that the United States might be invited to sample the *Halliard* cloud, using the American-built Canberras already deployed for their own *Operation Hardtack*, but there was too little time to arrange this.

Flagpole

Meanwhile at Christmas Island practice flights for *Flagpole* had begun and three high-explosive shots were dropped by Valiant bombers between 26 and 30 August.

Fall-out from *Flagpole* was expected to be insignificant, but post-shot radiological surveys were to be made as a matter of routine. Before the firing, predictions were made of fall-out distribution in the unlikely event of two hypothetical accidents. For the first – a crash of the bomber on take-off followed by a low-yield nuclear burst – the predicted fall-out contours would determine the course to be taken by vessels during an emergency evacuation operation. For the second hypothetical accident – a full-yield surface burst at ground zero – the predicted distribution of fall-out would be used to determine whether the forecast meteorological conditions were suitable for firing. Predictions on 27 August for the six days to D-Day, 2 September, indicated unfavourable conditions on 29 and 30 August. A rapid improvement then followed and the actual winds on 28 August gave very favourable conditions which were maintained up to and including D-Day.

The live *Flagpole* round was dropped on the morning of 2 September, and it exploded at 8.24 am local time, at a height of 9,440 feet. The fire-ball expanded to a diameter of 8,500 feet, and the yield was estimated at Christmas Island as 1.21 megaton. Three Canberra bombers sampled the cloud at intervals after the burst. The third one spent over 11 minutes making six passes through the cloud at an altitude of 53,700 feet and, owing to an instrument failure which was not realized at the time, the crew received a gamma dose above 100 milliSieverts.[9] The fault was found and rectified before the *Burgee* shot.

The post-shot radiological survey covered an area of sea of 60 nautical miles radius, and the survey Shackleton took off at 4.20 pm, just under seven hours after hours after the burst, to traverse the sector at increasing distances from ground zero. On its return, the equipment was found to have been faulty and a second Shackleton took off two hours later to get the true figures. Apart from a slight rise in radioactivity over ground zero, no excess above the background count was detected.

Flagpole was a success. There was no reason to suppose that, with *Pendant* as a primary (instead of the unboosted *Indigo Hammer* primary), it would not give at least as good a yield as the test result. Aldermaston now had the basis of a lightweight (1 ton) immune megaton weapon.

Halliard

To meet the American request, *Halliard 1* was to be the next shot. The components began to arrive in instalments. The Tom reached Christmas Island on

2 September and was promptly radiographed. Charlie, the novel component, arrived next day and was left sealed in the transit container until wanted. On 4 September practice flights began, and the Dick was delivered, still in its own section of the lightweight *Halliard 3* weapon casing.

The same day, at Aldermaston, Cook told the WDPC that the Prime Minister had agreed to firing *Halliard* and *Burgee*, and had congratulated the director on the successful work of the establishment which had made possible such a fruitful outcome to the Washington talks. The Americans had confirmed that they would supply information on lightweight megaton weapons and Cook had immediately signalled Christmas Island to convert *Halliard 3* into *Halliard 1*. Unfortunately, the Hastings aircraft carrying the conversion equipment had been forced to return to Aldergrove airfield in Northern Ireland, but it was hoped that the delay would not be more than 12 hours, and the equipment would only be a day late.

The yield of *Halliard 1* was predicted as 0.75 megaton. Theoretical fall-out predictions were made in the same way as for *Flagpole* but with somewhat different assumptions about yields in the two hypothetical accidents – a ground burst at ground zero or a crash on take- off. Of the six days for which predictions were made, conditions were only unfavourable on one, 8 September.

The delay in receiving the *Halliard* conversion kit had cut the time available for modifying the weapon from four days to only 20 hours. The trials planning branch had suggested starting work before all the equipment arrived on the delayed Hastings, but the weapon assembly team had decided against it; as the conversion had been planned with the minimum of equipment, starting without all of it might endanger the successful completion. The decision was amply justified by the smooth progress of the modification. Work began on it in the weapon assembly area at 3.00 pm on Sunday 7 September, under the direction of Dr Catherall. Dick was taken out of its *Halliard 3* casing and fitted into the Dick section of the *Halliard 1* casing. This was then bolted to the other section of casing which contained Tom and Charlie. Assembly was completed at 6.00 am on Monday 8 September, in only 15 hours. The completed warhead was fitted into the *Blue Danube* bomb case, finished off with liberal applications of the indispensable plasticine. The unwanted section of the *Halliard 3* casing was then filled with surplus lithium hydride blocks[10] and crated for return to the United Kingdom.

After the usual practice runs, the live *Halliard* device was fired on 11 September. The Valiant's run began at 11.30 am, and the device was dropped from 46,000 feet. Exploding at a height of 8,500 feet, it produced a fire-ball some 8,000 feet in diameter. The yield was subsequently assessed as 0.8 megaton, close to the 0.75 predicted.

The cloud reached a high altitude. Four aircraft were used for sampling, and the third Canberra spent a total of 12 minutes in the cloud at heights of up to

54,600 feet. The doses received by the sampling crews were calculated by multiplying dose rates by sampling time; one RAF officer who handled the active filters before radiochemical analysis received a dose of more than 30 milliSieverts, and his total gamma dose for the operation was 39.8 milliSieverts (see Appendix 4). The post-shot radiological survey, carried out over a sea area of 65 nautical miles radius, began about four hours after the burst and continued for two hours. Again no reading above the previously measured background count was detected.

The *Halliard* cliff-hanger had come to a successful conclusion.

Burgee

Immediately after *Halliard*, rapid preparations for the *Burgee* test began at the balloon site. On 11 September the tritium gas generator, the incongruously named *Daffodil*, was delivered to Christmas Island, where it was taken to the weapon assembly area for some modifications and a function check. During this check, a microswitch failure caused an enforced stop, and the shock did some damage and bent the shaft that operated a valve. More robust replacements were manufactured and fitted on the spot. Further tests were satisfactory, and *Daffodil* was then taken to the balloon site.

Three days after *Halliard*, the *Burgee* assembly shed, with its air-conditioning plant, was ready to be handed over to the weapons groups. The four balloons that would be linked together had been inflated and all the balloon gear assembled in readiness for a practice hoist. The same day, 14 September, *Burgee*'s radioactive core arrived. It was routinely tested for radioactivity, radiographed and measured, and then taken to the explosives assembly group to be mounted in the supercharge. After assembly, the complete weapon was taken to the forward area and stored in a marquee on the balloon site. That afternoon, practice hoists began, and on 20 September a combined scientific and operational rehearsal took place.

Theoretical predictions of fall-out were made, as before, for five days. For the period beginning 18 September, the predicted conditions were unfavourable only on 18 September. D–1 Day was declared on 22nd. The *Daffodil* equipment was inspected, the balloons prepared, and test sequences carried out. The four linked balloons, with a cargo representing the weapon assembly to be fired next day, were hoisted to the correct height to test that all the equipment was working properly. At 12.30 pm, D–1 Day was confirmed and, at five minutes past one, everything stopped for lunch while the balloon array was left swaying in the sea breeze.

After lunch the balloons and cargo were winched down and the balloons moored separately. In the late afternoon, the weapon functioning group began final assembly of the weapon. The group worked on overnight installing the detonators and connecting the massive multi-point cable harness, and by 2.00 am on D-Day the work was complete.

At the balloon site, the balloons were connected together and the stacking process began. At 4.00 am the weapon stillage was taken to the balloon flying point, the control cable was connected, and the *Daffodil* device was installed on the weapon. After checks, the joint operations centre gave permission to begin the hoist. At 6.00 am, the four balloons and their strange cargo began rising into the cool dawn over Christmas Island. By 6.55 am they had reached the operational height. Evacuation of the remaining personnel began. When the helicopters arrived to collect the last few people, the safe/live switches were set to 'live' and *Burgee* was ready to go.

Meanwhile, all personnel had been assigned to specified areas according to their safety measure duties. Orders were then given over a public address system to all personnel, service and civilian, by an 'executive controller', who warned that failure to obey instructions might well result in damage to the eyes. Instructions for the safety of aircrew at the time of the burst were issued separately by the air task group commander, and other instructions, for the safety of personnel at sea and at Port London, including the Gilbertese villagers, came from the naval task group commander.

About 500 people were permitted to see the operation from a special 'observation area' on the north-east prominence of the island. There was no need to wear anti-flash suits, helmets or gloves, nor were plans necessary for aircraft and building safety, as the expected yield was only 25 kilotons. There were special procedures in case the weapon misfired or the public address system failed, and a team was on hand to repair the latter if it broke down. There were special safety procedures for those concerned in the re-entry phase. At 8.10 am a final check was made to account for all personnel and then a general announcement was made to explain the broadcast countdown procedure. At 'minus 40 minutes', the control phase began with the insertion of a master safety link into the control panel, and the firing was handed over to the automatically sequenced control system.

'Minus 30 minutes' was announced. Two minutes later, the *Daffodil* generator began to produce tritium gas; the correct pressure was reached less than two minutes later, and the 'no veto' phase had begun. The countdown continued – 'minus 20 minutes'. At 'minus 15 minutes' the previous announcements and instructions were repeated. At 'minus 10 minutes' all were instructed to turn away from ground zero. At 'minus 40 seconds' they were all told to close and cover their eyes. At 'one' the word 'flash' was heard. Everybody felt a momentary heat pulse as the weapon fired. The flash of the explosion was 'sensed' by the closed eyes of some observers as a yellow glare. It was between 8.59 and 9.00 am on 23 September.

Then the loudspeakers commanded everyone to turn, and they saw the red and orange fire-ball rising swiftly into the air, turning in on itself to form the familiar nuclear mushroom cloud. The blast wave, accompanied by the sound of the explosion, reached the observers harmlessly some 40 seconds after the burst. A towering column of dirt and sand was sucked up into the wake of the rapidly ascending fire-ball, reaching up towards, but never touching, the boiling cloud of incandescent gas. As its momentum was spent it fell back to earth in a cloud of dust while the fire-ball soared up.

Those who watched could not be quite sure of it at the time, but they had just seen Britain's last atmospheric nuclear test. The international moratorium began at the end of October and lasted until September 1961, and Britain never resumed atmospheric testing.

After *Burgee* the post-shot radiological survey covered an area of sea with a radius of 70 nautical miles of ground zero. Levels of radioactivity were similar to those found after *Pendant* – low, but, as was expected, higher than those after *Flagpole* and *Halliard*. No significant fall-out had been detected then, and no radioactivity above background level had been found in samples of sea water taken near ground zero.

With the *Burgee* test satisfactorily and safely accomplished with a yield of 25 kilotons, the Aldermaston scientists had succeeded in both gas boosting and solid boosting of fission weapons. They now had the possibility of making the invulnerable (or immune) 1-ton/1-megaton nuclear weapon that had been the ultimate objective of the four *Grapple* series. These cumulative advances had not only equipped them to produce strategic warheads for the services but had been of immense political significance for Britain (see Chapter 14).

Part V
A Special Nuclear Relationship

14
The Great Prize

Hope deferred

Successful H-bomb research and development provided the strategic deterrent potential that Britain wanted, but much more also. It was the major, if not the only, factor that enabled Harold Macmillan in 1958 to seize what he called 'the great prize' that three Prime Ministers before him had striven for. The background to the events of 1958 is outlined in the first part of this chapter.

For 12 years, ever since the 1946 United States Atomic Energy Act – the McMahon Act – had ended the wartime Anglo-American atomic relationship so abruptly, restoration of the relationship had been a prime objective of British governments, Labour and Conservative. Hopes rose during the 18 months from mid-1947 while co-operation was being generally renewed – though with uneven success – in economic and military fields and in foreign policy. A real advance in atomic collaboration seemed possible in late 1947 and talks in Washington led to a *'modus vivendi='*,[1] agreed on 7 January 1948. It confirmed the status of the existing Combined Policy Committee as the tripartite (Anglo-American-Canadian) 'organ for dealing with atomic problems of common concern', particularly the allocation of uranium. It also defined topics for technical co-operation.[2]

The scope of the *modus vivendi* was limited and even within these limits collaboration proved disappointing. Possibilities of improvement were hindered by serious internal disagreements in Washington among various parts of the Administration, officials with differing views, and members of Congress – and in particular the powerful Joint Committee on Atomic Energy (JCAE) set up by the McMahon Act.

However, during a momentous month – September 1949, when the pound was devalued on 18 September and evidence of *Joe 1*, the first Soviet atomic test, was received on 19 September – new tripartite talks began. They went on for three months and were dominated by American determination, in view of

Joe 1, 'to maximise the mutual defense effort'. The British wanted both full American co-operation and support and a balanced, independent atomic energy programme of their own. The Americans wanted raw materials supplies and production plants to be located for strategic reasons in the United States or Canada, and argued that, to get the best value from joint resources, the manufacture of nuclear weapons should be concentrated in the United States, where efficient production methods would ensure the most economic use of raw materials.[3] British scientists working in United States laboratories, they said, might well have a catalytic effect, and British brains would be a much more valuable contribution to the common effort than a few outdated and relatively inefficient British atomic bombs.

An integrated effort had certain attractions for the cash-strapped British, but also some obvious dangers. If their own programme were to be strictly limited, they would want a share of the weapons stockpile and some powerful guarantees (for example, that no future action of Congress could invalidate the agreement). But altogether there were great difficulties on both sides, especially for the Americans after their hydrogen bomb decision. The outlook for a satisfactory agreement looked poor, and its death blow came on 2 February 1950, with the arrest for espionage of Klaus Fuchs. The Combined Policy Committee did not meet again for two years, and though the *modus vivendi* lingered on, there was little to show for it.

A new approach

When a Conservative government under Winston Churchill replaced the Attlee government in October 1951, the old statesman believed that he could renew the transatlantic relationship in all its fullness, including the atomic relationship. He arranged to visit Washington in January 1952 and atomic matters were high on his agenda. Living in a time warp, in spite of Lord Cherwell's attempts to explain that atomic events had moved on, he had no doubt that he could regain a 'reasonable share of what they have made so largely on our initiative and substantial scientific contribution'.[4] The January visit did indeed produce some useful results, and created a far better and more sympathetic feeling in Washington towards Britain.

Looking ahead towards the first British A-bomb test in October 1952, Churchill thought that *Hurricane* would surely win Britain greater respect from the United States. But in the event the United States, alas, was not greatly impressed.[5] The Americans had greatly improved A-bombs and had already carried out their first H-bomb test, and the feeling in Washington was reported to be that the British programme was merely a propaganda effort to interest the United States authorities. Soon after *Hurricane* when an American newspaper polled Congressmen about atomic energy exchanges with Britain, one Congressman said 'We would be trading a horse for a rabbit.'[6] This was not to be the Washington view by 1958.

A most encouraging change in the Anglo-American situation came in 1953 with the election of President Eisenhower. Though with a genuine respect and affection for Churchill, he felt that the elder statesman 'had developed an almost childlike faith that all the answers are to be found in the British-American partnership' and that he was trying to relive World War II.[7] But Eisenhower believed strongly in close ties with Britain, with the qualification that in the post-war world no such special relationship could be maintained or even suggested publicly;[8] he was very conscious of the NATO dimension.

Eisenhower had long disapproved of the McMahon Act which he famously regarded as 'one of the most deplorable incidents in American history of which he personally felt ashamed'.[9] He was sympathetic to the idea of expanding the nuclear relationship with the major allies in Europe, with Britain – then the only other western nuclear power – clearly in a special position. However, the President's hands were firmly tied by the McMahon Act and by Congress.

The 1955 bilateral agreement

Atomic co-operation was discussed by President and Prime Minister at the three-power Bermuda Conference of December 1953 and again in Washington in June 1954, when Churchill repeated his pleas for the renewal of the wartime technical collaboration. At least, he argued, the British ought to be enabled to design their bomber aircraft with the essential knowledge of the weight, dimensions and ballistic characteristics of American nuclear bombs. Moreover, he said, until the British had their own stockpile of nuclear weapons the RAF would depend on American bombs, stored in Britain under American custody. Eisenhower could only assure Churchill that steps were being taken to amend the McMahon Act.

The new United States Atomic Energy Act passed into law on 30 August 1954.[10] It allowed for data on external characteristics of nuclear weapons, yield and effects – but not on design and fabrication – to be shared with NATO allies; Britain got preferential treatment, in receiving scientific and technical information on weapon test programmes. The subsequent negotiations were tortuous, but a bilateral 'Agreement for Co-operation Regarding Atomic Information for Mutual Defence Purposes' was finally signed on 15 June 1955.[11] (A multi-lateral agreement with NATO governments was signed a week later but not ratified until March 1956.)[12]

The 1955 bilateral agreement was certainly an advance, but gave the British much less than they wanted. It was of limited practical use, as the JCAE mistrusted the President's liberal attitude to the allies and was doubtful about

British security standards. Then too there were inter-agency disagreements about the amount of disclosure permitted under the bilateral, with differences of opinion between the AEC and the Department of Defense. Lewis Strauss, the chairman of the AEC, thought that disclosing even limited information about external features of weapons might reveal too much.

A period of estrangement

Eden, who succeeded Churchill as Prime Minister in April 1955, did not show the same drive to reach a better nuclear understanding with the United States.[13] During his premiership Anglo-American relations generally reached a critically low point with the Suez operation of October–November 1956; Eisenhower and his advisers were outraged by the Suez action, and applied severe economic pressures to end it. The situation was so serious that Harold Macmillan, then Foreign Secretary, even called it 'the Anglo-American schism'.[14] But at this time Britain still depended heavily on American goodwill and nuclear support since the British stockpile of A-bombs was still much too small to arm the 50 Valiant bombers due for delivery by the end of the year.

Friendship renewed

The Eden government fell and on 9 January 1957 Macmillan became Prime Minister. An immensely experienced statesman, he was an old friend of the President – a friendship dating back to his wartime service in North Africa as Minister Resident and liaison officer with General Eisenhower at Allied Headquarters. The most urgent, and the most delicate, task that confronted him was to repair and eventually to restore the old relationship. Eisenhower too was anxious to repair the damage. Another wide-ranging conference was quickly arranged, for March 1957 in Bermuda, and there the relationship was effectively renewed.[15] Eisenhower described it later as the most successful international conference that he had attended since the close of World War II.[16]

The British, acutely aware that during the Suez crisis the Soviets had threatened to intervene militarily and had even hinted at using nuclear weapons against the British Isles,[17] urgently wanted both to push forward their own nuclear weapons programme and meanwhile to have the protection of American nuclear missiles. Detailed arrangements for placing IRBMs in Britain were worked out at the Bermuda Conference.[18]

The *Sputnik* opportunity

In May/June 1957, the British carried out their first hydrogen bomb test series at Christmas Island (see Chapter 10), which interested but did not greatly impress the American scientists. A further trial was planned for the autumn, but before *Grapple X* in November 1957 (Chapter 11) a dramatic event occurred. *Sputnik I*, the first Soviet satellite, was launched on 4 October, and a second followed on 11 October. *Sputnik* caused near panic in the United States, and gave a profound psychological shock to American confidence in the country's technological superiority and also its invulnerability to direct Soviet attack. But *Sputnik* offered a wonderful opportunity[19] to Macmillan and, less obviously, to Eisenhower to promote Anglo-American *rapprochement*. After a discussion with Lewis Strauss – who was visiting London – and urged on by Harold Caccia, the British ambassador in Washington, Macmillan wrote to Eisenhower[20] on 10 October pleading for a new approach and a re-examination of the West's ability to meet the Russian challenge. The countries of the free world should pool their resources to meet the increasing threat; each country had its contribution to make and the United States must give the lead. If Anglo-American co-operation in the atomic field was to be resumed, it would necessitate repeal of the 1946 McMahon Act, which effectively prevented the development of any common programme, forcing the British scientists and technologists to trace a path already trodden by their American friends; they could do the job, but at a heavy cost.[21] (Unfortunately, at this very time an embarrassing fire occurred in one of Britain's two plutonium production reactors at Windscale in Cumbria.[22] Macmillan feared that it would adversely affect Britain's standing in the United States and hamper the negotiations, already facing 'rough going' in Congress.)

After informing the Commonwealth countries and French and German governments as a courtesy, Macmillan set out for Washington, accompanied by Selwyn Lloyd, the Foreign Secretary, Norman Brook, Powell of the Ministry of Defence, Dean of the Foreign Office, and Plowden, chairman of the AEA.[23] The talks (in part of which Henri Spaak, the NATO secretary-general, was involved) lasted three days, 23–25 October, and made excellent progress. A communiqué drafted by the American side was quickly agreed and published immediately as a 'Declaration of Common Purpose', and it was agreed to set up two groups to deal with collaboration on weapons and nuclear collaboration.

The Declaration of Common Purpose embodied all that British governments had hoped for since 1946, and in particular stated that 'the President of the United States will request the Congress to amend the Atomic Energy Act as may be necessary and desirable to permit of close and fruitful collaboration of scientists and engineers of Great Britain, the United States, and other friendly countries'.[24] However, the devil was in the detail and, while Eisenhower believed that the American attitude should be liberal, there were others involved – including Strauss – who were worried by the President's open-handedness and who would do their best in the coming months to impose their more restrictive views.

The small group set up to make recommendations in the nuclear field was led by Strauss and Plowden; the other – to make recommendations on defence co-operation and in particular on missiles – was led by Powell, head of the Ministry of Defence, and Quarles, the Deputy Secretary of Defense. Technical sub-committees got to work at once during November 1957 and in the beginning of December Strauss, Plowden, Quarles and Powell submitted interim reports to the President and Prime Minister.[25] Implementation would have to await United States legislative changes. During the first half of 1958 Washington and Whitehall were concerned with other nuclear matters besides the Atomic Energy Act and the exchange of nuclear weapons information. These included the stationing of American missiles in Britain and negotiation of the *Thor* agreement, and also the growing political pressures on both countries to end nuclear weapon tests. But here we are concerned with the amendment of the 1954 Atomic Energy Act and the new bilateral agreement.

The American officials were anxious that the new legislation should not appear too permissive, inviting opposition from the JCAE. They also wanted to ensure that the wording should effectively exclude any 'fourth power' but should not explicitly refer to Britain. The Act would permit not only weapon information exchanges but also the supply of non-nuclear components and the exchange of materials – uranium-235 and tritium from the United States for plutonium from Britain.[26] Thanks at least in part to *Sputnik*, Congress and the JCAE were not likely to present such formidable obstacles as previously, and the Eisenhower Administration could expect substantial support for its legislation. Strauss sent details of the proposed amendments to the JCAE at the end of January 1958. In the subsequent hearings the danger of proliferation was emphasized, and fears were expressed about the disclosure of H-bomb design information. By March the draft Bill had been revised to ensure that only nations that had made 'substantial progress' in the nuclear weapons field could be given atomic weapons data. At the time this description could apply only to Britain, and the British had already, by spring 1958, made considerable thermonuclear progress. The JCAE were told that only by opening up their own nuclear weapons secrets to some extent would the American scientists be able to discover how far the British had got, and perhaps to gain something from their expertise. The desirability of avoiding unnecessary duplication of effort and of increasing the collective strength was emphasized.

For the British, American legislation and renewed collaboration were urgent. At the end of March 1958 the Soviet Union, having just completed an important series of tests, announced a unilateral and indefinite ban on nuclear weapon testing, while reserving the right to resume testing if the United States and Britain continued.[27] Opposition leaders called on Macmillan to accept a moratorium. For Britain, with *Grapple Y* imminent (Chapter 12) this was a serious threat to the weapons programme. What would the American reaction be? The United States Administration thought the moratorium idea both impracticable and dangerous, and they were planning a big test series themselves, *Hardtack*, in the autumn. But they suggested that Russian and Western scientists should get together for technical discussions on methods of verification to obviate cheating during a possible moratorium. A committee of experts was set up, to meet in Geneva; during the summer of 1958 it was to occupy a substantial amount of Penney's time and attention.

After long discussions the amendments to the Atomic Energy Act were finally agreed, were placed before Congress on 10 June and became law on 30 June. Meanwhile, on 4 June Plowden arrived in Washington, followed shortly by a team of experts, and work began on drafting the necessary bilateral agreement.

Nuclear reunion – Washington 1958

By mid-June 1958 the bilateral agreement for co-operation on the uses of atomic energy for mutual defence purposes had been drafted,[28] and was awaiting approval by the AEC, the Department of Defense and British ministers. It would then 'lie on the table' in Congress for 30 days and, if all went well, would be approved before Congress recessed in early August. The next move, as already agreed with the Americans by Brundrett and Penney, would be a joint meeting, designed to provide a basis for early decisions on the division of effort and information exchanges and to establish procedures for further co-ordination and exchanges. This initial meeting, which was to be kept as small as possible, would specifically cover the atomic weapons of interest to both parties, described in a technical annex to the agreement. By then the American representatives hoped to be able to supply information about several existing weapon designs, and about others expected before, say, the end of 1961. This information would include external characteristics and yield; the special nuclear materials required for each weapon; the degree of safety, and how achieved; vulnerability to enemy action; and whether tested or needing further nuclear testing before fabrication. What the Americans could disclose would depend on further study of the position in United States law, but they thought that the major part could be immediately 'determined as transmissible'. However, it was not contemplated that the detailed design of specific weapons, or the more advanced theory or techniques, could be 'determined as transmissible' before the first meeting. The British representatives, for their part, hoped to provide similar data about their own designs and any other additional information appropriate to this stage.

Both sides would then try to define a possible basis both for division of research and development effort and for further exchanges. The objective of co-operation, as stated in the Technical Annex, was the development of the best designs and the most equitable distribution of effort in the design, development and fabrication of warheads for the following purposes:

(a)   lightweight, high-yield bombs for medium bombers;
(b)   low-yield warheads for air defence, anti-submarine and general tactical use;
(c)   lightweight warheads for intermediate-range ballistic missiles (IRBMs) and anti-missile missiles;
(d)   lightweight, high-yield warheads for long-range air-to-surface missiles to be delivered by medium bombers.

Only the first and last of these purposes directly concern the present book.

The British Embassy in Washington told London to expect an invitation to this first meeting by mid-August 1958, and Brundrett informed Penney (then in Geneva at a conference of experts on detection of nuclear explosions, which was studying techniques for verification to support a possible international agreement to ban or limit weapon tests).

A letter from the AEC was duly received on 21 August proposing meetings in Washington on 27 and 28 August. Initial exchanges, it suggested, should cover the general characteristics of the most satisfactory designs which each nation had developed or was developing for the uses (a) to (d) above. For each design the information should include external characteristics (dimensions, weight, shape); yield; compatible systems; amounts of weapons grade uranium and plutonium needed for each weapon; safety; whether in production or under development, and when production was expected; vulnerability; and what improvements – such as reduction in size, increase in yield, greater economy in use of materials – might be expected from R&D under way.

The American delegation for the talks was to include Dr Willard Libby (who had succeeded Strauss as chairman of the AEC), General Loper (assistant to the Secretary of Defense), Brigadier-General Starbird (director of Military Application, AEC), Dr Norris Bradbury (director of Los Alamos), Dr Edward Teller (director of Livermore); and Dr James McCrae (president of the Sandia Corporation).[29] It was not good news for the British, Penney thought; 'I cannot see this team straining at the leash to help us', he remarked. He was too pessimistic, for once.

As the five British representatives – Brundrett and Macklen from the Ministry of Defence, and Penney, Cook and Newley from Aldermaston – left England, the first round in the *Grapple Z* series had just been fired at Christmas Island; the second was due to be fired in a few days, on 2 September, with two more shots to follow (Chapter 13). Penney understood only too well what a tremendous load Cook[30] was carrying, but was most anxious that he should be in the negotiating team.

The first exchange – August 1958

The five went off to Washington well briefed by Aldermaston, where a special 'bilateral working party' had been busy since early July, and with a file of papers produced by the scientists. The team had also had a high level briefing in the Ministry of Defence, at a meeting on 25 August to review tactics, with Sir Richard Powell, the Permanent Secretary, Sir Edwin Plowden, chairman of the AEA, and Sir Patrick Dean of the Foreign Office. The delegation should, it was agreed, press as hard as possible for a full exchange of information on weapon design, in particular on lightweight (500–700 lb) megaton warheads for offensive ballistic missiles, lightweight kiloton weapons for tactical purposes, and techniques of ensuring nuclear safety in various types of warhead. The British representatives should base their requests on recent assurances given by the President to the Prime Minister; they should stress that a free exchange was greatly advantageous to the West at the moment; they should emphasise the importance of interdependence, and the need to avoid duplication by an equitable distribution of effort. The Americans could be given a broad indication of the British programme, and the British team would have to be fairly forthcoming, but the extent of disclosure of details would have to depend on how the talks went. Some of the many different United States agencies involved were not favourable to increased co-operation with the British, and the release of information under the bilateral agreement would inevitably be a gradual process. The British team should also sound out prospects for the supply of fissile and other special nuclear materials and, if possible, find out if the Americans were short of plutonium. The Combined Policy Committee,[31] long dormant, could provide machinery for negotiation.

Brundrett, Penney and Cook sent back their first impressions to London next day. The Americans expressed surprise at British progress, and Brundrett was confident that everyone was anxious for a good result and concerned that the visitors should not return to London dissatisfied. However, from preliminary conversations he inferred that the President's authorisation to the AEC for these negotiations was less extensive than the undertakings he had made to the Prime Minister. It seemed that procedures on the American side would be very rigid and too much should not be expected in the next three days.

Since the Americans did not yet know how much the British scientists knew – and therefore how much it was legal and permissible to tell them – they were obliged to feel their way cautiously in these talks, testing the ground and seeking further authorisations as they appeared to be needed. The procedures did indeed appear rigid. First, the President determined (that is, laid down in detail) which weapons the American side could disclose in outline. Any specific requests for detailed information within the President's determination – or for more general information outside it – had to be processed by the AEC, which then made a recommendation to the President, reporting at the same time to the JCAE; the latter had no power of veto but could make representations to the President. Finally the President made a new determination.

This process might have been very prolonged but on the very first day of talks there was some streamlining which reduced the time-lag from a week or more to less than 24 hours. Clearly this amelioration was possible because of the President's earlier assurances to the Prime Minister, which had apparently gone much further than his prior definition of the scope of the meeting.

On the first day, 27 August, the American side described in outline three designs of megaton, and four of kiloton, weapons and explained their uses. In general, Brundrett and Penney considered that the megaton weapons information did not take the British beyond where they expected to be after completing their next test,[32] except for the somewhat more efficient use the Americans made of fissile material; this was a noteworthy characteristic of their kiloton weapons. The American side was clearly constrained by the determination procedure but the atmosphere could not have been more friendly. The Americans very much hoped that the British would complete the present *Grapple Z* series – and not only because (on the principle of 'sharing the odium') they did not want to be alone in continuing their own current series, *Hardtack*. They went out of their way to express admiration for the British achievement in reducing the weight of their megaton warhead and genuinely believed that the remaining *Grapple Z* shots might produce something of value to the United States as well as Britain. Both sides agreed that, with a test moratorium looming, they needed to get as much information as possible to 'safeguard the future'.

Next day each side gave information orally about their nuclear weapons, drawing on two documents which were then formally exchanged. The British team explained their state of the art in respect of fission and thermonuclear design,[33] and also put forward some of their developmental requirements, including several types of kiloton weapon and an immune 1-megaton warhead for threefold use – as a propelled bomb, an IRBM and an anti-missile missile. The American side agreed to recommend that information should be given to the British about weapons which the United States had (or would shortly have) that would meet British requirements. It would include fabrication or design prints, material specifications and relevant theoretical and experimental data.

The United States side would also recommend full discussions of certain other topics, such as initiators and electrical and high-explosive components. The British team was told on a personal basis about nine American weapons, including three megaton warheads, and it was agreed that the British delegation would provide detailed information on seven warhead designs. These included *Green Grass*, the 'interim' weapon, a fission warhead yielding

0.5 megaton; *Flagpole*, the two-stage, 1-megaton device due to be fired on 2 September; the boosted devices *Pendant*, fired on 22 August, and *Burgee*, due to be fired on 23 September; and the light triple bomb, *Halliard 3*.

Finally, it was agreed that further exchanges should take place at the Sandia Laboratory, Albuquerque, during the week of 15 September. Plans for co-operation should include staff exchanges, where appropriate. Security standards and procedures were discussed and compared, and classification experts would meet in London in late September to discuss a joint classification guide for weapons data.

Before leaving Washington, Brundrett and Penney discussed two important matters with their hosts – the outstanding *Grapple Z* shots, which had not yet been approved by the Prime Minister, and the supply of special materials. The Americans were particularly interested in the last two *Grapple Z* shots – *Burgee*, the gas-boosted fission bomb, and *Halliard*. Of the three *Halliard* devices, 1 and 3 were triple bombs, and the Americans (as we saw in Chapter 13) were more interested in *Halliard 1*, the heavier version, than in the lighter *Halliard 3*. Brundrett and Penney sent an 'emergency' telegram to London urging an immediate decision on the remainder of the test series; it was essential to make the maximum contribution to the common pool of knowledge, and to safeguard the British position – especially as the AEC and the President had not yet approved the proposed Sandia meeting in September – and the Prime Minister should be asked urgently to authorize completion of *Grapple Z*.

Brundrett and Penney had informally broached the question of nuclear materials with Libby, Loper and Starbird, and had had some encouraging reactions both to the possible exchange of plutonium for uranium-235 and to the supply of tritium and enriched lithium. The matter should, they suggested, be pursued by Plowden with the AEC.

Back at Aldermaston, Cook called a special Sunday meeting of the WDPC on 31 August. He reported that the talks in Washington had been very successful. The information that the American representatives had indicated they could provide on lightweight megaton weapons made it unprofitable now to fire *Halliard 3*, the lightweight triple bomb. In response to their interest in *Halliard 1*, Cook had offered to alter the firing programme, and to arrange for an American observer to be invited; in return he asked for a guarantee by 1 September that American information on lightweight megaton warheads would indeed be available. Components for either *Halliard* weapon could be got to Christmas Island by 4 September to meet the earliest possible firing date, 11 September (Chapter 13).

Next day, 1 September, the Prime Minister met Penney and Cook to congratulate them on the successful work that had led to such a fruitful outcome of the Washington talks. He was extremely pleased, and understandably so, and he authorised the firing of *Halliard 1* and *Burgee* (see Chapter 13). His diary for that day read, 'In some respects we are as far and even further advanced in the art than our American friends. They thought interchange of information would be all *give*. They are keen that we should complete our series, especially the last megaton, the character of which is novel and of deep interest to them.'[34] He wrote later[35] that he was particularly glad to hear that, 'somewhat to the surprise of our friends', it was found that the specialist information was not all on one side.

This was not simply a euphoric delusion on the part of a British politician and a non-scientist. In reporting to the JCAE[36] on the highlights of the August meeting, the AEC wrote:

1. Our transmission to the United Kingdom consisted of a written report and more detailed oral statements concerning certain weapons we now have and will shortly have in production. Included were details of size, weight, shape, yield, amount of special nuclear material, method of nuclear safety, mechanical and electrical design, and vulnerability. The weapons described were: Mark 7, Mark 15/39, Mark 19, Mark 25, Mark 27, Mark 28, Mark 31, Mark 33 and Mark 34.

2. The United Kingdom representatives presented parallel information, together with an indication of weapons they intend to develop. Following completion of all items in the agenda, the United Kingdom representatives gave an oral presentation of their state of achievement in the nuclear weapons field, in which they described two rather sophisticated [deleted] small fission devices, one of which they had tested and the other which was to be tested ...

3. During the first meeting it became obvious that *the United Kingdom has achieved an advanced state of weapon research and development in both the fission and thermonuclear fields*. Moreover, it appeared that *certain advances made by the United Kingdom would be of benefit to the United States*. Despite these achievements, however, the British apparently do not have an appreciation that plutonium produced from uranium subjected to higher burn-up in their power reactors is usable in weapons. This knowledge would be of great significance to their civilian power programmes. In addition, they have apparently not exerted major effort towards making their weapons one-point safe.[37] [author's emphases.]

The Sandia meeting – September 1958

While Presidential approval was awaited, plans for the Sandia meeting in mid-September went ahead. The British delegation, led by Cook, was to number 10 to 12, and key staff members who were away were being traced and recalled – Corner (from Geneva), Curran, Pike, Armstrong and Challens. Relevant drawings and data on the British warheads listed at the Washington meeting were assembled, and an ENI unit was made ready to show to the Americans. There was much preparatory work to be done for Sandia, and the *Grapple Z* firing programme had to be changed, with little time to spare.

Besides preparing papers on the detailed information to be given to the Americans, the British scientists had to decide exactly what they wanted from the American side, to enable them to make the most efficient use of limited quantities of fissile material and to meet the weapon requirements of the services in the most sensible way. In particular, they wanted to keep the V-bomber force viable as long as possible, by producing an airborne propelled bomb in the megaton range, and to maintain the deterrent continuously in being by developing an IRBM. For the former they planned to use *Blue Steel*;[38] for the latter *Blue Streak*, a liquid-propelled rocket to be fired from underground, with a range of 2,500 miles. A much smaller missile than *Blue Streak* (possibly solid-fuelled) was desirable, but the British megaton warhead was too big and heavy; a lighter version was urgently required, but if tests were suspended there would be insufficient time to develop it, and American help might be invaluable.

Another vital need was an anti-missile missile for defensive purposes, with a lightweight megaton warhead, and the British had not got very far with this. There were some less urgent questions about kiloton warheads for various purposes. But the key questions were, did the United States have information on the design and functioning of an invulnerable megaton warhead weighing, say, 500–700 lb, and, if so, could this information be given to Britain?

There were a great many more detailed questions that the Aldermaston scientists wanted to ask the American team, about how American and British thermonuclear weapon designs compared. For example 'We use a 2-bomb technique – what is US practice?' 'We are attempting designs using 2-stage implosion of Dick to increase compression – have the Americans tried this and with what results?'. These and 20 other questions of varying detail and complexity were listed, with the comment that they might be irrelevant if American devices differed radically from the British. If that was the case it would be difficult to see how the British weaponeers could use information on radical new designs without doing new trials.

The meeting at Sandia on 17–19 September went extremely well. The atmosphere was very friendly, and General Starbird and General Loper went as far as they could to be helpful. The talks were something of a revelation to the weaponeers on both sides of the table, who had worked independently in their secret laboratories for 12 years. Though, as we saw, there had been some limited exchanges of information in the years since 1946 – on nuclear weapon effects and on the detection of distant nuclear explosions – each country had proceeded in virtually complete ignorance of the other's nuclear, and above all thermonuclear, designs. At Sandia, 12 years of history unrolled in a few hours.

The British side was much impressed by the design of the Mark 28 warhead, and by its engineering execution (which had taken two years). Cook thought Britain would do well to consider manufacturing it as a general purpose megaton warhead. The Mark 47 appeared much less impressive – a 'scrappy assembly', the British scientists thought at first; however, it had been tested and found to work with a yield of 400 kilotons. The American kiloton weapon information was very valuable – equivalent to another year of British tests. An American gas-boosted system almost identical to *Burgee* was due to be fired in a few days.

As the formal Sandia discussions concluded on 19 September, Cook reported back to London that there was

> no doubt that our technical achievements in thermonuclear warheads, invulnerability and component techniques with our resources and time-scale have considerably impressed US delegates and [have] been reason for a more forthcoming attitude than formal procedures would dictate. Starbird has been very co-operative and is genuinely anxious that exchange should be increased.

Cook deliberately broadened the discussion on specific thermonuclear warheads to show the Americans some ideas which the British had had no time to work on as yet. All the American representatives expressed admiration for the technical basis of the Aldermaston designs – especially Edward Teller, who was anxious that United States procedures should permit frank discussions of general physics problems in thermonuclear weapons. They were particularly keen to co-operate very closely on high explosives (in which the British seemed to have a lead), on electrical and electronic components, on neutron sources, and on multi-point initiation.

Both sides would gain by co-operation, as there were some problems which the Americans were meeting which the British had already solved, and vice versa.

The *Halliard 1* warhead – the triple bomb fired on 11 September – excited technical interest, and the untested double bomb, *Halliard 2*, was discussed and compared with Livermore's Mark 47, a design which the British scientists, with more information, were now more favourably inclined towards.

The American warheads, Cook noted, used a cylindrical second stage, which the Americans considered more amenable to calculation. (This was surprising to the Aldermaston scientists; it was partly because of the difficulties of computation and their lack of computing power that they had decided on spherical secondaries which, despite their limitations, reduced the need for complex implosion calculations.)

The most impressive of the American warheads was undoubtedly the Mark 28 which was just going into production. It was economical, apt for many uses – free-falling bombs, powered bombs, tactical bombs and IRBMs – and with a variable yield up to 1.1 megatons. The 0.4 megaton Mark 47, or a later version of it, would be suitable, Cook thought, for British ballistic missiles. (It was later to be used in the *Polaris* system.)

Cook was well satisfied with the Sandia meetings. 'Our staff was excellent', he cabled to Plowden, 'and played their hands magnificently. Roberts and Challens were particularly impressive and Newley made many friends. They have all worked extremely hard and well.' A great prize, Plowden said, had been deservedly won.

After Sandia there was much work to be done quickly and a great deal of information to be digested and analysed before the next stage of collaboration. It would take at least two weeks for each side to determine what aspects of further co-operation it would propose. Corner estimated that the new information advanced the British scientists' knowledge by about two years. As a result it caused a discontinuity in their development policy.

K.V. Roberts, the theoretical physicist, recorded his impressions after the meeting:

US double bombs are like ours – Tom → radiative implosion → Dick. But their Tom is immune, unlike ours, their Dick is cylindrical not spherical ...

We've always considered that with a spherical Dick a slight difference of time or pressure over the outer surface of Dick is unimportant and have not tried to correct for this. But with a cylindrical design the different sections of the Dick implode essentially independently and ... it is essential to calculate the pressure time curve accurately for several points along the axis and to allow for variation.

Teller, Hulme said, thought cylindrical geometry was the natural geometry to use; it had the advantage of allowing a greater volume of material to be imploded in a case of given dimensions. Case weights were lower in American bombs, yet calculated compressions were higher. One of the most striking conclusions, Hulme said, was that there was nothing revolutionary in the American designs. The British had considered many of the ideas – for example, cylindrical implosion and two-point detonation – but had not had the mathematical or engineering facilities to develop them (or the facilities for empirical tests that might be necessary). This did not mean that the American designs were not very superior to the British; their superiority had been achieved by careful optimisation of a design which offered more freedom.

The designs given to the British were, of course, not the American's latest ideas. Teller had said that they had taken 'the next step' and could only reveal what it was if the British scientists could tell them that they already knew what it was! Hulme did not think 'the next step' was revolutionary; he guessed that it was connected with producing even greater compressions by using implosion energy more uniformly in time. The American megaton designs combined very high compressions with very low case weights, an achievement of great interest to the British scientists. The American philosophy, Hulme thought, assumed a number of failures, and the Americans had obviously been able to make far more extensive use of testing than the British could. But with a moratorium imminent, British experience of developing bombs with many fewer tests might be helpful to the Americans.

After Sandia

Within a week of Sandia there was an Anglo-American meeting in the Pentagon with Duncan Sandys, the British Minister of Defence, leading a delegation which included Sir Richard Powell, Sir Frederick Brundrett and three very senior service officers.[39] The United States side, headed by Donald A Quarles, Deputy Secretary of Defense, included General Nathan Twining, chairman of the Joint Chiefs of Staff, Robert Murphy of the State Department, and Brigadier-General Herbert Loper of the Department of Defense.

General Loper reviewed recent events. The exchanges in August and September had, he said, been complete and successful and now a short period of digestion was needed while the British considered how far United States information met their requirements. If it did not, further American designs might have to be examined. In many cases, he noted, the American and British requirements had been different and so the 'fit' might not be exact. The exchange, he observed, had revealed that since 1946 the two countries had followed essentially the same paths and there was no basic principle known to one partner and unknown to the other. The larger effort available to the United States – and, he might have added, a rather longer time-scale – had produced a greater variety of weapon types whereas Britain had tried to make warheads fulfil a range of different requirements.

Duncan Sandys was encouraged and pleased by the way the technical talks had gone. He was sure the recent changes in United States law would lead to a most profitable working partnership. Despite the limited scale of Britain's effort, clearly it could contribute substantially. Donald Quarles affirmed his confidence in the future British contribution.

From September 1958 on, collaboration went forward pretty well. Penney envisaged four stages – the transmission of drawings, specifications and details of fabrication techniques; further scientific exchanges to elaborate specific weapon problems; discussions of future R&D of mutual interest, especially the development of a very lightweight megaton warhead; and intelligence discussions.

A high level US/USSR/UK meeting planned for 31 October 1958 might well agree to suspend tests for at least one year. However, until the test suspension was authorized, provisional preparations for a fifth *Grapple* trial in March 1959 continued.

Implementing the bilateral

The joint agreement signed by General Starbird and Sir William Cook at the end of the Sandia meeting in September 1958 had set out two objectives: (1) the improvement of the British production and stockpile; and (2) co-operation leading to greater overall combined progress. Cook lost little time in framing proposals regarding further co-operation with, and assistance required from, the United States. These were forwarded to the United States government on 6 October.

The proposals relating to objective (1), in so far as they dealt with megaton/thermonuclear weapons, expressed the wish, first, to produce the Mark 28 warhead, adapted to British use and as a complete weapon, in all versions including variable yield, for the earliest possible introduction to the British stockpile. Second, Britain wanted to produce the Mark 47 warhead for later introduction into the stockpile. As the performance of the Mark 47 was marginal, Cook said the British would like to collaborate in investigating improvements and in considering alternative designs to reach a higher yield, if possible more efficiently. This might perhaps be effected by seconding members of the Aldermaston theoretical group to work at Livermore for a period.

On objective (2), topics for further scientific co-operation and information exchange were suggested with a view to formulating complementary programmes. These included methods of calculating boosted and thermonuclear yields;[40] radiation hydrodynamics; electronic components; diagnostic techniques; the mixing of uranium and lithium-6 deuteride; and vulnerability of ballistic missiles to nuclear attack.

The United States government accepted the proposals on 29 October. It suggested that, to further the British weapons programme, two groups of American experts should visit Aldermaston the following month; visits by British specialists to American production facilities should follow in December. After discussions in Washington, high level talks in London with Dr Libby of the AEC and John McCone, JCAE chairman, dealt with lithium and tritium supplies and with major topics for future collaboration, for example, lightweight, high- yield weapons, three-stage systems and ABMs.

On 17–18 November in a meeting at Aldermaston on exchange of nuclear weapons design information, Penney and his senior staff[41] met a high powered American delegation including Brigadier-General Starbird, Norris

Bradbury and Edward Teller. They brought up to date the Sandia information of September 1958, in the light of the latest test series (*Hardtack II*). The Mark 47 and other, non-thermonuclear, warheads were discussed; so was the Livermore *Tuba* design for a double bomb with a spherical secondary, which Teller said was very similar to British designs. Various forms of testing were compared, using balloons or barges; the Americans thought balloon shots preferable to airdrops, which had proved inaccurate on at least two occasions. The British suggested numerous fields for useful exchanges of information such as materials (especially plutonium, tritium and plastics) and problems of materials compatibility.

On the suggested exchange of scientists, the American team explained that long-term exchanges would present great difficulties; the United States side had not disclosed all its weapon designs and there would be security and 'need-to-know' problems if British scientists were working in American laboratories. They therefore preferred programmes of visits between the two countries, an idea that later developed into the Joint Working Group (JOWOG) scheme.

A week later a second American team came to Aldermaston to discuss detailed plans for the production of an Anglicized Mark 28. This meeting agreed two programmes for AWRE visits to the United States. About 15 staff, in eight teams, concerned exclusively with information about Mark 28 production, were to spend ten days in December 1958 visiting Los Alamos, Livermore, Sandia, Savannah River, Rocky Flats, Bendix and Pantex. In January/February 1959 another 25 would visit the United States for two weeks.

On 8 December Macmillan discussed with Plowden and Penney the future of nuclear weapons research in Britain in the light of the new Anglo-American co-operation. Using the knowledge already obtained from the United States, they told him, the British were now in a position to build up a stock of kiloton and megaton nuclear weapons of up-to-date design, without continuing R&D into more advanced types of weapons. It would therefore be possible to effect an economy by curtailing work in that field, but the objections to such a policy were twofold. First, Britain would risk not having more advanced weapons which might be developed in the future (for example, very lightweight strategic weapons or perhaps anti-missile missiles). Secondly, the R&D effort could not be reduced without incurring criticism from the Americans, who intended to continue weapons research on a large scale, whether or not bomb tests were ended. They had now implemented the policy of nuclear interdependence to an extent which had brought Britain great benefit, but on the understanding (though never explicitly stated) that the British would continue to play their part in research. If the British failed this moral obligation they could not hope to maintain a special relationship with the United States in the key sector of defence, nuclear weapons. After being behind the Americans for so many years, the British had at last

(Plowden and Penney surprisingly said) gained equality in knowledge. But if they allowed themselves to fall behind again, the effect would not be confined to nuclear weapons; as in the past, they would find that information about other closely related defence matters would be denied to them, and the scope of interdependence would be seriously curtailed.

Conversely, with continued R&D effort in nuclear weapons they might expect relations with the United States in defence R&D generally to grow even closer and stronger than at present, and British effort would be increasingly integrated with American. Plowden recommended to the Prime Minister that the second alternative should be adopted, at a cost.[42] Macmillan was convinced by these arguments and Aldermaston and its R&D programme were saved from the economy cuts that the Treasury had clearly been hoping for after the bilateral.

All these visits to the United States proved very profitable though the December programme was rather too rushed, with insufficient allowance for travel times. The return visits paid to Aldermaston and Foulness appeared to be useful to American specialists. The topics covered included warhead design, assembly techniques, high explosives, and plutonium.

In many of the American drawings he saw, Shackleton, AWRE's design authority, encountered no uncertainties, and he decided that Aldermaston could begin to gain fabricating experience using simulated materials if necessary. Plans would be drawn up for prototypes by July 1959 and precise manufacturing drawings by September, with production beginning in October. The apparently wide tolerances which were a feature of the drawings were practicable in the United States because of large-volume American production and the IBM card index system which made it possible to mix and match components; this approach was neither possible nor desirable on Aldermaston's small production scale, which required tailor-made methods and very close tolerances.

Hopkin, the ingenious and much-tried chief of materials at Aldermaston, reported on his return from the United States that the American scale of fabrication of fissile materials precluded the use of their manufacturing methods in British production, but some principles might be applicable. He commented on the less strict criticality limits in the United States.

British production plans appeared in some danger of delay, however. The AEC had some 6,000 classified drawings to scrutinize and clear and, though staff returning to Aldermaston were convinced that American goodwill and readiness to supply information were unabated, legal and administrative bottlenecks were restricting the flow. Plowden, Penney and Strath were to visit Washington for talks at the end of February 1959, and questions for discussion would include these delays in transmitting data, as well as the supply of non-nuclear materials and the barter of British civil plutonium for American uranium-235. They would also express their disappointment that General

Starbird had turned down the offer to second Corner and Roberts to work at Los Alamos and Livermore, and had suggested joint working groups instead.

The Washington visit was successful and, at the end of February, four crates of drawings and papers were handed over by the AEC to British staff in Washington; samples of non-nuclear materials were to be provided shortly, and no problems were expected with bulk supplies. A bid for non-nuclear components for *Red Snow* (the Anglicized version of the United States Mark 28) had been favourably received. A second bilateral agreement was in an advanced stage of drafting.[43] A 'stock-take' meeting would be held in mid-April 1959, to develop the present exchanges and widen the field, and to study the proposal for joint working groups.

Pike and Schofield, visiting Los Alamos and Livermore in February 1959 to discuss weapon physics questions, returned with interesting information on 'mechanical safing', and calculations on the effects of varying the composition and thickness of the case of *Red Snow*, which confirmed the proposed British variations. The main American advantage, they considered, was in mechanical analysis and computer support. They noted that both the American laboratories had done calculations on the *Grapple Z Flagpole* shot, and had predicted substantially the same fusion and fission yields as had Corner's staff.

Anglicization

Before turning to the first stock-take, we comment briefly on the problems of turning a United States warhead design, Mark 28, into a British warhead, *Red Snow*. It was by no means the case – as is sometimes suggested – that, once given the American engineering drawings and specifications, it was a simple and relatively unskilled matter to produce 'Chinese copies'.

For one thing British engineers, as we saw, had to work to much stricter tolerances than their American counterparts because of the constraints of small-scale production. Then, too, American manufacturing techniques were sometimes unsuitable for British use. British materials had to be used wherever possible, and the specifications would often differ from United States specifications; they might perhaps be superior – for example, for high explosive components – or not. British manufacturing equipment had to be employed, and even extremely small variations between different dies, moulds, presses, and so on, could have significant effects on a product as unforgiving as a nuclear weapon.

Besides all these factors there were other problems, such as finding alternatives for materials not available from British sources; modifying engineering designs which might not comply with British standards of safety and compatibility; and meeting British service specifications, different from and sometimes more stringent than United States specifications. So there was a great deal of work to be done before the drawings for a Mark 28 warhead could materialize as a British *Red Snow*. Completion of the first production weapons was expected in March 1960, if all went well and according to plan. By the time of the first stock-take in mid-April 1959, the early stages of the *Red Snow* programme were under way, and there had been a flood of transatlantic visits on many aspects of nuclear weapons collaboration as well as practical production questions about *Red Snow*.

The balance of advantage in the exchanges was necessarily in Britain's favour but they were not entirely one-sided. In some areas, notably electronics and high explosives, the British were equal or perhaps even superior, and in many areas they had valuable ideas to contribute, as the American scientists, and notably Teller, appreciated. One of Aldermaston's aspirations was to identify a particular field in which the Americans had done little work, so that the British scientists could cultivate it to good effect themselves. On some topics they had perforce done much more work by means of minor experiments. (Teller thought that sometimes the Americans had not done enough work *before* going to full-scale testing.)

The first 'stock-take' – April 1959

The tasks of the first stock-take were to look back to survey and evaluate what had been done so far, both on specific weapons and on more general scientific collaboration; and then to look ahead to future collaboration and the widening of its scope. This general review meeting, the first of many, was held in London on 13–14 April 1959, less than nine months after the bilateral agreement of August 1958. Sessions were chaired by Brundrett, Loper, Libby and Penney and they covered an impressively wide range of topics, reviewing collaboration to date, examining operational requirements, and considering future exchanges. They discussed the nuclear materials agreement (then in preparation); problems of safety in storage and handling of weapons; co-operation on any future tests; scientific exchanges; 'clean bombs'; and the civil uses of nuclear explosions (Project *Plowshare*). They listed over 20 subjects for exchange of information by visits or reports; these included diagnostic methods and interpretation, radioflash, health physics, mechanical safing, interpretation of yield measurement data and physical metallurgy of plutonium. They agreed to set up 15 joint study groups and joint working groups, to deal with *inter alia* anti-missile missile defence systems, a 500–600 lb 1-megaton warhead, external neutron sources, vulnerability, safety of high explosives, compatibility of materials, and underground and outer space testing.

The JOWOG idea – a scheme which continues to this day – had been put forward earlier by the Americans, as we saw, as an alternative to British proposals for staff exchanges or secondments. The April 1959 stock-take agreed that before joint working groups began, joint study groups should survey the particular fields; JOWOGs would then convene as soon as possible and meet as often as necessary to consider progress in their own fields, to 'block out' further avenues for investigation, and to propose how work should be divided. Individual scientists (though not seconded or attached) would move back and forth between laboratories. JOWOGs should report formally to stock-take members. Future review meetings would be held at intervals of six to nine months, the next to be in Washington in October 1959.

Collaboration and information exchange would also be through *ad hoc* visits and the transmission of reports (EIVR). The transfer of materials, including some non-nuclear components, would have to await final amendments to the 1958 bilateral agreement, soon to be submitted to Congress for approval. Then a British representative would be posted to Albuquerque to facilitate operations.

By mid-April 1959, the exchange of weapon design information had already materially improved. Work was going on, too, on drafting a joint nuclear weapon classification guide and a guide to procedures under the bilateral agreement.

An agreed record of the stock-take meeting was signed on 14 April 1959 by Libby, Loper, Brundrett and Penney. This was to be given to the JCAE, and an abridged unclassified version was to be presented to Congress. Both sides considered the meeting a success, and the British certainly were delighted. Penney minuted Plowden on 17 April:

> The meeting was extremely satisfactory. There was an obvious wish on the part of the Americans to co-operate warmly and generously. In conversation outside the meetings, the leaders of the American party expressed the opinion that it would only be a matter of time before collaboration became complete over the whole field. There were still sections which at present had not been revealed to us, and we were told what to ask for in order to remove the remaining barriers. The present state on materials was reviewed. ... The AEC wish to publish a statement about the benefits to both sides of this materials agreement in order to assist Congress and public opinion to appreciate the mutual advantages.

Plowden passed these impressions to the Prime Minister on 20 April with a summary report of the stock-take meeting, a copy of which Brundrett had already sent to the Minister of Defence.

The second stock-take – October 1959

By October 1959, when the second stock-take took place in Washington, the arrangements for collaboration – both JOWOGs and EIVR – were running smoothly and both sides appeared well satisfied with their operation. A little pruning of JOWOGs was carried out at this stock-take, but a new one was set up on detection of nuclear tests. The AEC was clearly maintaining a lively interest in further development of serviceable weapons and wanted Britain to collaborate in all phases. But there was no relaxation in the United States legal control, and the flow of information was closely watched to ensure that the exchange remained within the areas covered by 'Presidential Determinations'. A British request for a list of areas covered by PDs was refused because there was no PD on PDs!

By the time of the second stock-take, too, the 1959 bilateral agreement[44] was in being and the materials exchange programme had already started. American tritium was being sent in exchange for British plutonium, and initial shipments of lithium and some non-nuclear components were just about to begin. The necessary procedures and techniques were agreed for manufacture, inspection, testing and acceptance for materials assemblies and components, for quality assurance, and for evaluation of safety and reliability, and the United States side had asked for firm forecasts of long-range British requirements.

Aldermaston after the bilateral

The 1958 bilateral had a very marked effect on Aldermaston's role and organization. The Treasury had certainly hoped that access to United States nuclear weapons information and designs would lighten Aldermaston's load and permit some staff reductions. But the work-load was altered rather than reduced. As noted earlier, the Prime Minister had recognized the need to maintain Aldermaston's research and development effort at about its previous scale, and we have already seen how much effort had to be devoted to weapons production and to Anglicization of the new designs.

Then, in March 1959, Penney asked the Atomic Energy Executive for more staff in the next two years. Weapons were now required more quickly and in greater numbers than originally. Much effort would have to be applied to absorbing new knowledge and developing new techniques, and bringing the new designs into service. These new designs were of much greater refinement and performance than the old ones, which affected all aspects of the warhead – design, manufacture, inspection, assembly, and so on. R&D effort was therefore being re-directed, first, to studying the American warhead designs and preparing drawings for British manufacture. Secondly, new knowledge had to be acquired to support the new warhead programme; strong teams were required to reproduce or match American techniques in practically every field, including theoretical calculations, nuclear and non-nuclear components, explosives and electronics. Thirdly, a large research programme must be applied to the development of new and improved devices if the British scientists were to be able to foster collaboration and enlarge its scope.

In bilateral discussions, Penney said, the British were endeavouring to obtain every possible benefit from the United States – ready-made weapon components, bulk materials and samples. The British needed to know the best techniques, and to carry out advanced research. They should be able to produce the new weapons from resources under their own control; what was obtained from the United States would save time but would hardly affect Aldermaston's manpower situation. Most of its R&D staff would be fully loaded; a few sections would even need more people to cope with the new warhead programme.

Moreover, warhead production, as well as R&D, would involve a major increase of staff and facilities. Larger uranium and plutonium buildings were needed. To produce two new types of warhead and put them into service, 20 more designers were wanted immediately; temporarily, staff would be shifted from other work. The design teams would be employed for some years on these new weapons. And more was involved than weapon design: inspecting and testing of components and materials; environmental tests (for example, on vibration and temperature); designs for safe transport and handling – all were essential before a weapon was ready for acceptance by the services.

Advanced theoretical calculations which were the basis of these new warheads had to be studied; about six additional scientific assistants would be required, and improved computing facilities, since current American thinking depended on at least 10 times more computation than anything the British scientists had previously encountered.

For production of nuclear and other special components, new and more complex techniques had to be developed. In order to establish alternative methods, and to cope with an increased rate of production, bigger buildings were needed, and over 200 more staff to maintain and operate them. New non-nuclear materials were used in American warheads, and Aldermaston was trying to get them from American sources, while investigating British equivalents for some 20 different materials – plastics, polyurethane, various rubbers and adhesives. More staff might be required if the American supply proved difficult. Further work was needed on beryllium and lithium oxide, which the Ministry of Supply would be responsible for producing. Another new area of work would be studying British equivalents of American explosives, and the use of improved British explosives in American types of weapon. A new bomb chamber would be required to study implosion – an area in which Britain was highly skilled.

In electronics too an increased range of systems had become necessary. The Americans were having difficulties in producing some systems and the British did not want to copy unsatisfactory designs or production methods; it would be cheaper and quicker to proceed with British designs that had been under development before the bilateral. Another important change resulting from the bilateral was that a warhead and its firing circuit had to be developed as a single package, so that AWRE had to take over responsibility from the Royal Aircraft Establishment (RAE Farnborough) as design authority. This meant 24 more professional staff and ten more industrials at Aldermaston.

Apart from the weapons programme, major research installations planned some time previously – Allen's Van der Graaff accelerator and the *Herald* light water reactor – were about to come into commission, needing 60 extra staff, including 10 professionals. New buildings and site maintenance alone called for additional clerks, police, cleaners and messengers.

Though the end of atmospheric overseas trials yielded some staff savings, many people released from major trials work were fully occupied with minor trials[45] at Maralinga (which continued during the moratorium and did not end until 1967).

So in March 1959, when the AWRE strength was 8,828 (including 1,272 professionals) Penney wanted 500 more (96 of them professionals).

Whatever Aldermaston's overall success in the weapons programme, how was its success achieved and what were its strengths and weaknesses? John Corner, an acute observer whose experience went back to the beginning in 1947, thought that it was much more competent as an establishment than the outside world realised. Many errors made by individuals, he recalled, were quickly retrieved by teamwork. There was unusual competence at the top, and a special project-mindedness deriving from some exceptional people, dominantly Penney and Cook. The quality persisted in the organization and in the individuals whom it moulded. Corner believed it was important to understand this particular corporate excellence lest it should be destroyed inadvertently. Did it persist, he wondered, because the laboratory tended to promote from within? Would it survive sudden massive changes in top people?

After the bilateral agreement of 1958 Corner felt that, in spite of limited future activities, it would be wrong to reduce the scientific staff and dismiss scientists. A greatly diversified scientific programme was desirable. Aldermaston needed good theoretical and experimental scientists for four reasons: to maintain a standard that would ensure continued Anglo-American collaboration; to preserve in Britain the knowledge and special skills needed for nuclear weapons work; to advise on weapon applications and properties; and to devise new weapons.

A diversification programme strongly advocated by Aldermaston's chief nuclear scientist, Dr (later Sir) Sam Curran, was CTR (controlled thermonuclear reactions) research. Harwell too had a CTR programme, but Curran was convinced there was ample scope for an expanded Aldermaston programme. However, a high-level decision was made instead to set up a new CTR establishment at Culham, near Harwell, in 1960, drawing staff from both Harwell and Aldermaston. This was a great disappointment to Curran who left soon afterwards, and to others. Allen too was deeply disappointed by the reduction of nuclear physics at Aldermaston after the bilateral, as the emphasis moved from fundamental science to engineering and materials sciences. He, with Roberts and Taylor, transferred to Culham and he later returned to academic life in Oxford.

Postscript

Britain's megaton quest was over in 1958, and by 1959 the Anglo-American nuclear partnership was already being closely integrated. After 12 years of isolation and independence, a unique and lasting nuclear relationship was beginning which – through many vicissitudes and through changing world conditions – continues to the present day.

15
Some Questions and Answers

We have asked ourselves – and have been asked – many questions about the British H-bomb, and have found some answers. Future research, we hope, may find many more; there is room for much more work.

The questions have included: Did the H-bomb decision represent a rational choice or a delusion? Was the development programme a success or a 'thermonuclear bluff'?[1] Who was 'the father of the British bomb'?[2] How safe were the Christmas Island tests, and what was the cost in human health? What did the H-bomb cost in money terms?

A rational choice?

Was the 1954 H-bomb decision simply, as is sometimes alleged, due to a desire for national prestige and to self-flattering delusions of a waning great power? A study of the decision-making process persuades us that, whether right or wrong, it was a realistic and carefully reasoned decision. It was derived – to quote a later Minister of Defence[3] – from 'a cold analysis of the facts of the situation', and the circumstances of the time made it almost unavoidable.

After the appalling destruction of two world wars, the all-important objective of British politicians and the Chiefs of Staff was the avoidance of major war. To most of those responsible in Britain in the 1950s a minimal but effective nuclear deterrent appeared to be a vital contribution to that objective. But the deterrent, though not seen as a means of fighting a war, had to be credible – *as if* for use – so it inevitably appears ambiguous. As an existential threat, from the spring of 1958 when the V-bombers became operational, the British deterrent force was far from insignificant and was soon to become a small but formidable force 'capable of inflicting an absolute – not a relative – level of damage on a potential attacker sufficiently great to deter him from nuclear aggression'.[4]

Equally important was the leverage that this strategic deterrent gave Britain *vis à vis* the United States, and the 'incentive to the United States to include Britain in her strategic plans and her deterrent orbit'.[5] Indeed, in 1957 a Ministry of Defence official told American officials in London that British nuclear weapon production was largely for political reasons.[6] For this purpose, as for its strictly deterrent value, the British force had to have credibility. 'Great Britain's search for a nuclear deterrent' (in the opinion of an American defence historian) was 'waged with a purposeful dedication' and was 'never a quest for privilege or status, ... never sought as an end in itself'.[7]

Were the 1957 trials successful, or were they just a 'thermonuclear bluff'?

An article in October 1992, already mentioned,[8] suggested that none of the four British nuclear tests in the Pacific in 1957 was a hydrogen bomb test, but that they took the Americans in and led to the special nuclear defence relationship. These 1957 tests, the authors infer, were of two versions of boosted fission bombs and high-yield fission bombs, none of which would have yielded as much as 1 megaton.[9]

However (as seen in Chapter 10), the first and third shots at *Grapple* (*Short Granite* and *Purple Granite*) were certainly two-stage H-bombs which made use of X-rays from an exploding primary to implode a thermonuclear secondary. They were disappointing in yield but were successful as proofs of principle,[10] and they were also operational successes for the RAF who dropped them accurately on target to detonate at the required altitude. It was not a bad start, going straight from the drawing-board to an airdropped test device; the first American H-bomb test, *Ivy Mike*, had not been an airdrop, or a solid-fuelled device.

As for *Orange Herald*, it was not a failed H-bomb; and never had any pretensions to being an H-bomb. It was a huge fission bomb, only slightly boosted,[11] that could be relied on to give a very big explosion. (The *Granites* were more advanced but more experimental.) At 750 kilotons, *Orange Herald* was somewhat bigger than *Ivy King*. *Orange Herald* was regarded as a dependable type, in the megaton range, that could if necessary be used as a warhead for purposes to which the *Granite* type, even if successful, might not be adaptable – for example, for a powered guided bomb or a ballistic missile. The fourth Pacific shot, *Grapple X* in November 1957, was a double bomb device with a simplified secondary, and was the best to date, yielding 1.8 megaton (Chapter 11). Britain then had an effective, two-stage, megaton plus, design. The next objective was to improve it and make it lighter, more compact and more economical.

The British achievement was real enough, if at first tentative. *Grapple X*, in November 1957, had quickly picked up the partial success of *Grapple* and had erased its disappointments. But even if the British had wanted to deceive the Americans about the results it would have been futile to try, since American observers were present and, as we saw, American scientists were monitoring the tests and exchanging information with the British about measurements and yield estimates.

As to the success of the British programme, the comparative time-scale, alongside the United States and Soviet time-scales in Chapters 2 and 3, is as follows. From the first A-bomb explosion to the first two-stage, solid-fuelled, radiation implosion device:

United States	*Trinity* to *Bravo*	103 months
Soviet Union	*Joe 1* to *Joe 19*	63 months
United Kingdom	*Hurricane* to *Grapple*	55 months
	or *Hurricane* to *Grapple X*	61 months

If we compare the times from the Government decision to the first test, the periods for the United States and Britain are:

United States	Presidential directive to *Bravo*	49 months
United Kingdom	Cabinet decision to *Grapple*	33 months
	or to *Grapple X*	39 months

There are various other possible bases for comparison, but the picture is not of British scientific inferiority.[12]

The question of the independence of the British development arises. As mentioned earlier, only the world's first H-bomb can be considered completely independent, because nations that follow know it is possible, even if they know little else. And once atmospheric tests begin, it is open to other nations to learn by monitoring them, provided they have the operational capability and the advanced scientific skills to do so; Britain undoubtedly obtained some useful information from foreign tests, especially *Joe 19*. Another question is whether the British scientists benefited from hints picked up by Penney from friends on his many visits to the United States.[13] The consensus is that they did not. Their general feeling was that, whatever snippets he gave them when he returned, however hopefully awaited, were not useful. It was often fragmentary information that he did not really understand, one Aldermaston scientist thought, given to him by people who probably should not have done so. One even suspected it might be 'disinformation'.

So it seems clear that British H-bomb development was independent of such assistance, and various features of it certainly surprised and interested the American scientists in 1958. Scientifically, the British development was hardly inferior to the American, though in 1958 the engineering development was far less advanced: partly because of the later British start and the short time they had had to weaponize the designs, but certainly also because of the United States' vast resources and greatly superior engineering strengths.

Who was 'the father of the British H-bomb'?

Unlike Teller, Ulam or Sakharov, none the of the British weaponeers – neither Penney nor Cook, nor any of the Aldermaston scientists – wrote personal accounts of their work. Though Penney has been called 'the father of the H-bomb', he never made any such claim himself and would certainly have deprecated it.

Few contemporary documents give any consecutive account of the nuclear weapon programmes (one account is reproduced at Appendix 3), and they are brief and impersonal. Exactly how and when Aldermaston discovered the three essential ideas of the H-bomb is still something of a mystery.[14] In trying to elucidate it, we have had to depend on collating many miscellaneous documents, often scrappy, sometimes ambiguous, frequently unsigned and undated and barely identifiable. Fortunately, we were able to talk to several participants[15] who were close to the origins of the British H-bomb, though, regrettably, not to four who were at the heart of it – Penney, Cook, Hulme and Roberts.

It does not seem to have occurred to any of the scientists to regard their work as anything other than a corporate effort, nor did they appear to take a personal or proprietorial view of their achievements. An exception was Dr John Ward who, as we saw in Chapter 6, worked at Aldermaston for six months in 1955 and who, many years later, claimed to be the inventor of the British H-bomb (see Appendix 5).

The consensus among all the scientists we have been able to talk to is that the essential insights came from Keith Roberts and Bryan Taylor, and that very important contributions were made by Ken Allen, especially to the *Grapple Y* design. These three, and Corner (perhaps also Hulme), were thought to be the most creative minds.[16] Corner himself considered Roberts and Taylor to have played the most valuable part. But he, and everyone else, agreed that 'without Cook we shouldn't have had the H-bomb',[17] while Cook himself said that 'Penney led us to the H-bomb'.[18]

The British H-bomb was truly the work of many people. Even the conceptual design was a corporate achievement rather than the inspired work of a single person. And it would never have materialized without the dedicated and often brilliant work of the chemists, metallurgists, engineers and craftsmen who transformed concepts into designs and then into hardware.[19]

This was a complex process (not then as highly formalized as later) which might involve a thousand or more detailed drawings between the theoreticians' conceptual sketch and a test device – not yet a finished production weapon – to be exploded at Christmas Island.

Why should the H-bomb have had a 'father'? It is a misleading metaphor, like so many metaphors, and to ask about its 'father' is a meaningless question.

What was the cost to the health of the participants?

Test hazards

The emergencies for which careful contingency plans had been made – aircraft crashes on take-off or landing with a test device on board – did not occur, and there were no fall-out disasters such as *Bravo*. There was some unforeseen blast damage to buildings and equipment at *Grapple X* but no one was injured. The island hospital had no cases of radiation sickness caused by high radiation exposures, and the medical staff's chief worries had been dysentery and sunburn. The main health hazard to trials personnel was from low level radiation exposure (equivalent to that then normal in the nuclear industry). The radiation exposure limits that applied during the trials were similar to the internationally agreed limits for radiation workers in industry and hospitals, and similar well-tried principles of radiological protection were employed, including safety distances, personal monitoring of potentially exposed individuals, air and ground monitoring, and strict health physics control of contaminated areas and of personnel movements.

Local radioactive contamination at Christmas and Malden Islands was minimal because there were no ground or tower bursts (which draw up large quantities of soil and rock, much of which return to earth as heavy particles of local fall-out). All seven big shots were high airbursts, and the debris was mostly carried very high into the upper atmosphere, to be slowly diffused over great distances. Even the two smaller shots, *Pendant* and *Burgee* at *Grapple Z*, were detonated on balloon arrays at a height of 450 metres – much higher than a 31-metre tower–mounted shot. The avoidance of ground and sea contamination had been an important consideration in planning the tests.

Thus there was less likelihood of personnel being exposed to radiation during the Pacific trials than during the kiloton trials in Australia. For the early trials in Australia, nearly all the test personnel were badged, but this policy was reviewed for the later Pacific trials and, where it was judged that measurable exposure would not occur, individual monitoring was not carried out.[20] Even so, it was found that, of the participants who were individually monitored, many had 'zero doses'. This indicates, though it does not prove, that most or all of those who were thought not to require film badges had 'zero doses' also.

The radiation record

There are two possible ways to assess how well the health and safety measures protected the test participants from long-term damage. The first and simpler is to look at the radiation record – how well were exposures contained within the authorized limits, and were they kept as low as reasonably possible? The second, more satisfactory and much more difficult, way is to look at the subsequent health record of the participants; this inevitably takes years because of the long latent periods that may be involved in cases of radiation damage.

Some data from the radiation record are given in Appendix 4. Much the highest radiation exposures in the Pacific trials were to 84 RAF aircrew officers engaged in Canberra sorties to collect high-altitude cloud samples. About half the total dose for the entire population of test participants was received by the Canberra aircrews. The only instance where the 'special high integrated level' (SHIL) – which could be authorised only by the task force commander in an emergency – was exceeded, was when a Canberra encountered 'unexpected and abnormal conditions'.[21] The two officers involved received a total dose slightly above the 'accident limit' given by the International Commission on Radiological Protection (ICRP) in its 1958 Recommendations.

Next to the Canberra aircrews, the Aldermaston scientists were the most exposed group because of the various special tasks they had to carry out. Most of the other test personnel were not 'potentially exposed' and were not individually monitored; of those 971 that were, nearly half had exposures 'at or below threshold' (that is, too small to be measurable). Some film badges recording 'zero dose' were destroyed by health physics staff as useless; though this was perhaps unfortunate by hindsight, in trials conditions it is hardly surprising. But some test participants may have been worried about their missing film badges, or because they were not monitored. Most of them had very limited information at the time about the duties they carried out at various locations, and thus their scope for assessing the possibility of any unrecorded exposure was poor.[22]

The health record

Radiation standards are sometimes changed, usually becoming stricter; moreover no system, however efficient, is ever perfect. Therefore, the best evidence of success is less the radiation record than the actual health record of the test participants. A retrospective study is a complex undertaking because it is necessarily long-term and because the late effects – mainly cancers – which may be caused by low-level radiation are not specific to radiation. (By contrast, asbestosis, for example, has an unambiguous cause.)

Since one in three people in this country will contract cancer during their lives, many test participants would have done so over time in the ordinary course of events. To determine whether any individual case is, or is not, due to radiation exposure in the Pacific trials is generally impossible; it is a question of probability.

The health of the test participants can only be assessed statistically, compared with the experience of a control group closely matched in terms of age, employment, service in the armed forces, and time spent overseas in tropical or sub-tropical conditions (but *not* on nuclear weapons trials).

A very comprehensive study of 21,358 test participants (estimated at 85% of the total) and 22,333 controls was carried out by an independent expert team, led by the eminent epidemiologist Sir Richard Doll. Two reports were issued in 1988 and 1993.[23] The study examined the mortality rates, the incidence of leukaemia and 26 other forms of cancer, and 15 other causes of death. It found that there was no significant difference between the participants and the controls, and that mortality was lower than in the nation generally (except that cancer mortality among naval personnel was similar to the national rate). The team detected little evidence to relate cancer incidence to recorded dose; indeed, incidence tended to *decrease* with higher recorded dose.

The general conclusion of this authoritative investigation and analysis[24] was that 'participation in the nuclear weapon testing programmes has not had a detectable effect on the participants' expectation of life, nor on their risk of developing cancer or other fatal diseases'.

What did the H-bomb cost?

In 1953 it had seemed that to develop an H-bomb would be too difficult and too expensive for Britain. In 1954 it appeared both necessary and affordable. In the next four years the bomb was developed with very limited resources at comparatively low cost. We do not attempt to estimate the overall expenditure,[25] nor the opportunity cost. Certainly, cost was a serious matter for a relatively poor nation, and one Whitehall official[26] commented anxiously on 'the British subscription to the hydrogen club'. He wrote:

At present ... R&D is costing us about £30 million per annum, or nearly 20 per cent of our total expenditure on defence R&D (two-thirds being spent on developing the means of delivery) ... Expenditure on the ballistic rocket is estimated at £1.9 million this year, £3.7 million next year and £5.5 million in 1957/58, and rising steeply after that. Development of V-class bombers is estimated to cost £6.9 million next year, £6.8 million in 1957/58. ... Costs of production are very high both for megaton weapons and for means of delivery. We are embarking on an R&D programme which is financially crippling. ... It is recommended that the UK subscription to the H-club be kept as low as possible.

As we have seen in earlier chapters, Aldermaston certainly did so.

But most of the costs detailed by that worried civil servant were not for warhead development but for delivery systems. Would there have been a saving if the H-bomb decision had not been taken, if Britain had opted out of the 'hydrogen club' but had planned to retain an A-bomb deterrent? This is impossible to assess, but the answer is probably no. Production demands might well have been greater, more fissile material would have been needed, and the need for delivery systems – much the most costly element in the deterrent – would not have been reduced. Above all, without the bilateral agreement, the all-important economies of Anglo-American co-operation would have been lost.

Postscript

Back in post-war Cambridge, Chadwick[27] reflected that 'the H-bomb can hardly be classed as a weapon at all. Its effect in causing suffering is out of all proportion to the military effect. The H-bomb does not offer any improvement in the waging of war, and it brings with it a risk of making the world uninhabitable'. On another occasion, considering a major conventional war with perhaps a final recourse to nuclear weapons, he surmised that 'the development of these fantastic weapons of destruction means the end of the great wars we have known in the past'.

Penney and Cook, intensely aware of the H-bomb's terrible potential and of the actual horrors of two world wars, did not seek an 'improvement in the waging of war'. Their purpose, and that of Aldermaston, was to prevent future wars. The 'end of the great wars' had been Penney's fervent hope and belief ever since the days that he and Leonard Cheshire[28] had waited together for the Nagasaki raid in August 1945.

Appendix 1
Technical Note

It is hoped that this technical note, written by a non-scientist, will be useful for non-scientist readers, and that any scientist readers will find it not inaccurate (though much simplified).

A-bombs and H-bombs

Fission and fusion

1. An A-bomb – an atomic or fission bomb – derives its immense explosive energy from the *fission* or splitting of atoms of a very heavy element, uranium or plutonium. A hydrogen or H-bomb (or fusion bomb) derives a large part of its explosive energy – but not all – from the *fusion* of atoms of hydrogen, the lightest element. Since H-bombs require A-bombs in order to function, this note begins with fission and A-bombs.

Sub-atomic particles – protons, neutrons and electrons

2. Atoms – like unimaginably small solar systems about one hundred-millionth of a centimetre in diameter – are mostly empty space. Each has at its centre a nucleus – the analogue of our sun – made up of sub-atomic particles called nucleons. The most important are protons (with a positive electrical charge) and neutrons (electrically uncharged); thus the nucleus as a whole carries a positive electrical charge.
3. The number of protons in an atom varies from one in the hydrogen atom to 92 in uranium, the heaviest element in nature. There are even more protons in the so-called transuranic elements (including plutonium) which do not exist in nature.
4. In the nuclei of the lighter elements the number of protons and neutrons is generally about equal. But in nuclei of the heavy elements the proportion of neutrons is greater; for example, a uranium nucleus has 92 protons but more than 140 neutrons. It is this neutron surplus that makes nuclear fission possible (see paragraph 10 below).
5. The number of protons in the nucleus determines the chemical properties and identity of an element. So, for example, an atom with 6 protons – whatever the number of neutrons – must be carbon; an atom with 26 protons must be iron; one with 92 must be uranium. This proton number is called the atomic number, denoted by the symbol Z.
6. The total number of nucleons – protons plus neutrons – is the atomic mass number (symbol A). So if N denotes the number of neutrons, then Z plus N = A.
7. An element has only one atomic number Z and a single chemical identity; if Z changes it becomes a different element. But the atomic mass (A) may vary because the number of neutrons may vary. Thus, an element may contain atoms of varying atomic mass; 99.3% of natural uranium is uranium-238 and 0.7% is uranium-235.
8. These variants of different atomic mass are called isotopes, and they may be stable or unstable. The latter are called 'radioisotopes', because they are radioactive.
9. Outside the nucleus, sub-atomic particles called electrons move round it like planets orbiting round the sun. Electrons are, 1850 times lighter than protons. They carry a

negative electrical charge, equal to the positive charge on the nucleus, so that generally the atom is electrically neutral. But it can, in various ways, acquire a net charge, negative or positive, and it is then called an ion.

Nuclear fission

10. The neutron is highly effective in inducing nuclear changes. Being uncharged and relatively very heavy, it is extremely penetrating, and it can move freely, unchecked by forces of electrostatic attraction or repulsion, until it collides with an atomic nucleus.

11. If certain heavy unstable elements, of which the most important are uranium (but see paragraph 16 below) and the man-made element plutonium, are bombarded by neutrons, some atoms may split into roughly equal fragments, creating new atoms of lighter elements. Because lighter nuclei contain lower proportions of neutrons, some neutrons then become surplus and are ejected from the nucleus at a speed of 10,000 miles per second. The number of surplus neutrons per fission in uranium-235 averages 2.5 and these free neutrons may go on to collide with other uranium nuclei, causing further fissions, and creating a chain reaction.

12. At each fission, a large amount of energy is released, mainly in the form of kinetic energy of the neutrons and the fission fragments. Heat is generated as they are slowed down by interaction with the surrounding material. The fission products released (mostly radioisotopes from the middle of the periodic table) include strontium-90, caesium-137 and iodine-131, which are important constituents of fall-out.

13. If every fission results in one new fission – if the multiplication rate (k) is 1 – then criticality is achieved and a chain reaction will be maintained at a steady rate. If k is *less* than 1, the reaction will die out. To keep it going, each free neutron must liberate enough new neutrons to replace itself and to compensate for unproductive neutrons (see paragraph 16 below).

14. If k is *more* than 1 and each fission yields enough neutrons to cause more than one new fission, then the neutron population and the number of fissions will increase exponentially in a 'divergent chain reaction'. The rate of growth will depend upon the excess k; if each fission leads to 1.5 new fissions on average, the multiplication factor, k, is 1.5 and the excess k is 0.5.

15. Since atoms are mostly space and nuclei are so small, looking for a nucleus in an atom is like looking for a needle in an empty house. It is quite astonishing that a free neutron ever does hit a nucleus. Some nuclei present better targets than others, and the probability of a nucleus being effectively hit is called the nuclear cross-section. This differs from element to element, and from isotope to isotope, and each nucleus has several different cross-sections (for different particle velocities and for different types of encounter – fission, absorption, elastic collision, and non-fission neutron capture: see paragraph 17 below).

16. The chance that a free neutron may be unproductive is therefore high. It may miss the target altogether. It may bounce off it, be absorbed, or be lost to the system by 'neutron escape' – a surface effect dependent on size and shape, being greater from a flat plane than a sphere and from a small sphere than a large one. Density of the fissile material is an important factor; when compressed, less material is required for criticality. The amount in which fission can produce enough free neutrons to maintain the neutron population is called the critical mass. Below this critical mass no chain reaction is possible.

17. In elastic collision the neutron's initial speed of 10,000 miles per second is slowed down to, say, one mile per second. The slow-moving, so-called thermal, neutrons

are most likely to cause fissions in uranium-235 but cannot fission U-238. In natural uranium (or uranium with a high U-238 content) it is only the U-235 constituent that makes a chain reaction possible. However, U-238 atoms may absorb free neutrons by non-fission neutron capture to form a new element, plutonium (Pu). The isotope Pu-239, like U-235, is a fissile material. U-238 is *not* fissile itself but is called fertile because fissile material can be produced from it.

A-bombs: atomic or fission bombs

18. Both nuclear reactors and atomic bombs use fission reactions in uranium and/or plutonium. In reactors, controlled chain reactions are needed to produce a steady energy release, and they can operate on natural uranium or uranium slightly enriched in U-235. But a fast, uncontrolled, chain reaction in pure or almost pure fissile material can be used as a super-explosive.

19. Assembling U-235 or Pu-239 in a more than critical mass can initiate a divergent chain reaction which releases tremendous amounts of energy in a period of time measured in fractions of micro-seconds. The super-critical mass can be created either by bringing two sub-critical pieces of fissile material together very rapidly in a gun-like device, or by implosion. The implosion method uses high explosive to compress a sub-critical mass of fissile material to an extremely high density at which it becomes super-critical. All this must be done with very great rapidity. Timing is crucial for, as we saw, the neutron population, and the number of fissions, increase exponentially in a divergent chain reaction so that most of the energy release occurs in the last few generations of fission. Therefore, the total yield will be disappointingly small if the system is blown apart by a premature explosion before the designed fission process is complete. There are various technical devices – such as neutron reflectors and heavy casing – which are used to delay disassembly and maximise the neutron population growth.

20. Atomic (or fission) bombs have vastly greater explosive power than chemical bombs. It would take 22,000 tons of conventional high explosive to produce an explosion equal to the Nagasaki bomb 'Fat Man', which contained only a few kilograms of Pu-239 and only consumed about 1.25 kg of it. However, there is a limit to the explosive power obtainable from a fission bomb, because the critical mass imposes a limit on the amount of fissile material that can be used. But there is no theoretical limit to the power of fusion bombs, which can have multi-megaton yields.

H-bombs: hydrogen, thermonuclear or fusion bombs

21. H-bombs work not just by fission in the heaviest elements but by fusing nuclei of the lightest element, hydrogen. For them to fuse, the forces of electrostatic repulsion between the positively-charged nuclei have to be overcome and so fusion is accompanied by the release of these forces, from which the H-bomb derives much (not all) of its power. Hydrogen comes in three different forms: the commonly occurring form H_1, with one proton and no neutrons; and two heavier isotopes – deuterium (D or H_2) with one proton and one neutron, and the artificially produced tritium (T or H_3), with one proton and two neutrons.* Fusion is almost impossible to achieve in ordinary hydrogen (H_1).

---

* Thus for H, D and T, Z = 1, but A is, respectively 1, 2 and 3.

22. It is thermonuclear fusion that provides the energy of our sun and the other stars, and fusion can only occur in conditions of heat and pressure – temperatures of tens of millions of degrees Celsius – comparable to those in the sun. Such conditions, continuously maintained in the sun, are created on earth for an infinitesimal fraction of time by the explosion of an atomic bomb. So the advent of A-bombs made the development of H-bombs theoretically possible.

23. There are four possible fusion reactions in D and T. The easiest to achieve and the one which releases the greatest amount of energy is that in which T and D fuse to create helium and eject a fast neutron. (T + D = He + n).*

24. There are severe practical problems in handling both tritium – a highly reactive gas – and deuterium – which has to be kept in a liquid state by cryogenic means. So an ingenious solution was found: to create these materials within the bomb, at the instant of explosion, by incorporating a solid thermonuclear fuel, lithium deuteride (LiD) – a compound of the light metal, lithium and deuterium. This use of solid thermonuclear fuel was a very important feature in H-bomb development.

25. It was soon realized by weapon scientists that the idea of placing the LiD round the A-bomb – the 'layer cake' concept – was unsatisfactory, because the weapon would be blown apart before more than a small amount of the thermonuclear fuel had been ignited. It was essential to be able to initiate the thermonuclear reaction more rapidly than the system would be disassembled. The solution found was twofold. First, the fission bomb (the primary) was separated from the thermonuclear component (the secondary) in a two-stage design, and the best geometry had to be calculated. Secondly, an efficient means had to be found of conveying the energy from the exploding primary to the secondary in order to implode the latter. The hydrodynamic shock of the primary explosion would not convey it fast enough, because that same shock would blow the system apart almost as fast. But there was another possibility. Much of the energy released by exploding A-bombs is in the form of X-rays, and radiation travels at practically the speed of light. Perhaps radiation pressure could carry the energy from the primary to the secondary fast enough for the latter to function before the weapon was blown to pieces.

26. The weapon's yield could be greatly increased by having a uranium tamper in the secondary. As noted (paragraph 7), uranium is mostly U-238 which, unlike U-235, is not normally fissile, but is fissioned by the very fast (14 Mev) neutrons produced in thermonuclear reactions. So H-bombs were designed to derive a very considerable part of their yield from fission in the secondary (and, of course, in the primary) as well as from fusion. These bombs are described as fission–fusion–fission (or F–F–F). Typically, the fission-fusion ratio may be considered as 50/50.

27. All these basic ideas for H-bomb design were developed during the 1950s by the weapon scientists of the (then) three nuclear powers. The possible variations in design are almost unlimited.

---

* Lithium (Z = 3) is the least dense solid element. Natural lithium (Li) consists of two isotopes, Li_6 and Li_7. In the H-bomb, lithium deuteride, LiD, produces tritium, T (in the reaction $Li_6 = He_4 + H_3$). The H_3(T) then reacts with the D in the compound (see paragraph 23).

Boosted bombs

28. In boosted bombs, thermonuclear reactions are used – but not as a major source of the yield, as in H-bombs. They are used to enhance the yield of fission bombs, or to improve their efficiency, so making it possible to reduce the size of a bomb for a given yield.

Appendix 2
Summary of Nuclear Weapon Tests, 1945–58

Test series, or individual shots, of especial interest in H-bomb development are
marked*.

	USA	USSR	UK
1945 July	*Trinity* 21 kT		
1946 June/July	*Crossroads* 2 shots of 21 kT		
1948 Apr./May	*Sandstone* 3 shots 18–49 kT		
1949 Aug.		RDS A (*Joe 1*)- 22 kT	
1951 Jan./Feb.	*Ranger* 5 shots 1.8–22 kT		
Apr./May	**Greenhouse* 4 shots including **George*, 225 kT, 8 May and **Item*, 45.5 kT, 24 May		
Sept./Oct.		RDS B&C (*Joe 2* and *3*) 38 and 40 kT	
Oct./Nov.	*Buster–Jangle* 7 shots 0.1–31 kT		
1952 Jan./May	*Tumbler–* *Snapper* 8 shots 1–19 kT		
Oct./Nov.	**Ivy* including **Mike* 10.4 MT, 31 Oct. and *King* 500 kT, 15 Nov.		*Hurricane* 25 kT, 3 Oct.
1953 Mar./June	*Upshot–* *Knothole* 11 shots 0.2–61 kT		

Test series, or individual shots, of especial interest in H-bomb development are marked*. – *continued*

	USA	USSR	UK
Aug./Sept.		7 shots 20–400 kT including *RDS F (*Joe 4*) 12 Aug.	
Oct.			*Totem* 2 shots 10 and 8 kT
1954 Feb./May	*Castle* 6 shots including *Bravo*. All were H-bombs – 110 kT–15 MT		
Sept./Oct.		8 shots 4–150 kT	
1955 Feb./May	*Teapot* and *Wigwam* 15 shots, all kT		
July/Nov.		7 shots including *Joe 18*, 215 kT, 5 Nov. and *Joe 19*, 1.6 MT, 22 Nov.	
1956 Feb./Dec.		9 shots including *2 T/N shots, 150 kT and 1.5 MT	
May/Jun.	*Redwing* 17 shots including 6 MT, 1.1–5 MT *Cherokee*, 20 May, was first US MT airdrop		*Mosaic* 2 shots 15 and 60 kT
Sept./Oct.			*Buffalo* 4 shots 1.5 – 15 kT
1957 Jan./Dec.		*13 shots including T/N shots on 24 Sept. and 6 Oct.	
May/July	*Plumbbob* 29 shots up to 44 kT. Included first underground test		

Test series, or individual shots, of especial interest in H-bomb development are
marked*. – *continued*

	USA	USSR	UK
May/June			*Grapple* 3 shots including 2 H-bombs. 0.2–0.72 MT
Sept./Oct.			*Antler* 3 shots 1–25 kT
Nov.			*Grapple X* 1 shot, 1.8 MT
1958 Feb./Nov.		25 or 26 shots, 8 probably in MT range	
Apr./Sept.	*HARDTACK I 34 shots including 8 in MT range (up to 9.3 MT). *Argus* 3 shots, each 1.2 kT		*Grapple Y* 1 shot, 3MT
Aug./Sept.			*Grapple Z* 4 shots including 2 H-bombs 0.8 and 1 MT, 2 and 11 Sept.
Sept./Oct.	*Hardtack II* 14 shots up to 22 kT		

Appendix 3
The History of British R&D on Atomic Weapons

(The following document in AWE archives, dated September 1958, is unsigned but was probably written by Dr John Corner. It was apparently prepared to be given to the American representatives at the bilateral meeting at Sandia in September 1958. Several lines of the original are omitted here for reasons of classification.)

The British government decided to develop 'the atomic bomb' in the summer of 1947. The work was begun in special sections of ARE, and exceptional secrecy measures were taken in order that there would be no leak that work was starting on the bomb. Only work on weapons effects could be done overtly within the secrecy limits of normal armaments work. Slowly the various divisions were created and makeshift facilities were provided. It became apparent that a special establishment for weapons work was essential, and site work began at Aldermaston in February 1950. Preparations for the *Hurricane* trial (October 1952) absorbed nearly the whole of the limited effort available. As more and more facilities became available at Aldermaston, the tempo rapidly increased. The divisions began to work as an integrated team, and scientific and industrial staff were rapidly recruited. The vast possibilities in the range and type of nuclear weapons began to be realized.

Until 1953 we had never thought that the United Kingdom would have the financial and technical resources to make a hydrogen bomb. Our objective was to produce pure plutonium and mixed fission bombs. The early work on the air lens (1952) gave promise of considerable reduction in size and weight. However it became clear in early 1953 from stories in the American Press that a very large explosion (perhaps 10 MT) had been achieved in 1952. We began to think of high yield weapons – first, of a pure fission weapon using U-235 with a yield approaching 1 MT. We also began to think about thermonuclear weapons.

It was obvious that the fastest known thermonuclear reaction, T+D, must play an important part in a thermonuclear bomb, and we also began to think of the possibilities of making tritium in the bomb from lithium-6. Arrangements were made for the production of experimental quantities of tritium and lithium-6. At this stage our ideas of quantities were very much influenced by what we remembered from Los Alamos about the superbomb. Requests were therefore made for a production of the order of 100 g of tritium per year by January 1958, with 10 g quantities some 18 months earlier. The original request for Li-6 (late 1953) was for 10 kg a year, but later this was increased to about 100 kg a year.

Work on MT thermonuclear weapons was authorised by the Government in 1954. Ideas were at first strongly influenced by the 'classical' superbomb and the tendency was to think of propagation along a stick or tube using Li-6D and U-238. This would be started by heat or compression arising essentially from blast or a neutron pulse from a trigger bomb.

The first *Castle* shot in the spring of 1954, and the contamination of a Japanese fishing boat which followed, revealed that there were large quantities of fission productions in the thermonuclear shots of the 10 MT class. This seemed to imply that tons of uranium had been irradiated by neutrons, giving of the order of 0.5 ton of fission products. We did not see a military requirement for 10 MT bombs, and we thought that they would weigh at least 10 tons, which was more than our planes would carry. Therefore we tried to think of 1 MT weapons, weighing 2 or 3 tons. The result was that we began to think about uranium concentrated in a bomb. By late 1955 we were working on a simple system by which a trigger bomb and a thermonuclear bomb were placed inside a common outer case with a radiation-transmitting material surrounding them. Some work was also being done on double bombs in which the second bomb was compressed by a hydrodynamic wave from the first bomb. Devices of this type were designed but never tested.

Meanwhile two possible routes to a MT airburst weapon were being followed. The first of these was merely a large fissile weapon with a very thin HE layer. The control of scabbing in this weapon took up a large part of our effort, but otherwise did not contribute to our thermonuclear work. The second route was the scheme of using a Li-6D layer just outside the U-235 of a big fissile bomb. The first deliveries of Li-6D were made early in 1956 and it was planned to do two tests on kiloton weapons to check the boosting by this material in such a position. As it happened, by the end of 1955 AWRE opinion had already come to the conclusion that no really worthwhile boost could be obtained in this way. This was verified by the first test [*Mosaic, G1*] and, in view of the importance of the conclusion, a second test was fired [*Mosaic, G2*] giving an even higher temperature and compression in the Li-6D layer, but again without producing more than a few per cent change in the yield. Thus it became clear by mid-1956 that we had really only two routes to the MT airdrop weapon, these being a straight fission weapon in which we had confidence and the problematical double bomb, which we doubted if we would have sufficient time to develop before nuclear tests were stopped by international agreement.

A major effort was then made to find the points at which the double bomb might fail, and to correct them. *Short Granite*, which was dropped in the spring of 1957, did, in fact, work correctly as a double bomb and all stages did operate. However the yield was not enough for a service MT weapon and a last minute attempt to improve it by eye led to the lower yield of *Purple Granite*. This demonstrated that we did not understand the working of the final thermonuclear stage in Dick. Post-mortems on these two rounds were hampered by the layered structure which arose from the U-238/Li-6D cycle which was being used for the thermonuclear reaction but we already suspected that we were working on the wrong cycle.

It was decided therefore that a further double bomb should be fired towards the end of 1957, in which the outer case and the trigger bomb would use the components proved by *Short Granite*. Dick would be of the very simplest possible type. This would make it possible to predict the results and to see where the theory went wrong. ...

In the summer of 1956, statements by American officials made it clear that thermonuclear bombs could be clean or nearly clean. These statements strengthened our suspicions that it must be possible to get away from the U-238/Li-6D cycle, and work began on other multiplicative processes. ... At about this time, in the summer of 1957, our [IBM] 704 was really coming into full operation, cutting down first the time taken to do Monte Carlo and then later the time for implosion by a factor of order 20. When these techniques were applied to the Dick that had been chosen for the *Grapple X* test it was found that compressions of order 25 were going to be obtained. ... From this point AWRE really began to have confidence in these weapons. The next development was the demonstration in *Grapple Y* that a considerably less enriched lithium could be used. ...

Although supplies of tritium adequate for generous use in trials were not expected until 1958, the first couple of grams became available in the middle of 1956. Meanwhile the idea had grown up that we might do well to use this first material as a demonstration that one could boost ordinary kiloton weapons with the aid of a gram or two of T. This first amount of T was therefore put in one of the weapons to be fired at *Buffalo* [at the Maralinga Range, South Australia, in October 1956]. Unfortunately the *Buffalo* weapons used a central initiator, and the presence of the deutero-tritide in the centre of the fissile core lowered the unboosted yield by a factor of order 2. ... This reluctance to redesign completely a weapon for the use of T persisted into 1957, when T was used on a fairly massive scale ... without, on balance, improving on the result we would have got if a core had been used which contained no tritide (and no empty space for tritide).

The desire to develop a strong source weapon with a yield of order 15 KT led to a study of hollow gadgets. ... It was found theoretically that such a weapon would be extremely suitable for boosting with T, either as a deutero-tritide or as gas. This has led to the *Pendant* and *Burgee* rounds.

Summary

The period 1947 to mid-1952 was spent in developing what was thought to be essentially a single object, namely 'the atomic bomb'. In 1953, we were still thinking only in terms of fission bombs, but great reductions in size and weight became possible (for example, *Red Beard*). In 1953 it became clear that a very large thermonuclear explosion had been made by the Americans. In 1954 it became clear that uranium in large amounts was involved in these weapons. By mid-1956 it had become clear that a Li-6D layer around a fissile core with HE implosion was not the route to a MT bomb. The double bomb and the simple MT fission bomb were both demonstrated in the spring of 1957. The aftermath of this trial and the 1956 newspaper story about clean bombs, and the increasing speed and competency of the Establishment, combined in late 1957 to give our first effective multi-megaton device.

Appendix 4
Health and Safety Aspects of Weapon Trials

Radiological protection

1. Since ionizing radiations – alpha and beta particles, neutrons, X-rays and gamma rays – can have damaging biological effects in living organisms including man, radiological protection measures are essential at nuclear weapon tests, as in the nuclear industry.

Measurement

2. The units of radiation dose used in the 1950s (rad and rem) were superseded in 1978 by the gray (Gy) and the sievert (Sv). Here the original figures have been converted (generally into millisieverts (mSv)).

Radiation effects

3. It was known from an early date that whole-body exposures of 0.25–1 Sv received within, say, 24 hours, might cause slight nausea and some blood changes. 1–2 Sv might cause nausea, vomiting and diarrhoea. Exposures of 3–4 Sv in less than 24 hours would be fatal within about 60 days in 50% of cases. The same doses spread over days or weeks would carry a much lower risk.
4. The cause of the damage would be clear in such cases. It is not so for long-term effects of low levels of exposure.
5. For a few long-term effects (such as eye cataracts) there is a threshold dose. For most long-term effects (leukaemia and other cancers) it is assumed that no threshold exists and that the risk of damage – though not its nature or severity – is proportional to the exposure, however small the dose.
6. Latent periods before the effects are seen may be years or decades.
7. Cancers which may be radiation-induced are not specific, and are not recognizably different from other cancers.
8. For the above reasons a causal link with low level radiation is virtually impossible to establish in individual cancer cases. However, epidemiological and other studies over many years have made it increasingly possible to calculate *statistical* risk factors.

Radiation standards

9. In the 1950s, guidelines set by the International Commission on Radiological Protection (ICRP) were designed to ensure that health risks for radiation workers, over a working lifetime, were 'small compared to the other hazards of life'.
10. In 1956 ICRP's occupational limit was 3 mSv a week. It was changed in 1958 to 30 mSv a quarter (and an annual average of 50 mSv).

240

11. The British Medical Research Council set standards for test participants equivalent to these ICRP occupational standards. No unnecessary exposures were to be permitted, and all exposures must be as low as possible. The normal working level (NWL) was limited to 3 mSv a week.
12. Exceptionally, a lower integrated level (LIL) of 30 mSv, for the duration of the whole operation, was permissible if necessary for the smooth running of the operation. (This was comparable to the ICRP's quarterly limit of 30 mSv.)
13. Two further exceptions could be permitted, in case of necessity or extreme necessity, with the approval of the scientific director and task force commander. The higher integrated level (HIL) was 100 mSv and the special higher integrated level (SHIL) was 250 mSv; the latter was allowed only for persons not normally occupationally exposed.

Monitoring test personnel

14. The chief means of monitoring personnel were individual film badge dosimeters (FBD). They measured radiation dose with considerable accuracy. For men working in 'active' – that is, radioactive – areas, badges were issued before each sortie and were developed and read, and the doses recorded, daily.
15. Entry to active areas was strictly controlled. Health escorts, with additional monitoring instruments, accompanied working parties into active areas and managed their movements so as to keep radiation exposures within prescribed limits.
16. Quartz fibre dosimeters (QFD) were sometimes issued with FBDs. Though less reliable they could be operationally useful in some circumstances because they gave instantaneous readings.
17. For most trials personnel, not working in active areas, radiation exposure was so low that an FBD could be worn throughout the whole trial period before being read, or might not be necessary at all.

The radiation record

18. The degree of success in complying with standards is shows by the radiation record. Tables A4.1–A4.3 below summarize the radiation records of 13,950 participants in the four *Grapple* trials.

Table A4.1   Number of men involved at each operation by service or employer

| | \multicolumn{5}{c}{*Service or employer*} |
	RN	*Army*	*RAF*	*AWRE*	*Total*
Grapple	1,722	638	1,038	117	3,515
Grapple X	597	625	1,009	107	2,338
Grapple Y	851	1,331	1,426	114	3,722
Grapple Z	738	1,438	2,017	182	4,375
Total	3,908	4,032	5,490	520	13,950

Table A4.2   Numbers of men mentioned in health physics (HP) records as a percentage of all participants

Operation	Total test participants	Number of men		
		Total mentioned in HP	Mentioned in HP with zero dose	Mentioned in HP with non-zero dose
Grapple	3,515	83 (2%)	4	79
Grapple X	2,338	179 (8%)	53	126
Grapple Y	3,722	114 (3%)	18	96
Grapple Z	4,375	618 (14%)	395	223

Note: The numbers with zero recorded dose may be an under-estimate, as some lists of men who wore radiation dosimeters, but for whom no dose was recorded, have been destroyed.

Table A4.3   Exposures in excess of 30 mSv

	Grapple	Grapple X	Grapple Y	Grapple Z	*Total*
No. of participants above 30 mSv	14	12	9	37	72
No. of participants above 100 mSv	0	3	6	8	17
No. of participants above 250 mSv	0	0	0	2	2

The health record

19. The radiation record is promptly available, the health record, of course, is not. It is on the long-term health outcome that the effectiveness of protection standards and procedures will eventually be assessed.
20. Table A4.4 summarizes the latest available mortality statistics (a) for participants at all the weapon tests and (b) for a matched control group. Observed (O) and expected (E) deaths are compared and standardized mortality ratios (SMRs – based on national rates adjusted for various factors including age and sex) are given.
21. Table 4.5 (*Grapple* participants only) shows mortality from leukaemia and other cancers. Observed (O) and expected (E), and SMRs are shown.

Table A4.4   Observed deaths (O), deaths expected from national rates (E) and standardized mortality ratios (SMR) among test participants and controls

Cause of death (ICD codes 9th Revision)	Test participants			Controls		
	O	E	SMR	O	E	SMR
All neoplasms	762	921.99	0.83	850	992.06	0.86
Other diseases	1,564	2,048.12	0.76	1,662	2,218.13	0.75
Accidents and violence	372	305.28	1.22	359	302.72	1.19
Unknown	55	–	–	68	–	–
All causes	2,753	3,275.40	0.84	2,939	3,512.92	0.84

Table A4.5   Mortality from leukaemia and other neoplasms among *Grapple* participants

Operation	Cause of death	O	E	SMR
Grapple	Leukaemia: whole follow-up period	6	4.90	1.22
	Leukaemia: 2–25 years	4	2.61	1.53
	Other neoplasms: 10+ years	112	138.85	0.81
Grapple X	Leukaemia: whole follow-up period	4	3.23	1.24
	Leukaemia: 2–25 years	2	1.75	1.14
	Other neoplasms: 10+ years	80	91.22	0.88
Grapple Y	Leukaemia: whole follow-up period	5	4.69	1.07
	Leukaemia: 2–25 years	2	2.64	0.76
	Other neoplasms: 10+ years	115	123.44	0.93
Grapple Z	Leukaemia: whole follow-up period	6	5.63	1.07
	Leukaemia: 2–25 years	4	3.20	1.25
	Other neoplasms: 10+ years	125	150.85	0.83

22. The health record reveals 'no detectable effect on the participants' expectation of life, nor on their risk of developing cancer or other fatal diseases'.

Appendix 5
A 1985 Claim

A letter to the prime minister

In 1985, when new scientific talent was being so urgently sought for the British H-bomb project, Dr John Ward was a brilliant acquisition. He came to Aldermaston with outstanding recommendations. Born in 1924, by 1950 he had already won an international reputation in physics and had given his name to a basic theorem of quantum electrodynamics (the 'Ward Identities').

In May 1985 – an FRS, winner of the Royal Society's Hughes Medal and the American Danny Heineman prize, with a distinguished scientific career in the United States and Australia – he wrote to Prime Minister Margaret Thatcher as follows:

> In the spring of 1955 advertisements were prominently displayed for theoretical physicists to join the staff at Aldermaston ... I was offered a position but decided to refuse ... When I telephoned William Cook to tell him of this decision, he was so upset that I said I would come if the matter was sufficiently urgent. He said it was indeed most urgent ...
>
> To my amazement, when I reached Aldermaston I was assigned the improbable job of uncovering the secret of the Ulam-Teller invention, an idea of genius far beyond the talents of the personnel at Aldermaston, a fact well-known to both Cook and Penney.
>
> Under great stress, and with no assistance whatever, I came up with the correct scheme within six months, minor modifications excepted (and also obvious precautions). When presented at a subsequent meeting, a crucial one, judging by the full-dress uniform of the visiting Admiral, my proposal (with working drawings of a primary), the only one offered, was peremptorily rejected by Penney, who declared the matter not to be urgent anyway! I was supported barely pro-forma, if at all, by Cook. Afterwards Penney demonstrated his complete lack of understanding of the problem in a private talk with Cook and myself. I was not invited to subsequent meetings held to discuss the project.
>
> I therefore quite correctly and naturally resigned forthwith, and returned to the US taking the first job I could get.

This letter was later quoted by Hansen in 1988 in *US Nuclear Weapons* and in 1994 was published in Volume V of *Nuclear Weapons Databook*.

Publicity

Meanwhile, the story had been publicized in 1992 by a long interview in a Portuguese newspaper (*O Publico*) which was picked up by the British press ('I'm father of the British H-bomb', in *The Independent*, 19 April 1992). The story then featured in a three-page article in the *London Review of Books* of 22 October 1992 ('Britain's Thermonuclear

Bluff', by the theoretical physicist, Norman Dombey, and Eric Grove, historian and defence analyst).

This article, in a conjectural account of the *Grapple* tests, suggested that one of the four devices tested in 1957 was a large fission bomb and three were boosted devices intended to bluff the Americans.* It went on to argue that, without Dr Ward's invention in 1955, Britain would have had no H-bomb tests in 1958, so that recent British history might well have been very different. (It is not explained why the 1955 invention was used in 1958 but not 1957.)

Sources of information

In seeking evidence we have had three sources: (1) the archives at Aldermaston; (2) information given to us by Dr Ward; and (3) discussions with former Aldermaston scientists who were closely involved in H-bomb research at the time.

1. A thorough archives search revealed no weapon design but yielded the following information. In the summer of 1955 Dr John Ward was appointed to Aldermaston's theoretical physics division and his immediate superior was Dr Herbert Pike, who had five groups under him: Ward was group leader of 'new devices' and his colleagues were Roberts, a principal scientific officer, and Russell, a scientific officer; the other groups dealt with implosion (9), experiments (2), Ferranti (6), and special problems (2). During 1955 the 82-strong theoretical physics division produced 123 scientific reports (TPNs); none was by Ward but his name occurs in the last one (TPN 123/55 – see Chapter 7). Ward was recorded as present at ten meetings of the Astrophysics Committee (see Chapter 6) and at the second meeting of the Radiation Committee set up in November 1955 to co-ordinate work on radiation hydrodynamics. There is little sign of interaction, except with Roberts.
2. Dr Ward was most helpful in providing information, both by mail and in person when visiting Oxford. When asked if he could recall his blackboard drawing of 1955 (see Chapter 7) he readily drew his conceptual sketch from memory. It seemed clear from his answers and the sketch that the Ward concept, whatever its intrinsic value, had not been the basis for the various *Grapple* devices (a fact he could not have known without access to later British work after he left Aldermaston).
3. We were too late to talk to Sir William Cook or, most unfortunately, K. V. Roberts. Of other physicists who worked on H-bomb problems in the 1950s, some did not remember John Ward and a few recalled personal details and events. Only John Corner had a distinct memory of his scientific ideas. (Clearly Ward – though he had a high regard for Pike and Roberts – worked, as he said, almost entirely alone; Corner commented that he did not 'fit in'.) Corner's enquiring mind found Ward's ideas original and interesting, and he himself apparently continued speculating on rather similar lines for years. However, he said, the British designers found a different solution, of limited potential but more immediately appropriate to Britain's urgent low-megaton requirement.

---

* This was answered by John Baylis in an article in *Contemporary Record* (see Bibliography).

Conclusion

The weapon concept Dr Ward produced at Aldermaston in 1955 was perhaps an advanced concept of much scientific interest. However, it was not developed, and was not the basis of the British H-bomb. That fact, as well as the lack of documentary evidence, puts it beyond the scope of a book concerned with what actually happened, not what might have happened. It is a tantalising subject.

Notes and References

This book is based predominantly on material in files still in the AWE (formerly AWRE) archives at Aldermaston. As these files are (at present) closed, they have not been cited. However it is hoped to compile a booklet of references as was done for earlier official atomic energy histories.

Various documents that we have seen in Aldermaston files, and not cited, are undoubtedly also to be found in Whitehall files, some of which may be in the Public Record Office. However it was not practicable for us to trace them to other sources.

Preface

1. J. Carson Mark, 'The Purpose of Test Explosions', in J. Goldblatt and D. Cox. *Nuclear Weapon Tests: Prohibition or Limitation?*
2. N. Bradbury in L. Badash *et al.* (eds), *Reminiscences of Los Alamos 1943–1945*, pp. 161–75.
3. Conversation with the late V. H. B. Macklen, 3 Sept. 1982.
4. Conversation with the late Dr F. Morgan, 21 March 1983.
5. G. A. Goncharov, 'Thermonuclear Milestones', *Physics Today*, Nov. 1996, 44.

1 Stellar Forces

1. A. S. Eddington quoted by J. H. Hendry in 'The Scientific Origins of Controlled Fusion Technology', *Annals of Science*, 44, 1987, pp. 143–86.
2. See *inter alia* E. Teller, 'The Work of Many People', *Science*, 25 Feb. 1955, and *Better a Shield than a Sword*, p. 66; R. Rhodes, *The Making of the Atomic Bomb*, pp. 370–1.
3. See J. H. Hendry, (op. cit.).
4. S. M. Ulam, *Adventures of a Mathematician*, p. 51; H. F. York, *The Advisors*, p. 20.
5. Heavy water (D_2O) contains heavy hydrogen atoms (deuterium – D). Heavy water was discovered by the American chemist Harold Urey in 1932 and the first sample of heavy water was produced in the United States in 1933 by Gilbert Lewis.
6. R. Rhodes, *Dark Sun*, p. 247.
7. Bethe was also working on reactions between hydrogen and carbon which are not relevant here.
8. S. M. Ulam, op. cit., p. 150.
9. R. Rhodes, *Dark Sun*, pp. 247–8.

2 The First Superbomb Project – the United States

1. R. G. Hewlett and O. E. Anderson, *The New World: a History of the US Atomic Energy Commission, Vol. I 1939–1946*, p. 104, R. Rhodes, *Dark Sun*, p. 248; D. Hawkins *et al.*, *Project Y: The Los Alamos Story Part I*, p. 86; L. Hoddeson *et al.*, *Critical Assembly: a Technical History of Los Alamos during the Oppenheimer Years, 1943–1945*, 1993, pp. 45–6.

2. R. G. Hewlett and O. E. Anderson, op. cit., p. 240, D. Hawkins, op. cit., p. 87.
3. D. Hawkins, op. cit., p. 87.
4. R. G. Hewlett and O. E. Anderson, op. cit., pp. 625–7; H. F. York, op. cit., pp. 16–19; D. Hawkins, op. cit., pp. 267–8, 356–68.
5. D. Hawkins, op. cit., p. 308, S. M. Ulam, op. cit., pp. 172–89, H. F. York, op. cit., pp. 22–5. R. Rhodes, op. cit., pp. 252–5. J. Carson Mark, 'A Short Account of Los Alamos Theoretical Work on Thermonuclear Weapons 1946–50.
6. R. Rhodes, *Dark Sun*, pp. 252–4. G. A. Goncharov, 'Beginnings of the Soviet H–bomb Program', *Physics Today*, special issue, Nov. 1996.
7. G. A. Goncharov, 'The American Effort', *Physics Today*, Nov. 1996.
8. S. M. Ulam, op. cit., p. 150.
9. D. Hawkins, op. cit., pp. 305–6. J. Carson Mark, op. cit. Bethe worked at Los Alamos for two months a year in 1949, 1950 and 1951 and 11 months in 1952–53. Fermi worked there for 2–10 weeks a year for 10 years, and Gamow for several months during 1949–50. Teller was there for nine months in 1946–49, and full time from June 1949 to October 1951.
10. H. F. York, op. cit., p. 55.
11. H. F. York, op. cit., p. 34, R. G. Hewlett and F. Duncan, *Atomic Shield: a History of the United States Atomic Energy Commission, Volume II 1947/1952*, pp. 362–4, R. Rhodes, op. cit., pp. 368–73.
12. R. G. Hewlett and F. Duncan, op. cit., pp. 373–4. H. F. York, op. cit., pp. 40–6, R. Rhodes, op. cit., pp. 381–408.
13. R. G. Hewlett and F. Duncan, op. cit., pp. 373–4.
14. Ibid., p. 375.
15. Ibid., p. 376.
16. Ibid., p. 380.
17. Ibid., p. 379.
18. Ibid., p.380.
19. Ibid., p.380.
20. Ibid., pp. 381–5, R. Rhodes, op. cit., pp. 395–402.
21. R. G. Hewlett and F. Duncan, op. cit., pp. 382–3.
22. Ibid., p. 384.
23. Ibid., p. 385.
24. Ibid., pp. 385–8. H. F. York, op. cit., pp. 56–9. R. Rhodes, op. cit., p. 404.
25. D. Holloway, *Stalin and the Bomb: The Soviet Union and Atomic Energy 1939–1956*, pp. 99, 318.
26. R. G. Hewlett and F. Duncan, op. cit., p. 388.
27. Ibid., p. 388.
28. Ibid., p. 393.
29. Ibid., p. 392.
30. Ibid., pp. 393–4.
31. Ibid., p. 395, R. Rhodes, op. cit., pp. 406–7.
32. R. G. Hewlett and F. Duncan, pp. 396–7.
33. Ibid., p. 396.
34. Ibid., pp. 403–5.
35. Ibid., p. 405.
36. Ibid., p. 403.
37. H. F. York, op. cit., p. 69, R. G. Hewlett and F. Duncan, op. cit., p. 415.
38. R. G. Hewlett and F. Duncan, op. cit., pp. 406–9. H. F. York, op cit., pp. 65–9.
39. R. G. Hewlett and F. Duncan, op. cit., p. 408, H. F. York, op. cit., pp. 69–70.

40. H. Bethe, 'Comments on the History of the H-bomb', *Los Alamos Science*, autumn 1982, p. 49.
41. R. Rhodes, op. cit., pp. 252, 304–5, 400.
42. Ibid., pp. 418–19.
43. R. G. Hewlett and F. Duncan, op. cit., pp. 439–40, R. Rhodes, op. cit., pp. 422–4, 455–6.
44. R. G. Hewlett and F. Duncan, op. cit., p. 440, R. Rhodes, op. cit., p. 424.
45. R. Rhodes, op. cit., pp. 455–6.
46. R. Rhodes, op. cit., pp. 456–7, R. G. Hewlett and F. Duncan, op. cit., pp. 441, 539–40.
47. R. Rhodes, op. cit., p. 457.
48. R. G. Hewlett and F. Duncan, op. cit., pp. 529–31, R. Rhodes, op. cit., pp. 459–61.
49. R. Rhodes, op. cit., pp. 462–72, R. G. Hewlett and F. Duncan, op. cit., pp. 536–7.
50. R. Rhodes, op. cit., p. 463. H. F. York, op. cit., p. 79, S. Ulam, op. cit., pp. 219–21.
51. R. Rhodes, op. cit., pp. 466–7.
52. Ibid., pp. 469–70.
53. Ibid., p. 470.
54. Ibid., p. 412. G. A. Goncharov writes of the Fuchs-von Neumann patent:

So in spring 1946 the principle of radiation implosion was born ... Fuchs' design, the first physical scheme to use the radiation implosion principle, was a prototype for the future Teller-Ulam configuration. Fuchs' proposal, truly remarkable in the wealth of ideas that it embodied, was far ahead of its time. Indeed, mathematical modelling of the physical processes involved was not yet advanced enough to further develop Fuchs' idea. It would take another five years in the US for the enormous conceptual potential ... to be fully substantiated. (G. A. Goncharov, 'The American Effort', *Physics Today*, special issue, Nov. 1996.)

55. Ibid., pp. 467–8.
56. Ibid., pp. 471–2.
57. The title of a 1955 article by Teller (*Science*, 1955, pp. 121–267). see Rhodes, op. cit., pp. 466–71.
58. H. F. York, op. cit., p. 77, R. G. Hewlett and F. Duncan, op. cit., pp. 541–2. F. Shelton, *Reflections of a Nuclear Weaponeer*, pp. 4/14–37, R. Rhodes, op. cit., pp. 473–4, B. C. Hacker, *Elements of Controversy*, pp. 53–9.
59. H. F. York, op. cit., p. 77, R. G. Hewlett and F. Duncan, op. cit., pp. 542–5. R. Rhodes, op. cit., pp. 475–7. F. Shelton, op. cit., p. 4/37.
60. R. Rhodes, op. cit., pp. 477–9.
61. R. Rhodes, op. cit., pp. 484–5.
62. This excellent phrase is Richard Rhodes's (op. cit., p. 486).
63. R. Rhodes, op. cit., pp. 486–7, 489–96.
64. Ibid., p. 485.
65. Ibid., pp. 494–5.
66. Ibid., pp. 497–8.
67. Ibid., p. 503.
68. R. Rhodes, op. cit., pp. 498–512, F. Shelton, op. cit., pp. 5/30–44, H. F. York, op. cit., pp. 82–3, B. C. Hacker, op. cit., pp. 86–9.
69. H. F. York, op. cit., p. 83–4.
70. R. Rhodes, op. cit., p. 541, R. G. Hewlett and J. M. Holl, *Atoms for Peace and War 1953–1961*, pp. 164–6.

71. R. G. Hewlett and J. M. Holl, op. cit., p. 170. B. C. Hacker, op. cit., pp. 131–52. F. Shelton, op. cit., pp. 6/34–43.
72. R. Rhodes, op. cit., p. 541.
73. R. G. Hewlett and J. M. Holl, op. cit., p. 173.
74. R. Rhodes, op. cit., pp. 541–2.
75. R. G. Hewlett and J. M. Holl, op. cit., pp. 174–5.
76. R. Rhodes, op. cit., p. 542, R. G. Hewlett and J. M. Holl, op. cit., pp. 175–7. R. A. Divine, *Blowing on the Wind: The Nuclear Test Ban Debate 1954–60*, pp. 3–9. R. E. Lapp, *The Voyage of the Lucky Dragon*, B. C. Hacker, op. cit., pp. 149–52.
77. R. A. Divine, op. cit., p. 13.
78. R. A. Divine, op. cit., pp. 21–2.
79. R. A. Divine, op. cit., pp. 20–1.
80. Ibid., p. 23.
81. Ibid., pp. 23–4.
82. Ibid., pp. 27–33.
83. R. G. Hewlett and J. M. Holl, op. cit., pp. 173–4. B. C. Hacker, op. cit., pp. 152–8.
84. R. G. Hewlett and J. M. Holl, op. cit., pp. 179–80.
85. Ibid., p. 331, F. Shelton, op. cit., pp. 7/30–41.
86. R. G. Hewlett and J. M. Holl, op. cit., pp. 456–7, 482–3.

3 The Second Superbomb Project – the Soviet Union

1. G. A. Goncharov, 'Beginnings of the Soviet H-bomb program', *Physics Today*, Nov. 1996.
2. R. Rhodes, *Dark Sun*, p. 121.
3. H. Bethe *et al.*, 'Did Bohr share nuclear secrets?', *Scientific American*, May 1995, pp. 65–70, G. A. Goncharov, 'Beginnings of the Soviet H-bomb program', *Physics Today*, Nov. 1996, pp. 50–4; D. Holloway, *Stalin and the Bomb*, p. 142; R. Rhodes, *Dark Sun*, pp. 217–21.
4. G. A. Goncharov, 'Beginnings of the Soviet H-bomb program', *Physics Today*, Nov. 1996, pp. 50–54.
5. D. Holloway, *Stalin and the Bomb*, p. 295; G. A. Goncharov, 'Beginnings of the Soviet H-bomb program', *Physics Today*, Nov. 1996; R. Rhodes, *Dark Sun*, p. 256. Goncharov gives the date as 1945 but this must be an error.
6. S. Leskov, 'Dividing the Glory of the Fathers', *Bulletin of the Atomic Scientists*, May 1993.
7. H. Bethe quoted in D. Holloway, 'New Light on Early Soviet Bomb Secrets', *Physics Today*, Nov. 1996.
8. G. A. Goncharov, 'The American Effort', *Physics Today*, Nov. 1996.
9. G. A. Goncharov, 'Beginnings of the Soviet H-bomb Program', *Physics Today*, Nov. 1996.
10. Ibid.
11. See D. Holloway, 'Soviet scientists speak out', and R. Sagdeev, 'Russian Scientists save American Secrets', *Bulletin of the Atomic Scientists*, May 1993.
12. T. Reed and A. Kramish, 'Trinity at Dubna', *Physics Today*, Nov. 1996.
13. Boris Vannikov administered the Soviet nuclear weapons programme from 1945 to 1953.
14. G. A. Goncharov, 'Beginnings of the Soviet H-bomb program', *Physics Today*, Nov. 1996.

15. Autobiographical essay quoted in S. D. Drell and S. P. Kapitza, *Sakharov Remembered*, p. 87.

16. D. Holloway, *Stalin and the Bomb*, p. 298; R. Rhodes, *Dark Sun*, pp. 334–5; G. A. Goncharov, 'Beginnings of the Soviet H-bomb program', *Physics Today*, Nov. 1996; Y. A. Romanov, 'The Father of the Soviet H-bomb', and H. Bethe, 'Sakharov's H-bomb' in S. D. Drell and S. P. Kapitza (eds), *Sakharov Remembered*.

17. The 'second idea' may or may not have been wholly independent. It may have owed something to an intelligence report from Los Alamos to Moscow a year earlier.

18. J. Albright and M. Kunstel, *Bombshell*, pp. 186–7.

19. S. D. Drell and S. P. Kapitza (eds), *Sakharov Remembered*, p. 93.

20. D. Holloway, op. cit., p. 305.

21. A. Sakharov, *Memoirs*, p. 158, said that snow that had been collected for analysis in the laboratory was accidentally thrown away. D. Holloway, op. cit., p. 312.

22. D. Holloway, op. cit., p. 314. A. Sakharov, *Memoirs*, pp. 169–73. R. Rhodes, *Dark Sun*, pp. 523–4.

23. D. Holloway, 'Soviet scientists speak out', *Bulletin of the Atomic Scientists*, May 1993; D. Holloway, *Stalin and the Bomb*, p. 312.

24. Y. Khariton and Y. Smirnov, 'The Khariton Version', *The Bulletin of the Atomic Scientists*, May 1993.

25. D. Holloway, *Stalin and the Bomb*, pp. 313–14; A. Sakharov, *Memoirs*, pp. 182–6; G. A. Goncharov, 'The Race Accelerates', *Physics Today*, Nov. 1996.

26. D. Holloway, *Stalin and the Bomb*, pp. 313–14. A. Sakharov, *Memoirs*, pp.183–90.

27. A. Sakharov, *Memoirs*, p. 190.

28. Ibid., p. 191.

29. Ibid., p. 192.

30. A detailed account of 'the third idea' is given by G. A. Goncharov in 'The Race Accelerates', *Physics Today*, Nov. 1996. A scientific report of 23 June 1955 listed 37 scientists and mathematicians as contributors to the theory of the two-stage H-bomb (RDS 37). Lenin Prizes were awarded to Kurchatov, Sakharov, Khariton and Zeldovich (see S. D. Drell and S. F. Kapitza, *Sakharov Remembered*, p. 131)

4 What Must Britain do?

1. M. Gowing, *Independence and Deterrence*, vol. 1, pp. 440–50.

2. See R. G. Hewlett and O. Anderson, *The New World*, pp. 714–22; M. Gowing, op. cit., pp. 104–12 and *passim*; J. Simpson, *The Independent Nuclear State*, pp. 38–9, 76–9; A. J. R. Groom, *British Thinking about Nuclear Weapons*, pp. 29–30, 115; J. Baylis, *Anglo-American Defence Relations*, pp. 24–8 and *Ambiguity and Deterrence*, *passim*.

3. S. Duke's *US Defence Bases in the United Kingdom* is indispensable.

4. R. Rhodes, *Dark Sun*, p. 347.

5. J. Baylis, *Ambiguity and Deterrence*, p. 71 and *Anglo-American Defence Relations*, pp. 34–5.

6. N. Wheeler, 'British Nuclear Weapons and Anglo-American Relations 1945–54', *International Affairs*, winter 1985–86, p. 72, cites DEFE 7/516 'US air force groups in the UK', 4 Jan. 1950.

7. J. Baylis, *Ambiguity and Deterrence*, p. 118, cites DEFE 4/32, COS(50)17, 27 July 1950.
8. S. Dukes op. cit., pp. 13 and 223, and L. Freedman *The Evolution of Nuclear Strategy*, pp. 69–70.
9. J. Baylis, op. cit., p. 118.
10. S. Duke, op. cit., p. 50–61, Baylis, op. cit., p. 119.
11. J. Baylis, op. cit., pp. 119–20; M. Gowing, op. cit., pp. 316–17.
12. J. Baylis, op. cit., pp. 140–2.
13. M. Gowing, op. cit., p. 450.
14. For a full account of Sir James Chadwick's work as head of the British Mission to the Manhattan Project see A. Brown, *The Neutron on the Bomb*. See also M. Gowing, *Britain and Atomic Energy 1939–45, passim*, and F. M. Szasz, *British Scientists and the Manhattan Project*.
15. Sir John Anderson, later Lord Waverley, was a scientist–politician who played a key role in British wartime and post-war atomic affairs, and in the 1950s chaired the committee which led to the setting up of the UKAEA.
16. Lord Portal, a Marshal of the Royal Air Force, served in World Wars I and II, commanded Bomber Command, and was later Chief of the Air Staff. For his atomic energy role see Gowing, *Independence and Deterrence*, vol. 1, ch. 2 and *passim*.
17. See R. C. Williams, *Klaus Fuchs, Atom Spy*; R. Rhodes, *The Making of the Atomic Bomb, passim*, and *Dark Sun, passim*; B. Cathcart, *Test of Greatness*, pp. 99–107; M. Gowing, op. cit., vol. 2, ch. 16.
18. Sir Christopher (later Lord) Hinton, a distinguished engineer from ICI, had played a key role in armament production during World War II, and was then appointed to head Britain's post-war atomic production organization.
19. There is an excellent account of him in P. Hennessy, *Whitehall*.
20. The *modus vivendi* is reproduced in full in M. Gowing, *Independence and Deterrence*, vol. 1, pp. 266–72.
21. The papers and minutes of this series of meetings under Brook's chairmanship were numbered retrospectively, not at the time of issue, and some error seems to have been made in the sequence of numbers. We therefore refer to the meetings simply as GEN. 465 with the date.
22. R. A. Divine, *Blowing on the Wind*, p. 6.
23. *Daily Herald*, 17 March 1954.
24. R. A. Divine, *Blowing on the Wind*, p. 8.
25. R. A. Divine, op. cit., pp. 7–8.
26. This paper, with a separate intelligence report, was later submitted to the (ministerial) Committee on Defence Policy set up in April 1954 'to review, in the light of the recent development of nuclear weapons, the strategic hypotheses underlying current defence policy and the scale and pattern of defence programmes, military and civil'. The Prime Minister (who chaired the committee) wished it to keep prominently in mind the aim of securing a saving of £150 million in the defence expenditure forecast for 1955. (NB There had been a differently constituted committee of the same name in 1954 'to consider the future level of defence expenditure'.)
27. *Reynolds News and Sunday Citizen*, 28 March 1954.
28. HC Deb., 30 Mar. 1954.
29. Headline in *Daily Mirror*, 1 Apr. 1954.
30. *Daily Express*, 3 Mar. 1954.
31. HC Deb., 5 Apr. 1954.
32. The text of the 1943 Quebec Agreement is published in M. Gowing, *Britain and Atomic Energy 1939–45*, pp. 439–40.

33. Churchill said that Senator McMahon told him that 'if we had seen this agreement there would have been no McMahon Act'. This is discussed in A. Pierre, *Nuclear Politics*, pp. 117–20.
34. The typed copy is unsigned but a MS version is signed by Dolphin and dated both March and April 1954. It bears a note 'One copy typed for DAWRE [Penney] only.'
35. It started as a very small group, with meetings carefully minuted but with very few copies made. The membership increased but was always variable. Penney attended twice. Its purpose was to exchange scientific ideas and the discussions were wide-ranging. Many of the scientific papers circulated as TPNs were discussed. The committee held its last meeting in 1956 about the time that the WDPC was set up – see chapter 6.
36. GEN 464/1st meeting. Those present were the Prime Minister, the Foreign Secretary, the Chancellor of the Exchequer, the Lord President, the Minister of Defence, the Commonwealth Secretary, and Sir Norman Brook.
37. D. A. Rosenberg, *Origins of Overkill*, p. 38.
38. Ibid.
39. They were organised and catalogued in detail by Corner personally – a very busy division head – so he must have regarded them as especially important. Their destruction at some later date leaves a most unfortunate gap in our nuclear weapons history.
40. A subordinate committee of the Chiefs of Staff. The chairman was Sir Frederick Brundrett (chief scientific adviser to the Ministry of Defence). Members were: General Sir Frederick Morgan (Controller of Atomic Weapons, Ministry of Supply); the Deputy Chiefs of Staff; the scientific advisers of the Service ministries; Cockcroft and Penney.
41. The British guests present were the Prime Minister, Lord Cherwell, Christopher Soames, General Nye, and John Colville (who took notes).

5 A General Instruction from the Government

1. On 27 July 1954. See Chapter 4.
2. *In the Matter of J. Robert Oppenheimer – Transcript of Hearing before Personnel Security Board Washington DC 12 Apr. 1954, through 6, May 1954* was published by the USAEC in 1954. Aldermaston scientists had a pre-publication transcript which had been sanitised by deletion of classified words and passages. They studied the scientific evidence with minute attention, sometimes deducing clues from the length of the deleted words.
3. See Chapter 6.
4. *Statement on Defence*, HMSO, Cmd 9391, 1955.
5. See Chapter 3.
6. HC Deb., vol. 537, cols 1894–1905, 1 Mar. 1955.
7. HC Deb., vol. 537, col. 2175, 2 Mar. 1955.
8. See A. J. R. Groom, *British Thinking about Nuclear Weapons*, pp. 146–54.
9. From Lord Moran's diaries, quoted in J. Baylis, *Ambiguity and Deterrence*, pp. 178–9.
10. Ibid.
11. For the *Mosaic* and *Buffalo* trials see L. Arnold, *A Very Special Relationship*, chs 7 and 8.
12. *Bulletin of the Atomic Scientists*, vol. XI, no. 5, May 1955. See L. Arnold, op. cit., p. 79.
13. See Chapter 6.

6 Aldermaston and the Weaponeers

1. Edwin Plowden (now Lord Plowden) worked in the wartime Ministries of Economic Warfare and Aircraft Production, then at the Cabinet Office, and as Chief Planning Officer in the Treasury before being appointed as Chairman of the UK Atomic Energy Authority, a post he held for five years, 1954–59.

2. For convenience, the name Aldermaston is used to refer to the main site, the Atomic Weapons Research Establishment itself (AWRE) or to the Weapons Group as a whole, especially as we are most often concerned with what was happening at the main site.

3. He worked on bombing effects during the Blitz and then on the design of the Mulberry harbours which played such an important part in the Allied landings in Normandy in 1944.

4. See M. Gowing, *Independence and Deterrence*, vol. 2, p. 218 and ch. 13 *passim*.

5. B. Cathcart, *Test of Greatness*, p. 130.

6. Penney wrote of him '. . . a most capable man with excellent personal qualities ... He is very self-reliant and not perturbed by a job, however heavy and complex it may be'. He 'imbued his team with an excellent spirit of co-operation', B. Cathcart, op. cit., p. 68.

7. In 1952, Penney's own salary was £3,400; those of Hinton and Cockcroft were £4,500. The Director-General of Works, Ministry of Works, was paid £3,250.

8. M. Gowing, *Independence and Deterrence*, vol. 2, p. 72.

9. These included James Tuck and Ernest Titterton.

10. At Los Alamos, Peierls and Fuchs provided two-thirds of the team which made the implosion development possible and contributed to all phases of weapon development (including the Super). The solid implosion gadget invented by Peierls and Christy is commonly called the Christy gadget but was Peierls' idea. Tuck, independently and with the US scientists Neddermeyer and von Neumann, suggested the lens system for implosion and worked with Bethe on the initiator. Frisch made many contributions, especially to critical mass assembly studies. Bretscher made considerable contributions to Super feasibility studies. Titterton did outstanding work, particularly on electronic circuit developments. Rotblat worked with several others in the field of experimental nuclear physics. See F. Szasz, *British Scientists and the Manhattan Project*, pp. 148–51.

11. As in, for example, N. Dombey and E. Grove, 'Britain's Thermonuclear Bluff'.

12. In early 1950, a collection of his papers was sent from Harwell to Aldermaston (see Chapter 4, n. 40). In 1963, when Corner asked to look at the catalogue he had made, he discovered that they had been transferred to London and later destroyed.

13. L. Arnold, *A Very Special Relationship*, ch. 4.

14. Senior posts vacant included deputy director, assistant director (science), two deputy chief engineers and head of radiation division.

15. One was Ernest Titterton, the telemetry expert, who decided to go to the new Australian National University (ANU).

16. This refutes the idea, sometimes suggested, that Cook was imposed by Whitehall on an unwilling Penney.

17. Transcript of interview Cook/Gowing, 10 March 1976 (now in AWE historian's office).

18. Interview Curran/Arnold, 21–2 February 1995 (now in AWE historian's office).

19. See P. Hennessy, *Whitehall* Chapter 3 *passim*.

20. See n. 18.

21. Interview Corner/Arnold, 18 Sept. 1992.

22. Lord Penney and V.H.B. Macklen, 'William Richard Joseph Cook 1905–1987', *Biographical Memoirs of Fellows of the Royal Society*, vol. 34, 1988.
23. See n. 17.
24. See n. 18.
25. See n. 21.
26. See n. 18. A study of family and educational backgrounds would be interesting. Most of the nuclear scientists and engineers, like Penney, were 'scholarship boys', unlike many of the politicians, military men and civil servants involved.
27. Also called, at various times, the radiation division or the radioactive measurements division.
28. Though Cook thought highly of Egon Bretscher's work at Harwell.
29. See n. 21.
30. A. Sakharov, *Memoirs*, p. 84.
31. Reasons suggested are extreme security-consciousness, lack of time and overload, or even a desire to protect 'under the counter' information. Corner said that he did not get data on foreign weapons debris until 1956. We were told that Cook organised 'a raid' on Penney's safe in 1955 or 1956.
32. See n. 18.
33. Interview Roberts/Hendry, 21 Sept. 1981.
34. Under E. F. Newley (later Director of AWRE) and J. W. High.

7 The Megaton Mission

1. A Service opinion expressed by Sir William Dixon was that, in any case, it seemed improbable that Type B, as then envisaged, could be used effectively as a strategic weapon.
2. The potential of lithium deuteride had been remarked on early in 1953 by Aldermaston chemist D. T. Lewis but was more or less ignored. *Joe 4* confirmed its importance.
3. See Appendix 5.
4. It is not clear when the name *Green Granite* first came into use, or exactly what it denoted originally. *Granite* was the word associated with a double bomb device but may not have been so when first used.
5. J. B. Taylor came to Aldermaston in Aug. 1955 so that meeting cannot have been earlier.
6. Interview Ward/Arnold 24 Aug. 1995. See also Appendix 5.
7. There was apparently no record of this meeting, and we do not know the precise date. This account is based on information from Dr Corner, Dr Pike and Dr Allen.
8. Interview Allen/Arnold, 30 Apr. 1993 and conversation 26 June 1995.
9. Letter Pike/Arnold, 9 June 1995.
10. No record appears to exist. We are dependent on the memory of Dr Ward (see Appendix 5) and of Dr Corner, who remembered the blackboard drawing as showing a staged device which appeared to use radiation implosion of a spherical secondary.
11. In particular, a great deal of complex computation is required.
12. At the *Mosaic* test (2 shots) off the NW coast of Australia in May 1956. See Arnold, *A Very Special Relationship*, ch. 7.
13. TPN 123/55. TPN stood for Theoretical Physics Division Note; many 'notes' were big reports of 50 pages or so.

14. No record of the colloquium has been found so far.
15. Uranium-233, 234, 235, 236 and 238.
16. This was a Nuclear Physics Branch Note, NPBN 56/1 of 14 February 1956.
17. This was a transcript of the hearings, 'in the matter of J Robert Oppenheimer', by the United States Atomic Energy Commission (USAEC) Personnel Security Board, 12 Apr.–6 May 1954. A vast amount of scientific evidence was taken.
18. This was not the design used for the *Granites* fired at *Grapple* (they had many shells in Dick) but seems to resemble the simpler *Grapple X* device (see Chapters 10 and 11).

8 Captain Cook's Coral Island

1. W. E. Oulton, *Christmas Cracker*, p. 7.
2. This Whitehall committee, chaired by the Controller of Atomic Weapons in the Ministry of Supply, was the Atomic Weapons Trials Executive when dealing with weapons and trials in general but in dealing with individual trials became Totex, Mosex, Grapex, and so on.
3. W. E. Oulton, op. cit., p. 321.
4. See also L. Arnold, op. cit., pp. 79–80, 83–6.

9 Racing Against Time

1. R. A. Divine, *Blowing in the Wind*, p. 9.
2. Ibid., pp. 9–13; B. C. Hacker, *Elements of Controversy*, pp. 139–48; L. Arnold, *A Very Special Relationship*, pp. 77–80.
3. R. A. Divine, op. cit., p. 19.
4. Ibid., p. 4.
5. Ibid., p. 20.
6. T. J. Botti, *The Long Wait*, ch. 15.
7. R. G. Hewlett and J. M. Holl, *Atoms for Peace and War* p. 275.
8. R. A. Divine, op. cit., pp. 29–31.
9. J. Baylis, *Anglo-American Defence Relations 1939–1984*, pp. 85–6.
10. R. G. Hewlett and J. M. Holl, op. cit., pp. 264–6, 329–30; B. C. Hacker, *Elements of Controversy*, pp. 181–2.
11. R. G. Hewlett and J. M. Holl, op. cit., pp. 286–97; R. A. Divine, op. cit., pp. 36–57.
12. R. A. Divine, op. cit., p. 41.
13. Cmd 9391, 'Statement on Defence 1955', see A. J. R. Groom, *British Thinking about Nuclear Weapons*, pp. 99–108.
14. HC Deb., vol. 537, 1 Mar. 1955.
15. He became Prime Minister on 6 Apr. 1955 and called a general election in May. Harold Macmillan succeeded him in July 1957.
16. *Bulletin of the Atomic Scientists*, vol. X, nos 8 and 9 (October and November 1954); see L. Arnold, op. cit., p. 79.
17. R. G. Hewlett and J. M. Holl, op. cit., pp. 294–5.
18. J. Rotblat, *Scientists in the Quest for Peace*, pp. 1, 2, 137–40.
19. HC Deb., 29 Mar. 1955; L. Arnold, op. cit., pp. 79, 83–4.
20. Set up by the UN General Assembly in November 1956 to 'receive, collate and publish information on radiation levels and the effects of radiation on man and his environment'. UNSCEAR is still in operation.

21. HC Deb., vol. 546, 30 Nov. 1955.
22. L. Arnold, op. cit., p. 81.
23. Ibid., p. 82.
24. Ibid., p. 83.
25. We have found no record of a visit by the Archbishop.
26. L. Arnold, op. cit., p. 83.
27. Ibid., pp. 83–4.
28. Ibid., p. 85; R. A. Divine, op. cit., p. 120.
29. L. Arnold, op. cit., pp. 84–6.
30. Ibid., pp. 83–4.
31. HC Deb., 16 July 1956.
32. R. G. Hewlett and J. M. Holl, op. cit., pp. 345 and 368–9.
33. Ibid., pp. 346–8.

10 The First Trial – *Grapple*

1. See L. Arnold, *A Very Special Relationship*, ch. 7.
2. L. Arnold, op. cit., pp. 38–41, 233–41, 290–300 and 310–13.
3. See Appendix 4.
4. This contradicts the idea that *Grapple* was a 'bluff' intended to deceive the Americans.
5. Contained within latitudes 3.5° North and 7.5° South and longitudes 154° and 163° West.
6. L. Arnold, op. cit., ch. 7.
7. L. Arnold, op. cit., ch. 9.
8. Sometimes known as *Green Granite II*, but the nomenclature was rather careless and *Green Granite II* was also used for yet another variation which Cook proposed but which could not be made ready in time.
9. Cf. the Russian experience, Chapter 3.
10. Taylor instability (or more correctly 'Rayleigh-Taylor instability') occurs at 'the interface separating two fluids having different densities when the lighter fluid is accelerated toward the heavier fluid'.
11. See W. E. Oulton, op. cit., p. 202.
12. Ibid., p. 206.
13. Ibid., p. 209.
14. Ibid., pp. 336–9.
15. Ibid., p. 356.
16. Code-named *Windmill* at this time.

11 'We shall have to do it all again' – *Grapple X*

1. See N. Dombey and E. Grove, 'Britain's Thermonuclear Bluff', *London Review of Books*, October 1991.
2. Beryllium has the advantage of being highly transparent to radiation (but it is difficult to work with and very toxic).
3. At the best the series would be one or two shots, A and B; at the worst, only A. The sequences would be:
Round A successful → Round B (if ready).

or Round A moderately successful → Round C → Round D?
or Round A markedly poor → abandon?
4. L. Arnold, *A Very Special Relationship*, ch. 9.
5. L. Arnold, *Windscale 1957*, p. 66.
6. W. E. Oulton, *Christmas Cracker*, pp. 386–8.
7. L. Arnold, *A Very Special Relationship*, pp. 67–8.

12 Britain's Biggest Explosion – *Grapple Y*

1. Conversation with K. W. Allen at Aldermaston, 12 July 1995.
2. See ch. 6. The same epidemic affected Windscale at the time of the reactor fire in early October 1957.
3. The actual height of burst (in metres) for *Grapple Y* compares with other *Grapple* shots as follows: *Short Granite* 2200, *Orange Herald* 2400, *Purple Granite* 2400, *Grapple X* 2200, *Grapple Y* 2500, *Flagpole* 2800, *Halliard* 2600.
4. By contrast, a participant in the American *Ivy* trials in 1952 (quoted by R. Rhodes, *Dark Sun*, p. 503) wrote 'The nice thing about being overseas is that they feed you very well. They understand that if you want to have happy guys, you ration the booze ... but you serve very good food; shrimp, steak, ... lots of ice cream.'
5. By agreement with the United States and New Zealand governments.
6. K. Hubbard and M. Simmons, *Operation Grapple*, p. 114.

13 Mission Accomplished – *Grapple Z*

1. The two Windscale production reactors had both been closed after the October 1957 fire in one of them, and the new reactors at Calder Hall were only just coming into production.
2. L. Arnold, *A Very Special Relationship*, pp. 185–6.
3. Scientists not privy to super-secret information about 'RI' concluded that 'DP' stood for 'dirty plutonium' and that these bombs contained more highly irradiated plutonium than normal.
4. The difference between the two was in the amount of U-235 in the secondary.
5. The design is usually referred to as *Pendant* but the test is most often called *Pennant*. *Pennant* seems more appropriate than *Pendant*, in keeping with the other names used – *Flagpole*, *Burgee*, *Halliard* and *Ensign*.
6. The difference between the large and small versions of *Burgee* was not in the boosting but in the implosion and detonation systems.
7. *Grapple Z* sequence
    I   *If* (a) round 1 (*Pendant*) *or* round 3 (*Burgee*) yielded more than 14 kT *and* (b) round 2 (*Flagpole*) was successful *then* no *Halliard* round would be fired.
    II *If* the better of the two yields from rounds 1 and 3 (*Pendant* and *Burgee*) was intermediate, *then Halliard 2* (double bomb) would be fired as round 4.
    III *If* the better of two yields from rounds 1 and 3 (*Pendant* and *Burgee*) was poor then *Halliard 1* (triple bomb with thick case) would be fired as round 4.
    IV *If* rounds 1, 2 and 3 (*Pendant*, *Flagpole* and *Burgee*) were all successful *then Halliard 3* (triple bomb with thin case) should be made ready to fire as round 4. In the event, conditions I(a) and (b) were met and so no *Halliard* round was necessary. But *Halliard 1* was fired at American request.

8. Aldermaston collaborated on this innovatory design (see pp. 178, 185, 207) with SERL, the electronics research laboratory at Baldock, Hertfordshire.

9. This was not a dose which would lead to any perceptible symptoms. It was however equivalent to the 'higher integrated dose' permissible in exceptional circumstances with advance approval (see Appendix 4).

10. Not all the lithium hydride blocks apparently. Some were taken to a remote part of the south-west coast of Christmas Island, for a variety of *ad hoc* experiments. They were unwrapped and exposed to air, sprayed with water, and then completely immersed. Finally came an attempt to burn them on a bonfire, aided by two gallons of petrol. They were surprisingly reluctant to catch fire!

14 The Great Prize

1. M. Gowing, *Independence and Deterrence*, vol. 1, pp. 241–72.

2. In addition to those already listed as 'Topics for immediate declassification' the eight topics were, briefly, (1) health and safety, (2) radioisotopes, (3) fundamental nuclear and extra-nuclear properties, (4) detection of a distant nuclear explosion, (5) fundamental properties of reactor materials, (6) extraction chemistry, (7) design of natural uranium reactors, (8) general research experience with names low-power research reactors in the three countries. Only (4) related directly to weapons.

3. Fissile materials were very expensive, uranium was not yet abundant and supplies caused great anxiety to both the United States and Britain.

4. M. Gowing, op. cit., vol. 1, p. 407.

5. Ibid., p. 450.

6. Ibid., p. 450.

7. J. Melissen, *The Struggle for Nuclear Partnership*, p. 13.

8. Ibid., p. 13.

9. H. Macmillan, *Riding the Storm*, p. 324.

10. See, for example, J. Baylis, *Anglo-American Defence Relations 1939–1984*, p. 71; J. Melissen, op. cit., pp. 24–5; T. Botti, *The Long Wait*, pp. 140–1.

11. Cmd 9555. The text is in J. Baylis, op. cit., pp. 85–7; T. Botti, op. cit., ch. 15.

12. J. Melissen, op. cit., p. 25.

13. Ibid., p. 16.

14. H. Macmillan, op. cit., ch. IV; D. Carlton, *Anthony Eden: a Biography*, ch. XI; J. Baylis, op. cit., pp. 72–3, 103, 206; T. Botti, op. cit., pp. 171–4.

15. H. Macmillan, op. cit., pp. 240–61. A. Horne, *Macmillan 1957–1986*, pp. 23–7.

16. J. Horne, op. cit., p. 26; J. Baylis, op. cit., p. 90.

17. T. Botti, op. cit., p. 173; J. Simpson, *The Independent Nuclear State*, p. 124; R. Rhodes James, *Anthony Eden*, p. 572.

18. J. Baylis, op. cit., p. 90.

19. A. Horne, *Macmillan 1957–1986*, p. 53.

20. H. Macmillan, op. cit., pp. 314–6; A. Horne, op. cit., p. 53; T. Botti, op. cit., pp. 199–201; J. Baylis, op. cit., p. 92; J. Melissen, op. cit., pp. 43–4.

21. H. Macmillan, op. cit., p. 315.

22. See L. Arnold, *Windscale 1957*. A. Horne, op. cit., pp. 53–5.

23. H. Macmillan, op. cit., pp. 319–26 and 756–59 (text of 'Declaration'); A. Horne, op. cit., pp. 55–9.

24. H. Macmillan, op. cit., ch. X, entitled 'Honeymoon in Washington'; J. Melissen, op. cit., pp. 43–6.

25. J. Melissen, op. cit., p. 45.

26. T. Botti, op. cit., p. 210; J. Simpson, op. cit., pp. 130–1.

27. T. Botti, op. cit., p. 224–6; J. Simpson, op. cit., pp. 138–9; H. Macmillan, op. cit., pp. 481–2.

28. Published in Britain as Cmnd 470, July 1958; J. Baylis, op. cit., pp. 112–20.

29. The Sandia laboratories, near Albuquerque, New Mexico, are the premier nuclear ordnance facility of the United States. They developed out of the post-war Z Division of Los Alamos, located at Kirtland Base, Albuquerque; Z Division itself emerged from the Los Alamos wartime Division of Ordnance Engineering (O Division). It became an independent industrial corporation in November 1949. Lawrence Livermore, in California, was set up in 1952 as a second weapons laboratory to complement and compete with Los Alamos.

30. He had been appointed Board Member for Engineering and Production by the UKAEA in February 1958 but for some months was virtually doing two very demanding jobs, at Aldermaston and at Risley, and travelling between the United Kingdom, the United States and Christmas Island.

31. This committee had been set up under the Quebec Agreement in 1943 but had been dormant for many years.

32. This apparently means after completion of the *Grapple Z* trials, though another test was provisionally planned for March 1959.

33. This may have been the paper reproduced here as Appendix 3 ('The History of the British R&D on Atomic Weapons'.)

34. H. Macmillan, *Riding the Storm*, p. 563.

35. Ibid., p. 565.

36. 'Quarterly Progress Report: Part III, Weapons: July–Sept. 1958'. (Declassified copy from USDOE archives.) I am grateful to Professor Norman Dombey for a copy of this document.

37. A nuclear weapon is 'one-point safe' that is so designed that it will not produce a measurable nuclear yield if just one of its explosive charges is detonated.

38. A missile with a range of about 200 miles; to be extended in a later version to upward of 400 miles.

39. Admiral Sir Michael Denny, head of BJSM, Washington; Air Marshal Sir Geoffrey Tuttle, DCAS; and Lieutenant-General Sir Roderick McLeod, MOD. Plowden, Penney and Cook were apparently none of them present.

40. In this context the work by Roberts and Taylor on efficiency theory mentioned in chapter 13 was important.

41. Penney was now UKAEA Board Member for Research. The new director of AWRE, Dr N Levin, was present. Cook was not because of his commitments at Risley (he was now UKAEA Board Member for Reactor Development and Engineering).

42. Of perhaps £10 million over 3 to 4 years to provide additional research facilities, especially computing facilities.

43. Cmnd 859, May 1959. The text is in J. Baylis, op. cit., pp. 121–4.

44. See n. 43.

45. L. Arnold, *A Very Special Relationship*, ch. 10.

15 Some Questions and Answers

1. N. Dombey and E. Grove, 'Britain's Thermonuclear Bluff', *London Review of Books*, 22 Oct. 1992.

2. *Independent*, 1 Apr. 1992.
3. Francis Pym quoted by M. Greenberg, *Physics and Metaphysics of Deterrence*, p. 52, in a discussion of declaratory and operative policy.
4. Lord Orr-Ewing in a letter to *The Times*, 6 Feb. 1992 quoted by M. Greenberg, op. cit., p. 69. See also L. Freedman, *Britain and Nuclear Weapons*, p. 26. The question of credibility is interestingly discussed in A. Pierre, *Nuclear Politics*, pp. 173–86, 295, 306–7.
5. M. Greenberg, op. cit., p. 54 quoting M. Navias, *The Sandys White Paper and the British New Look*, pp. 51–2.
6. M. Greenberg, op. cit., p. 54.
7. Ibid., pp. 71–2.
8. See n. 1.
9. As to actual yields they guessed right. At the time they wrote the yields of various *Grapple* shots were not in the public domain; they were first published in 1993 in a National Radiological Protection Board report (NRPB-R266).
10. See Preface for an explanation of the various objectives of weapon tests.
11. *Orange Herald (Small)*, the version fired, contained a small quantity of thermonuclear material, but it was calculated later that the boosting effect had done little or nothing more than compensate for the fissile material it had displaced from the core.
12. But Corner was greatly impressed by the speed of the American development, from the Ulam-Teller breakthrough to the *Mike* shot. He thought the British lost too much time 'piddling about' (interview Mar. 1995).
13. Lord Sherfield, in his Royal Society biographical memoir of Penney, wrote, 'He kept in close touch with his American friends and was able to sit up drinking with them half the night. There is little doubt that he and he alone gleaned in this way much information about the American programme'. Unfortunately we have no evidence from Penney himself, except a reference in early 1954 to 'snippets of information'.
14. We have found no Eureka document. Perhaps in future K. M. Pyne (now technical historian at Aldermaston) may be able to find and interpret fresh evidence.
15. Including K. W. Allen, J. C. Challens, J. Corner, Sir Sam Curran, E. Pendlebury, R. Siddons and J. B. Taylor.
16. Corner was sometimes regarded by people who did not know him well as a 'number cruncher'. But his personal notes and memoranda (there is a large collection in the Aldermaston archives) show an original and penetrating mind. His contribution was clearly invaluable if not adequately appreciated. He wrote about the work of the establishment, and of his theoretical physics division staff, and not about his personal achievements.
17. A Corner dictum with which all the scientists would agree.
18. For what Cook thought, our only clue was a comment recorded by M. Gowing in 1977 that 'Penney led us to the H-bomb'. Unfortunately that remark was not followed up. (Confidential recorded interview in UKAEA historians' office.)
19. Behind them all, of course, was Hinton's complex of atomic production factories in the north-west of England
20. See NRPB-R266, p. 11.
21. See W. N. Saxby, 'Radiation exposure of participants at UK overseas atmospheric nuclear weapons tests and experimental programmes 1952-1957', *Journal of the Society for Radiological Protection*, May 1987.
22. NRPB-R266, p. 11.
23. NRPB-R214 and NRPB-R266.

24. It is the case that NRPB-R214 received some criticism but the later NRPB-R266 was able to be more complete and, so far as we know, no informed critic has faulted this study.

25. Estimating the costs is extremely difficult since they are divided among many departments and organisations, often with different accounting methods. Moreover defence budgets in that period were designed to conceal, not reveal, expenditure on the strategic nuclear force. Andrew Pierre's rough estimate for total expenditure 1945–70 is £3200 million (including nuclear facilities, warheads, bombers, missiles and cancelled projects). See A. Pierre, *Nuclear Politics*, p. 309.

26. Unsigned and undated typescript (? Apr. 1955).

27. A. Brown, *The Neutron and the Bomb*, p. 359.

28. Group Captain Leonard Cheshire was a VC and veteran RAF bomber pilot. He and Penney flew in the observer aircraft on the second A-bomb raid on Japan. Years later, Penney talked to Lorna Arnold about their long conversations in their tent at the Tinian airbase, about these new weapons and their meaning for the post-war world.

Select Bibliography

I Command papers and official publications

Cmd 8986, *The Future Organization of the United Kingdom Atomic Energy Project* (HMSO, 1953).

Cmd 9389, *A Programme of Nuclear Power* (HMSO, 1955).

Cmd 9391, *Statement on Defence: 1955* (HMSO, 1955).

Cmd 9555, *Agreement for Co-operation Regarding Atomic Information for Mutual Defence Purposes* (HMSO, 1955).

Cmd 9780, *The Hazards to Man of Nuclear and Allied Radiations* (HMSO, 1956).

Cmnd 537, *Agreement for Co-operation on the Uses of Atomic Energy for Mutual Defence Purposes* (HMSO, 1958).

Cmnd 733, *Amendment to Agreement for Co-operation on the Uses of Atomic Energy for Mutual Defence Purposes* (HMSO, 1959).

Cmnd 859, *Amendment to Agreement between the Government of the United Kingdom and Northern Ireland and the Government of the United States of America for Co-operation on the Uses of Atomic Energy for Mutual Defence Purposes of July 3, 1958* (HMSO, 1959).

Cmnd 1225, *The Hazards to Man of Nuclear and Allied Radiations: Second Report* (HMSO, 1960).

NRPB-R266, *Mortality and Cancer Incidence 1952–1990 in UK Participants in the UK Atmospheric Nuclear Weapon Tests and Experimental Programmes* (National Radiological Protection Board, 1993 – obtainable from HMSO).

II Books

Albright, J. and Kunstel, M., *Bombshell: the Secret Story of America's Unknown Atomic Spy Conspiracy* (New York: Times Books, 1997).

Arnold, L., *A Very Special Relationship: British Atomic Weapon Trials in Australia* (London: HMSO, 1987).

Arnold, L., *Windscale 1957: Anatomy of a Nuclear Accident* (London: Macmillan, 1992).

Badash, L., et al., *Reminiscences of has Alamas 1943–1945* (London, Baston and Dordrecht: D. Renold Publishing, 1980).

Baylis, J., *Anglo-American Defence Relations 1939–1984*, 2nd edn (London: Macmillan 1984).

Baylis, J., *Ambiguity and Deterrence: British Nuclear Strategy 1945–1964* (Oxford: Clarendon Press 1995).

Baylis, J. and Macmillan, A., *The Foundations of British Nuclear Strategy 1945–1960*, International Politics Research Papers 12 (Department of International Politics, University of Wales, Aberystwyth).

Botti, T. J., *The Long Wait: the Forging of the Anglo-American Nuclear Alliance 1945–1958* (New York: Greenwood Press, 1987).

Brown, A., *The Neutron and the Bomb: a Biography of Sir James Chadwick* (Oxford: Oxford University Press, 1987).

Campbell, D., *The Unsinkable Aircraft Carrier* (London: Michael Joseph, 1984).

Cathcart, B., *Test of Greatness: Britain's Struggle for the Atom Bomb* (London: John Murray, 1994).

Charmley, J., *Churchill's Grand Alliance: the Anglo-American Special Relationship 1940–57* (London: Hodder and Stoughton, 1995).

Charmley, J., *Churchill, the End of Glory: a Political Biography* (London: Hodder and Stoughton, 1993).

Clark, I., *Nuclear Diplomacy and the Special Relationship: Britain's Deterrent and America 1957–1962* (Oxford: Clarendon Press, 1994).

Clark, I. and Wheeler, N. J., *The British Origins of Nuclear Strategy 1945–55* (Oxford: Clarendon Press, 1989).

Clark, R., *The Greatest Power on Earth* (London: Sidgwick and Jackson, 1980).

Cochran, T. B., Arkin, W. M., Norris, R. S. and Sands, J. I., *Nuclear Weapons Databook*, Vol. IV, *Soviet Nuclear Weapons* (New York: Harper and Row, 1989).

Dimbleby, D. and Reynolds, D. J., *An Ocean Apart: the Relationship between Britain and America in the Twentieth Century* (London: Hodder and Stoughton for BBC, 1988).

Divine, R. A., *Blowing on the Wind: The Nuclear Test Ban Debate 1954–60* (New York: Oxford University Press, 1978).

Drell, S. D. and Kapitza, S. P. (eds), *Sakharov Remembered: a Tribute by His Friends and Colleagues* (New York: American Institute of Physics, 1991).

Driver, C., *The Disarmers: a Study in Protest* (London: Hodder and Stoughton, 1964).

Duke, S., *US Defence Bases in the United Kingdom* (London: Macmillan, 1987).

Freedman, L., *Britain and Nuclear Weapons* (London: Macmillan, 1980).

Freedman, L., *The Evolution of Nuclear Strategy* (London, Macmillan, 2nd edition, 1989).

Goldblat, J. and Cox, D. (eds), *Nuclear Weapon Tests: Prohibition or Limitation?* (Stockholm: SIPRI/Oxford University Press, 1988).

Gowing, M., *Britain and Atomic Energy 1939–1945* (London: Macmillan, 1964).

Gowing, M., *Independence and Deterrence: Britain and Atomic Energy 1945–1952*, 2 vol, (London: Macmillan, 1974).

Greenberg, M. A., *Physics and Metaphysics of Deterrence: the British Approach* (The Newport Papers 8, Naval War College Press, Newport, Rhode Island, 1994).

Groom, A. J. R., *British Thinking about Nuclear Weapons* (London: Pinter, 1974).

Hacker, B. C., *Elements of Controversy: the Atomic Energy Commission and Radiation Safety in Nuclear Weapons Testing 1947–1974* (Berkeley: University of California Press, 1994).

Hansen, C., *US Nuclear Weapons: the Secret History* (Aerofax/Orion Books, 1988).

Hawkins, D., Truslow, E. C. and Smith, R. C., *Project Y: the Los Alamos Story* (Los Angeles: Tomash Publishers, 1983).

Hennessy, P., *Whitehall* (London: Martin Secker and Warburg, 1989).

Hewlett, R. G. and Holl, J. M., *Atoms for Peace and War 1953–1961: Eisenhower and the Atomic Energy Commission* (Berkeley and Los Angeles: University of California Press, 1989).

Hewlett, R. G. and Anderson, O. E., *The New World: a History of the United States Atomic Energy Commission*, Vol. 1, *1939–1946* (Berkeley: University of California Press, 1990).

Hewlett, R. G. and Duncan, F., *Atomic Shield: a History of the United States Atomic Energy Commission*, Vol. II *1947–52* (Pennsylvania: Pennsylvania State University Press, 1969).

Hoddesdon, L., Hendrikson, P. W., Meade, R. A. and Westfall, C., *Critical Assembly: a Technical History of Los Alamos During the Oppenheimer Years 1943–1945* (Cambridge: Cambridge University Press, 1993).

Holloway, D., *Stalin and the Bomb: the Soviet Union and Atomic Energy 1939–1956* (New Haven: Yale University Press, 1994).

Horne, A., *Macmillan, 1891–1956* (London: Macmillan, 1988).

Horne, A., *Macmillan, 1957–1986* (London: Macmillan, 1989).

Hubbard, K. G. and Simmons, M. J., *Operation Grapple: Testing Britain's First H-bomb* (London: Ian Allan 1985).

Lapp, R. E., *The Voyage of the lucky Dragon* (New York, 1958).

Louis, W. R. and Bull, H. (eds), *The Special Relationship: Anglo-American Relations since the Second World War* (Newton Abbott: David and Charles, 1974).

Macmillan, H., *Tides of Fortune, 1945–1955* (London: Macmillan, 1969).

Macmillan, H., *Riding the Storm 1956–1959* (London: Macmillan, 1971).

Melissen, J., *The Struggle for Nuclear Partnership: Britain, the United States, and the Making of an Ambiguous Alliance, 1952–59* (Groningen: Styx, 1993).

Norris, R. S., Burrows, A. S. and Fieldhouse, R. W., *British, French and Chinese Nuclear Weapons*, Vol. V, *Nuclear Weapons Databook* (Oxford: Westview Press, 1994).

Oulton, W. E., *Christmas Island Cracker: an Account of the Planning and Execution of British Thermonuclear Bomb Tests 1957* (London: Thomas Harmsworth Publishing, 1987).

Pierre, A., *Nuclear Politics: the British Experience with an Independent Strategic Force 1939–1970* (London: Oxford University Press, 1972).

Rhodes, R., *The Making of the Atomic Bomb* (New York: Simon and Schuster, 1986).

Rhodes, R., *Dark Sun: the Making of the Hydrogen Bomb* (New York: Simon and Schuster, 1995).

Rhodes James, R., *Anthony Eden* (London: Weidenfeld and Nicolson, 1986).

Rosecrance, R. N., *Defence of the Realm: British Strategy in the Nuclear Epoch* (New York: Columbia University Press, 1968).

Sakharov, A., *Memoirs* (New York: Knopf, 1990).

Seaborg, G. T., *Kennedy, Khrushchev and the Test Ban* (Berkeley and Los Angeles: University of California Press, 1981).

Shelton, F. H., *Reflections of a Nuclear Weaponeer* (Colorado Springs: Shelton Enterprises Inc., 1988).

Shelton, F. H., *Reflections on the Big Red Bombs* (Colorado Springs: Shelton Enterprises Inc., 1995).

Simpson, J., *The Independent Nuclear State: the United States, Britain and the Military Atom* (London: Macmillan, 1983).

Szasz, F. M., *British Scientists and the Manhattan Project: The Los Alamos Years* (London: Macmillan, 1992).

Teller, E., *Better a Shield than a Sword: Perspectives on Defense and Technology* (New York: Free Press, 1987).

Ulam, S., *Adventures of a Mathematician* (New York: Scribners, 1976).

US Atomic Energy Commission, *The Effects of Atomic Weapons* (New York, Toronto, London: McGraw-Hill Book Company, Inc., 1950).

US Atomic Energy Commission, *In the Matter of J R Oppenheimer* (Washington: United States Government Printing Office, 1954).

Williams, R. C., *Klaus Fuchs: Atom Spy* (Cambridge, MA: Harvard University Press, 1987).

Wynn, H., *The RAF Strategic Nuclear Deterrent Forces: Their Origins, Roles and Deployment 1946–1969* (London: HMSO, 1994).

York, H. F., *The Advisors: Oppenheimer, Teller and the Superbomb* (San Francisco: W. H. Freeman, 1970).

III Articles

Adamskii, V., 'Dear Mr Krushchev', *Bulletin of the Atomic Scientists*, Nov./Dec. 1995.

Baylis, J., 'The Development of Britain's Thermonuclear Capability 1954–61: Myth or Reality?', *Contemporary Record*, 8/1, Sept. 1994.

Baylis, J., 'Exchanging Nuclear Secrets: Laying the Foundations of the Anglo-American Nuclear Relationship', *Diplomatic History* (to forthcoming).

Bethe, H. A., 'Comments on the History of the H-bomb', *Los Alamos Science*, autumn 1982.

Bradbury, N. E., 'The Los Alamos Laboratory', *Bulletin of the Atomic Scientists* vol. 10, 1954.

Carson Mark, J., 'A Short Account of Los Alamos Theoretical Work on Thermonuclear Weapons 1946–1950' (LA 5647 – MS, informal report issued July 1974).

Dombey, N. and Grove, E. 'Britain's Thermonuclear Bluff', *London Review of Books*, 22 Oct. 1992.

Goncharov, G. A., 'Thermonuclear Milestones (1) The American Effort (2) The Beginnings of the Soviet H-bomb Program (3) The Race Accelerates', *Physics Today*, Special issue, Nov. 1996.

Holloway, D., 'New Light on Early Soviet Bomb Secrets', *Physics Today*, Special issue, Nov. 1996.

Holloway, D., 'Soviet Scientists Speak Out', *Bulletin of the Atomic Scientists*, vol. 49, no. 4, May 1993.

Khariton, Y. and Smirnov, Y., 'The Khariton Version', *Bulletin of the Atomic Scientists*, vol. 49, no. 4, May 1993.

Leskov, S., 'Dividing the Glory of the Fathers', *Bulletin of the Atomic Scientists*, vol. 49, no. 4, May 1993.

Melissen, J., 'The Restoration of the Nuclear Alliance: Great Britain and Atomic Negotiations with the United States 1957–1958', *Contemporary Record*, 6/1, summer 1992.

Penney, Lord and Macklen, V. H. B., 'William Richard Joseph Cook', *Royal Society Biographical Memoirs*, 1988.

Reed, T. and Kramish, A., 'Trinity at Dubna', *Physics Today*, Special issue, Nov. 1996.

Rosenberg, D. A., 'A Smoking Radiating Ruin at the End of Two Hours', *International Security*, winter 1981–82.

Sagdeev, R., 'Russian scientists save American secrets', *Bulletin of the Atomic Scientists*, vol. 49, no. 4, May 1993.

Sawyer, R., 'The H-bomb Chronology', *Bulletin of the Atomic Scientists*, vol. 10, 1954.

Sherfield, Lord, 'William George Penney, OM, KBE, Baron Penney of East Hendred, 24 June 1909–3 Mar. 1991', *Royal Society Biographical Memoirs*, 1993.

Teller, E., 'The Work of Many People', *Science*, vol. 121, 25 Feb. 1955.

Wheeler, N. J., 'British Nuclear Weapons and Anglo-American Relations 1945–54', *International Affairs*, winter 1985–86.

York, H. F., 'The Debate over the Hydrogen Bomb', *Scientific American*, Oct. 1975.

Index